Data Virtualization for Business Intelligence Systems

Data Virtualization for Business Intelligence Systems

Revolutionizing Data Integration for Data Warehouses

Rick F. van der Lans

AMSTERDAM • BOSTON • HEIDELBERG • LONDON
NEW YORK • OXFORD • PARIS • SAN DIEGO
SAN FRANCISCO • SINGAPORE • SYDNEY • TOKYO

Morgan Kaufmann Publishers is an Imprint of Elsevier

Acquiring Editor: Andrea Dierna
Editorial Project Manager: Robyn Day
Project Manager: A. B. McGee
Designer: Mark Rogers

Morgan Kaufmann is an imprint of Elsevier
225 Wyman Street, Waltham, MA 02451, USA

Library of Congress Cataloging-in-Publication Data
Lans, Rick F. van der.
  Data virtualization for business intelligence architectures : revolutionizing data integration for data warehouses /
Rick F. van der Lans.
     pages cm
  ISBN 978-0-12-394425-2
1. Data warehousing. 2. Management information systems. 3. Virtual computer systems. 4. Business intelligence.
I. Title.
  QA76.9.D37L36 2012
  005.74'5–dc23

                                                                                            2012020776

British Library Cataloguing-in-Publication Data
A catalogue record for this book is available from the British Library

For information on all MK publications
visit our website at http://store.elsevier.com

Printed in the United States of America
12 13 14 15 16   10 9 8 7 6 5 4 3 2 1

Working together to grow
libraries in developing countries

www.elsevier.com | www.bookaid.org | www.sabre.org

ELSEVIER   BOOK AID International   Sabre Foundation

Dedicated to Diane Cools
for her life-saving gift

Contents

Foreword

The classic data warehouse and business intelligence architecture relies on a repository of quality, integrated data at its core. In the very early days of business intelligence, we struggled with manual processes to extract data from multiple operational systems, combine the data, fix any errors, fill in missing fields, remove duplicate data, and finally load the integrated data into a database, creating a physical data warehouse, or "single source of data," for reporting and analytics.

Shortly thereafter came the technological innovation of extraction, transformation, and load (ETL) tools, which automated many manual data integration tasks in a reliable and repeatable fashion. ETL tools greatly improved the overall process of creating a data warehouse. They included data quality technology to further improve the value of the integrated data for decision making. To this day, ETL tools remain a major mechanism for creating physical stores of *historical* data for business intelligence.

Recently, two significant trends are causing business intelligence architects to rethink their ETL and data management infrastructures: operational business intelligence and the advent of big data analytics. Let's look at operational business intelligence first. Most business intelligence environments start out producing historical reports and analytics about what has happened. Historical data can also be used for predicting what will happen, but it does not fully support real-time decisioning or operational business intelligence.

As enterprises started demanding the ability to make intra-day decisions based on current or low-latency data, we sped up the overall ETL process via change data capture, trickle feeds, and minibatches of operational data. These approaches reduced the latency of the data in our data warehouses from days and hours to minutes, but they were still not fast enough for true real-time decision making. Business intelligence implementers came to realize that classic ETL processing had reached its limits, and a new form of data integration was in order.

It is a similar story for big data and its associated analytics. Examples of big data include social and text analytics, sensor data, and event or in-motion data. Much of big data is unstructured or, more accurately, occurs in multiple formats. It does not have the traditional and predictable structures found in typical operational systems. It's also massive in volume, relative to previous standards. For many data warehouse implementers, big data poses significant integration challenges.

Truth be told, much big data may not need to reside in a formal data warehouse. Often, it is used for experimental or investigative analytics. Even so, there may be a need to combine some of this data with the data warehouse data. How can we effectively accommodate the demand for operational business intelligence and big data and extend business intelligence architectures without disrupting existing ETL processes? The answer is data virtualization.

I have known Rick van der Lans for many years. His articles and research papers often educate me because they *always* give me interesting alternatives and innovative twists to traditional thinking. Rick forces me to reevaluate all I held as true. And this is certainly true of his latest effort: *Data Virtualization for Business Intelligence Systems: Revolutionizing Data Integration for Data Warehouses.*

Data virtualization has become a must-have technology for today's business intelligence implementers. As with any new technology, there are many questions about how to implement it, when to use it, and what challenges and pitfalls to avoid. Rick covers these issues and more in this detailed and practical "how-to" guide. I will be referring to it for years to come. I know you will as well.

Claudia Imhoff
President of Intelligent Solutions, Inc.,
Founder of the Boulder BI Brain Trust (BBBT)

Preface

Introduction

Data virtualization is a technology that makes a heterogeneous set of databases and files look like one integrated database. When used in business intelligence systems, it can make the architectures dramatically simpler, cheaper, and, most important, more agile. New reporting and analytical needs can be implemented faster, and existing systems can be changed more easily. This increased agility is needed because, on one hand, business users demand more agility from their systems since their world has begun to change, and, on the other hand, because new forms of business intelligence, such as operational reporting, big data analytics, 360-degree reporting, self-service reporting, and exploratory analysis, are required. This book is dedicated to data virtualization and how to efficiently exploit that technology in business intelligence systems. But let's start with the beginning, and let's start with the term *virtualization*.

In the IT industry, we have entered the era of *virtualization*. Sometimes it feels as if anything in our industry can be virtualized, including memory, storage, networks, and data centers. Virtualization is hot. Look at the popularity of cloud technology, which can be classified as a virtualization technology as well. Virtualization is right in the spotlight, and it will stay there for some time.

What all these virtualization technologies and concepts have in common is that they encapsulate a certain resource. Any virtualization solution hides how much of the resource is available, its location, how much of the resource is available, what API is needed to get to the resource, and so on. But don't confuse virtualization with the term *virtual world* offered by some computer games. Those games do present something virtual, but they're not encapsulating a particular resource.

This book explains one particular form of virtualization: *data virtualization*. In a nutshell, data virtualization means making data available in an integrated fashion to applications regardless of whether all that data is distributed over multiple databases, stored in different formats, and accessible through different database languages. It presents all these different data stores to the applications as one logical database. Although data virtualization products and technologies have been around for some time, it's only since, roughly, 2009 that it's receiving the attention it deserves. Because of the effect it has on solutions—namely, increased agility—more and more organizations are adopting the technology. It looks like as if the 2010s will become the decade of data virtualization.

Data virtualization can be deployed in all types of information systems where data is being retrieved and manipulated, such as classic data entry systems, Internet-based systems, service-oriented systems, master data management systems, and business intelligence systems. The focus of this book is on business intelligence systems. Data virtualization can be used to integrate data from various data sources, including data warehouses, data marts, and production databases. It has the potential to revolutionize the way we develop business intelligence systems. Data virtualization can become the heart of most of these systems.

In short, data virtualization allows us to build business intelligence systems with simpler and more agile architectures. If you want to know how and why, this book is for you! It describes in detail how data virtualization products work, how the technology can be applied, what the do's and don'ts are, and the benefits of applying it in business intelligence systems.

Who Should Read This Book?

This book is recommend for the following:

- *Business intelligence specialists* who are responsible for developing and managing a data warehouse and business intelligence environment; for those who want to know how such systems can be simplified by applying data virtualization and how data virtualization can lead to a more agile business intelligence system.
- *Information management specialists* who want to know what the effect of data virtualization is on their profession and how it will impact activities such as information management, data governance, database design, data cleansing, and data profiling.
- *Master data management specialists* who are responsible for setting up a master data management system and want to know how they can benefit from deploying data virtualization.
- *Data architects* who are responsible for designing an overall architecture for data delivery to any part of the organization.
- *Database administrators* who have to understand the features and restrictions of data virtualization servers for determining how and where this technology can be applied effectively and efficiently.
- *Designers, analysts, and consultants* who have to deal, directly or indirectly, with data virtualization and want to know about its possibilities and impossibilities.
- *Students* who want to know what data virtualization is and what the difference is compared with other data-related technologies.

Prerequisite Knowledge

Some general knowledge of topics such as data warehousing, business intelligence, and database technology is required.

Terms and Definitions

Unfortunately, not all of the terms used in the worlds of data virtualization and data warehousing are perfectly defined, as will become clear in this book. To avoid confusion, we have tried to clarify and define most of them. However, we can't guarantee that the definitions in this book correspond with yours.

There are various reasons for this jumble. The first reason is that frequently the marketing wizards of the vendors come up with new terms purely to distinguish their products from those of the competition. But marketing people don't define terms; they just introduce them and describe them in general terms. And before everyone realizes, we all use that terminology that is badly defined or not defined at all. The second reason is that this field evolves very rapidly, allowing minimal time for inventing terms for new concepts and for coming up with well-balanced definitions. As a consequence, a term might have been picked too hastily that, on closer examination, doesn't really cover it.

And Finally ...

For me, writing a book feels like a solo project: sitting in my office for hours, days, and months, with a cup of tea and listening to my favorite music. But it's not a solo project at all. Many people contribute to a book, and that certainly applies to this book as well. Therefore, I would like to thank some of them for their help, contributions, ideas, comments, mental support, and patience.

- My thanks to Jim Bean and Richard Hackathorn for their technical reviews. Their comments were probably much more valuable than they realize. Their feedback came in while I was still writing, which made the whole project quite inspiring. I wish I had had technical reviewers like them on all my previous book projects.
- I would like to thank Claudia Imhoff, author and coauthor of various books on business intelligence, codesigner of the corporate information factory, author of numerous articles on business intelligence and related topics, founder of the Boulder BI Brain Trust, and speaker at countless events, for writing the foreword for this book. With her impressive track record in the business intelligence field, she was the most obvious person to do the job. Therefore, I was delighted that when asked, she said yes without hesitation. I still feel honored. Thank you, Claudia!
- From the first day I started working on the book, I had the full support of the following three vendors: Composite Software, Inc.; Denodo Technologies, Inc.; and Informatica Corporation. To the following specialists in particular, I am very grateful: David Besemer, Robert Eve, Kevin O'Brien, Ian Pestell, and Jean-Philippe Player of Composite Software; Suresh Chandrasekaran, Juan Lozano, and Alberto Pan of Denodo Technologies; and Diby Malakar, James Markarian, Bert Oosterhof, Ash Parikh, and Lalitha Sundaramurthy of Informatica. They all answered my technical questions expertly and patiently.
- For their willingness to share their thoughts on the future of data virtualization, I am also grateful to Composite Software's, Denodo Technologies', and Informatica Corporation's respective CTOs: David Besemer, Alberto Pan, and James Markarian.
- This is my first book for publisher Morgan Kaufmann. Now that the book has been published and is available both in bookstores and on the Internet, I must say I made a wise decision. Working with Andrea Dierna and Robyn Day, who guided me professionally through this project, was a pleasure. Thank you both for making it a readable book. It was a great experience, and I apologize for the fact that my writing process is quite unorganized.
- In the book, most of the examples relate to a sample database derived from the database designed by Roland Bouman and Jos van Dongen for their book *Pentaho Solutions; Business Intelligence and Data Warehousing with Pentaho and MySQL*. I would like to thank both authors for developing this database and for allowing me to use it in this book. I especially want to thank Roland for reviewing a part of the book. Every writer should invite him to be an editor.
- I would like to thank the hundreds of people across the world who attended my sessions at seminars and conferences on data virtualization and the data delivery platform over the past years. Their comments and recommendations have been invaluable for writing this book.
- Immensely useful were the discussions on business intelligence and data virtualization that I've had through the years with independent analysts and good friends Colin White and Mike Ferguson. I have known both for close to 20 years, and I have always respected and highly valued their views on new technologies.

- Without diminishing how hard all the people mentioned above worked on this book and how much they contributed, one person was vital to the entire project: my "personal editor" and, more important, my wife, Diane Cools. Already, we've worked on more than ten books together, and it's still great to work with her after all these years. In fact, without her, it is doubtful I would ever have written a book on data virtualization. As always, I'm very grateful, Diane!

Finally, I would like to ask readers to send comments, opinions, ideas, and suggestions concerning the contents of the book to info@r20.nl, referencing *Data Virtualization for Business Intelligence Systems*. Many thanks in anticipation of your cooperation. I hope you have as much fun reading this book as I had writing it.

Rick F. van der Lans
Den Haag, The Netherlands, March 2012

About the Author

Rick F. van der Lans is an independent consultant, lecturer, and author. He specializes in data warehousing, business intelligence, service-oriented architectures, and database technology. He is managing director of R20/Consultancy B.V.. Rick has been involved in various projects in which business intelligence, data warehousing, SOA, data virtualization, and integration technology were applied.

Rick van der Lans is an internationally acclaimed lecturer. He has lectured professionally for the last 20 years in many of the European and Middle East countries, the United States, South America, and Australia. He is regularly invited by major software vendors to present keynote speeches.

He is the author of several books on computing, including *Myths on Computing*. Some of these books are available in different languages. Books such as the popular *Introduction to SQL* and *SQL for MySQL Developers* are available in English, Dutch, Italian, Chinese, and German and are sold worldwide.

As an author for BeyeNetwork.com, a writer of whitepapers, a chair for the annual European Data Warehouse and Business Intelligence Conference, and a columnist in IT magazines, Rick has close contacts with many vendors.

You can get in touch with Rick via:

Email: rick@r20.nl

Twitter: http://twitter.com/Rick_vanderlans

LinkedIn: http://www.linkedin.com/pub/rick-van-der-lans/9/207/223

Introduction to Data Virtualization

1.1 Introduction

This chapter explains how data virtualization can be used to develop more *agile* business intelligence systems. By applying data virtualization, it will become easier to change systems. New reports can be developed, and existing reports can be adapted more easily and quickly. This agility is an important aspect for users of business intelligence systems. Their world is changing faster and faster, and therefore their supporting business intelligence systems must change at the same pace.

First, we examine the changes that are taking place in the fast-moving business intelligence industry. Next, we discuss what data virtualization is and what the impact will be of applying this technology to business intelligence systems. To get a better understanding of data virtualization, its relationship with other technologies and ideas, such as abstraction, encapsulation, data integration, and enterprise information integration, is described. In other words, this chapter presents a high-level overview of data virtualization. These topics are all discussed in more detail in subsequent chapters.

1.2 The World of Business Intelligence Is Changing

The primary reason why organizations have developed business intelligence systems is to support and improve their decision-making processes. This means that the main users of such systems are those who make the decisions. They decide on, for example, when to order more raw materials, how to streamline the purchasing process, which customers to offer a discount, and whether to outsource or insource transport.

This world of decision making is changing, and the biggest change is that organizations have to react faster, which means decisions have to be made faster. There is less and less time available to make (sometimes crucial) decisions. Studies are supporting this phenomenon. For example, the study by the Aberdeen Group in March 2011 shows that 43 percent of enterprises are finding it harder to make timely decisions (Figure 1.1). Managers increasingly find they have less time to make decisions after certain business events occur. The consequence is that it has to be possible to change existing reports faster and to develop new reports more quickly.

But this is not the only change. New data sources are becoming available for analysis and reporting. Especially in the first years of business intelligence, the only data available for reporting and analytics was internal data related to business processes. For example, systems had been built to store all incoming orders, all the customer data, and all invoices. Nowadays, there are many more systems that offer valuable data, such as weblogs, email servers, call center systems, and document

1

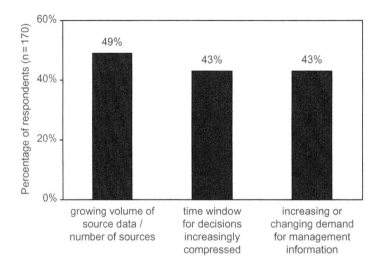

FIGURE 1.1

Study by the Aberdeen Group. The middle bar indicates that 43 percent of the respondents indicate that the time window for making decisions is shortening; see [2].

management systems. Analyzing this data can lead to a better understanding of what customers think about a firm's services and products, how efficient the website is, and the best ways to find "good" customers.

New data sources can also be found outside the boundaries of the organization. For example, websites, social media networks, and government data all might contain data that, when combined with internal data, can lead to new insights. Organizations are interested in combining their own internal data with these new data sources and thereby enriching the analytical and reporting capabilities.

As in every field—whether it's medical, pharmaceutical, telecommunications, electronics, or, as in this case, business intelligence—new technologies create new opportunities and therefore change that field. For business intelligence, new technologies have become available, including analytical database servers, mobile business intelligence tools, in-database analytics, massive internal memory, highly parallelized hardware platforms, cloud, and solid state disk technology. All of these new technologies can dramatically expand an organization's analytical and reporting features: it will support forms of decision making that most organizations have not even considered yet, and it will allow organizations to analyze data in only a few minutes that would otherwise have taken days with older technologies.

Another obvious change relates to the new groups of users interested in applying business intelligence. Currently, most users of business intelligence systems are decision makers at strategical and tactical management levels. In most cases these users can work perfectly with data that isn't 100 percent up to date. Data that is a day, a week, or maybe even a month old is more than sufficient for them. The change is that currently decision makers working at the operational level are attracted by business intelligence. They understand its potential value for them, and therefore they want to exploit the power of reporting and analytical tools. However, in most cases, they can't operate with old data. They want to analyze *operational data*, data that is 100 percent (or at least close to 100 percent) up to date.

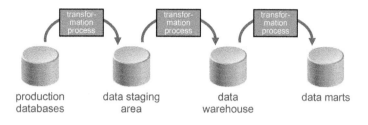

FIGURE 1.2

Many business intelligence systems are based on a chain of databases and transformation processes.

All of these changes, especially faster decision making, are hard to implement in current business intelligence systems because it requires a dramatic redesign. This is because most business intelligence systems that were developed over the last 20 years are based on a chain of databases (Figure 1.2). Data is transformed and copied from one database to another until it reaches an endpoint: a database being accessed by a reporting or analytical tool. Each transformation process extracts, cleanses, integrates, and transforms the data, and then loads it into the next database in the chain. This process continues until the data reaches a quality level and form suitable for the reporting and analytical tools. These transformation processes are normally referred to as *ETL* (Extract Transform Load).

This chain of databases and transformation processes is long, complex, and highly interconnected. Each change made to a report or to data can lead to a myriad of changes throughout the chain. It might take days, or even weeks, before an apparently simple change has been implemented throughout the chain. The effect is that the business intelligence department can't keep up with the speed of change required by the business. This leads to an application backlog and has a negative impact on the decision-making speed and quality of the organization. In addition, because so many transformation processes are needed and each of them takes time, it's hard to deliver operational data at an endpoint of the chain, such as a data mart.

What is needed is an agile architecture that is easy to change, and the best way to do that is to create an architecture that consists of fewer components, which means fewer databases and fewer transformation processes. When you have a small number of components, there are fewer things that require changes. In addition, fewer components simplifies the architectures, which also increases the agility level.

This is where data virtualization comes in. In a nutshell, data virtualization is an alternative technology of transforming available data into the form needed for reporting and analytics. It requires fewer databases and fewer transformation processes. In other words, using data virtualization in a business intelligence system leads to a shorter chain. Fewer databases have to be developed and managed, and there will be fewer transformation processes. The bottom line is that applying data virtualization simplifies business intelligence architectures and therefore leads to more agile business intelligence architectures that fit the business intelligence needs of current organizations: simple is more agile.

1.3 **Introduction to Virtualization**

The term *data virtualization* is based on the word *virtualization*. Virtualization is not a new concept in the IT industry. Probably the first application of virtualization was in the 1960s when IBM used this concept to split mainframes into separate virtual machines, which made it possible for one machine to run multiple applications concurrently. Also in the 1960s, virtual memory was introduced using a technique called *paging*. Memory virtualization was used to simulate more memory than was physically available in a machine. Nowadays, almost everything can be virtualized, including processors, storage (see [3]), networks, data centers (see [4]), and operating systems. VMWare and Cloud can also be regarded as virtualization technologies.

In general, virtualization means that applications can use a resource without any concern for where it resides, what the technical interface is, how it has been implemented, which platform it uses, and how much of it is available. A virtualization solution encapsulates the resource in such a way that all those technical details become hidden and the application can work with a simpler interface.

The first time I was involved in a project in which a resource was virtualized was very early in my career. An application had to be written that could work with different user interface technologies. One was called *Teletext* and was developed for TV sets, and another was a character-based terminal. Being the technical designer, I decided to develop an API that the application would use to get data on a screen and to get input back. This API was a layer of software that would hide the user interface technology in use for the rest of the application. Without knowing it, I had designed a user interface virtualization layer. Since then, I've always tried to design systems in such a way that implementation details of certain technologies are hidden for other parts of an application in order to simplify development.

1.4 **What Is Data Virtualization?**

Data virtualization is one of those forms of virtualization. As the term indicates, the encapsulated resource is data. In a nutshell, when data virtualization is applied, an intermediate layer is provided that hides for applications most of the technical aspects of how and where data is stored (Figure 1.3).

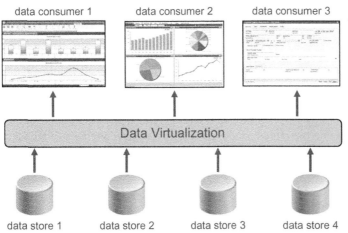

FIGURE 1.3

When data virtualization is applied, all the data sources are presented as one integrated data source.

Because of that layer, applications don't need to know where all the data is stored physically, where the database servers run, what the required API is, which database language to use, and so on. To every application using data virtualization, it feels as if it's accessing one large database.

If we apply the description used for virtualization in the previous section to data virtualization, we get this: Data virtualization means that applications can use data without any concern for where it resides, what the technical interface is, how it has been implemented, which platform it uses, and how much of it is available. A data virtualization solution encapsulates data sources in such a way that all those technical details are hidden and the application can work with a simpler interface.

In Figure 1.3 and throughout the book we use the terms *data consumer* and *data store*. The term *data consumer* refers to any application that retrieves, enters, or manipulates data. For example, a data consumer can be an online data entry application, a reporting application, a statistical model, an Internet application, a batch application, or an RFID sensor. Likewise, the term *data store* is used to refer to any source of data: a table in an SQL database, a simple text file, an XML document, a spreadsheet, a web service, a sequential file, an HTML page, and so on. In some cases, a data store is just a passive file and in others it's a data source including the software to access the data, such as a database server and a web service.

When a data virtualization solution is used, it resides between the data consumers and the data stores. The data consumers access the data through the data virtualization layer and the data virtualization layer hides the data stores.

1.5 Data Virtualization and Related Concepts

Data virtualization is closely related to some other concepts that are well known in the IT industry, such as encapsulation, information hiding, abstraction data federation, data integration, and enterprise information integration. In this section, these concepts and their relationship with data virtualization are explained.

Be aware that different definitions of all these concepts exist and that some people regard some of these concepts as synonyms. The reason for this mixup has been worded quite well by Edward Berard in [5]: "Abstraction, information hiding, and encapsulation are very different but highly related, concepts. It is not hard to see how abstraction, information hiding, and encapsulation became confused with one another."

1.5.1 Data Virtualization versus Encapsulation and Information Hiding

Forty years ago, in 1972, David L. Parnas wrote the groundbreaking article "On the Criteria to Be Used in Decomposing Systems into Modules" (see [6]). It has been republished a few times. In this legendary article he explains how important it is for applications to be developed in such a way that they become independent of the structure of the stored data. The big advantage of this concept is that if one changes, the other might not have to change. In addition, by hiding technical details, applications become more maintainable, or, to use more modern terms, the applications become more agile. Parnas called this *information hiding* and explains its purpose as "to make inaccessible certain details that should not affect other parts of a system."

Many years later, the term *encapsulation* became more common in the computing industry to refer to the notion of information hiding. Blair defines encapsulation as follows (see [7]):

Encapsulation (also information hiding) consists of separating the external aspects of an object which are accessible to other objects, from the internal implementation details of the object, which are hidden from other objects.

Here is an alternative and comparable definition by James Rumbaugh (see [8]):

Encapsulation (also known as information hiding) prevents clients from seeing its inside view, where the behavior of the abstraction is implemented.

If we translate this to the world of databases, encapsulation is about hiding the implementation aspects of some data store, such as its API, language, storage format, location, access mechanism, and so on. If this is done correctly, the *data consumers* see a simplified interface for accessing data. They don't have to concern themselves with all those technical details. These are encapsulated in the same way that the complex workings of my car's engine are encapsulated by a simple dashboard. Note that in both definitions encapsulation is seen as a synonym for information hiding. We will take the same stand on this.

This whole notion of encapsulation is also very similar to what the founder of the relational model, E. F. (Ted) Codd, called *physical data independence*. He used this term in an article he wrote when he received the ACM Turing Award in 1981 (see [9]). The objective of physical data independence is to hide for a data consumer how data is stored and how data is accessed. In a way, this is why in an SQL query we only have to specify *what* data we want and not *how* that data must be retrieved. The latter is the responsibility of the database server. SQL encapsulates all the technical details.

Data virtualization offers encapsulation. Data consumers accessing data via a data virtualization layer don't see all the technical details. Whether they are retrieving data stored in an SQL database, a spreadsheet file, or from an external website, all those particular technical details are hidden.

1.5.2 Data Virtualization versus Abstraction

As with encapsulation, many definitions of *abstraction* exist. We present the one of D. T. Ross (see [10]):

Abstraction is a process whereby we identify the important aspects of a phenomenon and ignore its details.

The easiest way to explain abstraction is by taking a database example. Imagine that a database consists of many tables, but it is likely that not all of those tables and their columns are relevant to every data consumer. For each data consumer it would be easier if only the relevant tables, columns, and rows are shown. When abstraction is applied, all the nonrelevant tables, columns, and rows are hidden. Abstraction in a database also means that if it's more convenient for a data consumer to process data in an aggregated way, it should only see the data in an aggregated way and it should not see all the detailed rows of data. Abstraction means that only the relevant data is presented in the form that the data consumers need, and the rest is hidden. Codd called this concept *logical data independence*. In most SQL database servers, abstraction is implemented with views.

Data virtualization offers abstraction. For each data consumer, it can present the data in the required form.

1.5.3 **Data Virtualization versus Data Federation**

Very often, the term *data virtualization* is associated with the term *data federation*. Some consider them synonyms, but others see data virtualization as an extended form of data federation. In this section we explain what the relationship is between these two and what the differences are.

Federation stems from the Latin words *foedus* and *foederis*, which both mean treaty, agreement, and contract. In most cases, if the term *federation* is used, it refers to combining autonomously operating objects. For example, states can be federated to form one country, or companies can operate as a federation.

According to businessdictionary.com, a federation is an organization that consists of a group of smaller organizations or companies that works to bring attention to issues that are of importance to all of its members. Each organization that comprises the federation maintains control over its own operations. For example, a group of small businesses in a related industry might form a federation in order to lobby the government for laws favorable to small businesses. And according to Merriam-Webster. com, a *federation* is an encompassing political or societal entity formed by uniting smaller or more localized entities. Each member (for example, an individual federate state) can operate independently as well.

If we apply this general explanation to the term *data federation*, it means combining autonomous data stores to form one large data store. From this, we can derive the following definition:

> *Data federation is an aspect of data virtualization where the data stored in a heterogeneous set of autonomous data stores are made accessible to data consumers as one integrated data store by using on-demand data integration.*

This definition is based on the following concepts:

- *Data virtualization:* Data federation is an aspect of data virtualization. Note that data virtualization doesn't always imply data federation. For example, if the data in one particular data store have to be virtualized for a data consumer, no need exists for data federation. But data federation always leads to data virtualization because if a set of data stores is presented as one, the aspect of distribution is hidden for the applications.
- *Heterogeneous set of data stores:* Data federation should make it possible to bring data together from data stores using different storage structures, different access languages, and different APIs. A data consumer using data federation should be able to access different types of database servers and files with various formats; it should be able to integrate data from all those data sources; it should offer features for transforming the data; and it should allow the data consumers and tools to access the data through various APIs and languages.
- *Autonomous data stores:* Data stores accessed by data federation are able to operate independently—in other words, they can be used outside the scope of data federation.
- *One integrated data store:* Regardless of how and where data is stored, it should be presented as one integrated data set. This implies that data federation involves transformation, cleansing, and possibly even enrichment of data.
- *On-demand data integration:* This refers to *when* the data from a heterogeneous set of data stores is integrated. With data federation, integration takes place on the fly, and not in batch. When the data consumers ask for data, only then is data accessed and integrated. So the data is not stored in an integrated way but remain in their original location and format.

Now that we know what data federation and data virtualization mean, we can make the following statements. First, data federation always implies multiple data stores, whereas data virtualization does not. Second, data federation can be seen as an aspect of data virtualization.

Final note: Until a few years ago, all the products available for data virtualization were called *data federation servers*. The main reason was that these products were primarily developed to make multiple databases look like one. Nowadays they are called *data virtualization servers*. The reason for the name change is that the "new" data virtualization servers offer much more functionality than the older ones. For example, some of those new products even support data modeling, data cleansing, and database language translation. Occasionally, this name change does cause confusion. In this book, we use the term *data virtualization server*.

1.5.4 Data Virtualization versus Data Integration

Data virtualization has a strong relationship with another concept that has already been mentioned a few times in this book: *data integration*. According to SearchCRM, integration (from the Latin word *integer*, meaning "whole" or "entire") generally means combining parts in such a way that they work together or form a whole. If data from different data sources are brought together, we talk about data integration:

> Data integration is the process of combining data from a possibly heterogeneous set of data stores to create one unified view of all that data.

Data integration involves, for example, joining data, transforming data values, enriching data, and cleansing data values. What this definition of data integration doesn't encompass is how the integration takes place. For example, maybe that original data is copied from its source data stores, transformed and cleansed, and subsequently stored in another data store. Another solution would be if the integration takes place live. For example, an application accesses multiple data sources, retrieves data from all those data sources, and integrates them. Another approach is that the source data stores are modified in such a way that data is transformed and cleansed. It's like changing the sources themselves in such a way that almost no transformation and cleansing are required when data is brought together.

But what exactly does data integration encompass?

- *Data joining:* Data joining refers to the process where data from different data stores are brought together. For example, data in the Customers table from one database has to be merged with data in the Orders table from another database. And let's assume both tables have a column called Customer Number, and every customer number in the Orders table appears also in the Customers table.
- *Data transformation:* Data transformation refers to the process where data values are transformed. Examples of data transformation are the dash separating the area code and the subscriber number in telephone numbers is removed, the first and last names of customers are concatenated into one string, and the state code is replaced by a state name. With data transformation, correct values are transformed into other correct values.
- *Data cleansing:* Data cleansing refers to the process where defective data values are corrected. For example, a column called Gender contains the values Woman, W, and F to indicate that certain employees are female. These values have to be changed into one standard code—for example, F. This is a simple example of data cleansing. Other examples are correcting misspellings of

customer names, filling up missing values, and deduplicating records. The essential difference between transformation and cleansing is that with the former, correct values are transformed into correct values, and with the latter, defective values are changed into correct values.

In many situations where data virtualization is applied, data integration is applied as well. But data virtualization does not require data integration. It depends on the number of data stores being accessed. For example, if all the data being virtualized come from one and the same data store, there is no need for data integration. Data federation, on the other hand, always requires data integration because data federation implies bringing data from different data sources together. Otherwise, there is no need for data federation.

Does that mean that data integration and data federation are the same thing? Are they synonyms? The answer is no. Data integration is an aspect of data virtualization. In many situations, with data virtualization, data has to be integrated, but not always. Maybe data virtualization is only used to transform the technical interface of a data store into one that is more suitable for a particular data consumer.

1.5.5 Data Virtualization versus Enterprise Information Integration

A term that is seldom used today is *Enterprise Information Integration* (EII). Wikipedia (on July 8, 2011) defines EII as follows:

> *Enterprise Information Integration (EII) is a process of information integration using data abstraction to provide a unified interface (known as uniform data access) for viewing all the data within an organization and a single set of structures and naming conventions (known as uniform information representation) to represent this data.*

According to this definition, the goal of EII is to make a large set of heterogeneous data sources appear as a single, homogeneous data source to a user or system. In other words, EII is quite synonymous with data virtualization. As data federation, it can be seen as an "older" term for data virtualization.

1.6 Definition of Data Virtualization

Data virtualization has been defined by several authors. In this book we use the following definition:

> *Data virtualization is the technology that offers data consumers a unified, abstracted, and encapsulated view for querying and manipulating data stored in a heterogeneous set of data stores.*

This definition leans on a number of concepts explained in the previous sections. We repeat them briefly here.

Data virtualization offers a *unified* view of the data, implying that data consumers don't see or have to know that the data they're accessing might be coming from multiple data stores. Data virtualization hides the fact that the data is being integrated to form that unified view.

Encapsulated means that the data virtualization technology hides the technical details for accessing the data. To data consumers, the location of the data, the storage structure, which API to use, which access language to use, the applied storage technology, and all the other technical details should be transparent.

Data virtualization offers an *abstracted* view of the data to the data consumers. They will see only relevant data, and they will see the data in a form that fits their needs. So data might be presented on a detailed level or on an aggregated level. It might be that data from different data stores is joined, values might be concatenated or transformed, and so on—whatever works best for the data consumers.

The definition contains the terms *querying* and *manipulating* to emphasize that data virtualization allows the data in the data stores to be queried, but it can also be deleted, inserted, and updated (if allowed by the data stores).

And finally, *heterogeneous* means that if multiple data stores are accessed, they might have different storage formats, database languages, and APIs. For example, in Figure 1.3, data store 1 could be an SQL database, number 2 an XML document, number 3 a NoSQL database, and number 4 a spreadsheet file. A data virtualization layer should still be able to present to the data consumers all the data in those data stores as one unified data store.

1.7 Technical Advantages of Data Virtualization

In most cases, accessing a data store directly is easy for a data consumer. For example, if a table in an SQL database is accessed, the data consumer supplies a user ID and a password, the name of the database, and some other technical details, and immediately it can access the data through SQL statements. The same applies when a data consumer needs to access an XML document or spreadsheet.

If accessing data stores is so easy, then why is data virtualization needed? Using a data virtualization layer offers numerous technical advantages. They are classified in three groups. The first group of advantages apply if only one data store is accessed by a data consumer:

- *Database language and API translation:* Maybe the database language and API offered by a data store are not ideal for the data consumers, or maybe it's a language not supported by them. Maybe the database server supports SQL through the JDBC API, while the data consumer would prefer to use the language MDX, XQuery, CQL, or a set of Java classes. A data virtualization layer is able to translate the language and API supported by the data store to the language and API convenient for the data consumer.
- *Data store independency:* Many SQL database servers support the SQL standard, meaning they have all implemented comparable SQL dialects. Still, differences exist. Data virtualization can hide those differences, making it possible to replace the current database server by another, if needed. This might be necessary if the database server in use is, for example, too expensive, too slow, or not secure enough. It could also be that a non-SQL-based data store has to be replaced by an SQL-based one. Again, if a data virtualization is in place, this might not be that difficult. Data virtualization makes data consumers independent of a particular data store technology, making the data consumers more portable. It will become easier to use the right data store technology at the right time.
- *Minimal data store interference:* A data consumer can cause *interference* (or *workload contention*) on the data store it's accessing. Its queries might be so resource intensive that other data consumers experience performance degradation. Most data virtualization products support a

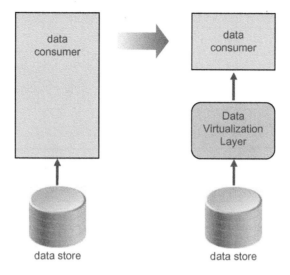

FIGURE 1.4

Data virtualization reduces the amount of code required for accessing data. The size of each rectangular box labeled data consumer represents the amount of code required.

caching mechanism. If this is switched on, a copy of the data in the data store is kept and managed by the data virtualization layer. From then on, the data consumer accesses the data in the cache instead of the data in the data store, thus minimizing interference on the source data store.

To summarize, data virtualization simplifies application development because it reduces the amount of code required for accessing the necessary data in the right way and form (Figure 1.4).

The second set of advantages relates to *meta data specifications,* such as the structures of tables, transformation and cleansing operations, aggregations, and so on. When data virtualization is used, meta data specifications only have to be implemented once, and it is not necessary to replicate them to multiple data consumers. In other words, data consumers share and reuse these specifications:

- *Simplified table structures:* The structure of a table implemented in a data store can be complex, making it hard for the data consumers to access the data. Complex table structures lead to complex queries for retrieving data, and that complicates application development. With data virtualization the transformation of a complex to a simpler and more appropriate table structure can be defined. This is done through meta data specifications which are defined only once and can be used by many data consumers. This simpler structure simplifies application development and maintenance.

- *Centralized data transformation:* Particular data values in a data store might have formats that aren't suitable for some data consumers. Imagine that all the data consumers prefer to process telephone number values as pure digits and not in the form where the area code is separated by a dash from the subscriber number. A data virtualization layer can implement this transformation, and all the data consumers can use it. These transformation specifications are regarded as meta data specifications.

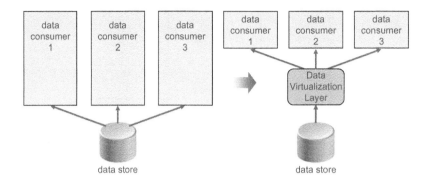

FIGURE 1.5

Multiple data consumers share the same specifications if data virtualization is applied, which simplifies application development and results in more consistent application behavior. The size of each recangular box labeled data consumer represents the amount of code required.

- *Centralized data cleansing:* Some data values in a data store might not be correct. Imagine that the column Gender in a table contains three different values to indicate Female. In that case, all the data consumers accessing these data values have to include code to transform those incorrect values to the correct ones. It would be better if this transformation is handled by a data virtualization layer that only shows the correct values to the data consumers. This solution is better than one where those data cleansing rules are replicated to all the data consumers.

If multiple data consumers use the same data virtualization layer, they share the same meta data specifications (Figure 1.5). This simplifies application development and will result in more consistent application behavior and more consistent results.

The third group of advantages relates to integrating data from multiple data stores:

- *Unified data access:* Different data stores might be using different storage formats. For example, some of the data might be stored in not processed yet SQL databases; some in Excel spreadsheets; some in index sequential files; some in NoSQL databases, such as Hadoop and MongoDB; some in databases supporting other database languages than SQL; and some in XML documents; some might even be hidden in HTML-based web pages. A data virtualization layer can offer one unified API and database language to access all these different storage formats, therefore simplifying data access for the data consumers. They will only have to support one language and one API.
- *Centralized data integration:* If multiple data consumers access multiple data stores, each and every data consumer has to include code responsible for integrating those data stores. The consequence of this is that many data integration solutions are replicated across data consumers (Figure 1.6). A data virtualization layer centralizes that integration code, and all the data consumers share that integration code.
- *Consistent reporting results:* If each data consumer includes its own integration solution, it's difficult to guarantee that data is integrated in the same way and according to the same rules. If this is not guaranteed, the odds are that data consumers will receive different and inconsistent results. If all the integration solutions are handled by a data virtualization layer, the chance increases that results are consistent.

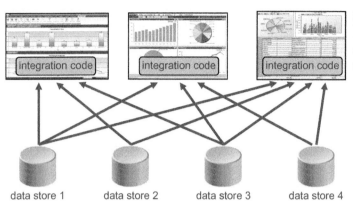

FIGURE 1.6

Integrating data stores without a data virtualization server leads to duplication of integration code.

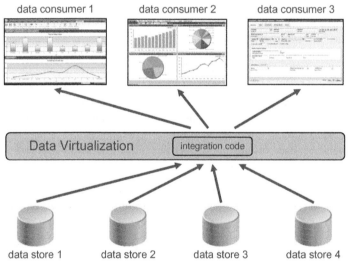

FIGURE 1.7

Integrating data stores using a data virtualization server leads to centralization and sharing of integration code.

- *Efficient distributed data access:* When data from multiple data stores is joined, a performance question is always where and how the join is processed: Is all the data first shipped to the data consumer, will the latter process the join, or should the data from one data store be shipped to another? Will that other data store process the join, or will some other processing strategy be used? A developer should not be concerned with such an issue. Therefore, this is a task taken over by a data virtualization layer.

All these advantages prevent meta data specifications for data integration being replicated across multiple data consumers (see Figure 1.6). Applying data virtualization centralizes these specifications, as indicated in Figure 1.7.

1.8 Different Implementations of Data Virtualization

Technically, many different alternatives are available for implementing a data virtualization layer. Here are a few examples:

- With a dedicated *data virtualization server*, multiple data stores look like only one. The applications see one large data store, while in fact the data is stored in several data stores.
- An *enterprise service bus* (ESB) can be used to develop a layer of services that allow standardized access to data. The data consumers invoking these services don't have to understand where and how the data is stored, its storage structure, its interface of the original source, or the other technical details. They will only see, for example, a SOAP or ReST (Representational State Transfer) interface. In this case, the ESB is the data virtualization layer. For more information on ESBs, see [11].
- Placing data stores in the cloud is also a form of data virtualization. To access a data store, the data consumers work with the cloud API and have no idea where the data itself resides. Whether the data is stored and managed locally or remotely is completely transparent.
- In a way, building up a virtual database in memory with data loaded from multiple physical databases can also be regarded as data virtualization. The storage structure, the API, and the location of the real data is transparent to the application accessing the in-memory database. This solution is sometimes referred to as *in-memory analytics*.
- *Object-relational mappers* (ORM) are tools that convert data structures from data stores to the concepts used in an object-oriented programming model, such as Java and C#. For example, an ORM might be able to convert the flat table structures of an SQL database to the object-oriented concepts used in Java. The effect is that the Java programmers don't have to understand and deal with the characteristics of the SQL concepts but purely with Java concepts. Examples of ORMs are Hibernate, NHibernate, and iBATIS.
- Organizations can also develop their own data virtualization layer that hides where and how data is stored.

Many more ways of developing a data virtualization layer exist, but because this book is aimed at business intelligence systems, the focus is on the first alternative: *data virtualization servers*. A data virtualization server is a dedicated product designed to support data virtualization, meaning it can present multiple heterogeneous data stores as one logical data store to data consumers. Accessing a data virtualization server is very similar to logging on to a database server. Without the data consumers knowing it, the data from different data stores is joined (even from data stores using different storage models), and the data is transformed, cleansed, aggregated, and so on.

The reason this book focuses on data virtualization servers is that internally these products have been optimized to handle large sets of data, not just record-for-record processing, and they are designed to process SQL queries. Both fit the requirements of typical business intelligence reports and tools well. But note that most of them can be deployed in other types of environments, such as service-oriented architectures (see Chapter 9), customer data integration applications, and Internet applications.

1.9 Overview of Data Virtualization Servers

Table 1.1 lists some of the data virtualization servers that are capable of supporting business intelligence systems. The expectation is that this market will grow now that organizations are becoming

Table 1.1 Overview of Data Virtualization Servers

Data Virtualization Server	Vendor
Composite Data Virtualization Platform	Composite Software
Dataflux Federation Server	SAS
Denodo Platform	Denodo Technologies
IBM InfoSphere Federation Server	IBM
Informatica Data Services	Informatica
Information Builders iWay Enterprise Information Integration Suite	Information Builders
Queplix Virtual Data Manager	Queplix
Red Hat JBoss Enterprise Data Services Platform	Red Hat
Stone Bond Enterprise Enabler Virtuoso	Stone Bond Technologies

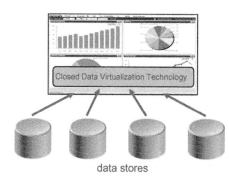

data stores

FIGURE 1.8

Closed data virtualization technology offers only one API for one particular tool or a restricted set of tools.

aware of the power and business value of data virtualization and begin to realize how these products can increase the agility of their business intelligence systems.

1.10 Open versus Closed Data Virtualization Servers

Many products are available that offer some form of data virtualization solution. Some of these products are stand-alone products, and some include data virtualization technology. For example, various analytical and reporting tools come with their own built-in data virtualization technology. For example, QlikTech's QlikView is more than capable of accessing and integrating data stored in a heterogeneous set of data stores. The same applies for the Universe concept in SAP/ Business Objects, which can be seen as data virtualization technology as well, and for the tools of IBM/Cognos, SAS, and many others. However, all the specifications entered in these products can only be used by the tools themselves (or tools from the same vendor); therefore, these specifications can't be shared.

Technically, these data virtualization technologies, although they support access to a heterogeneous set of data stores, usually offer only one API for accessing the data: the API required by that particular tool. Therefore, we refer to them as *closed data virtualization technologies* (Figure 1.8).

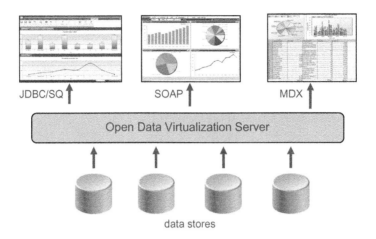

FIGURE 1.9

An open data virtualization server offers multiple technical interfaces for different data consumers.

An *open data virtualization server*, like closed data virtualization technology, can access many different data stores. However, the difference between the two is that an open solution supports multiple APIs for accessing the data (Figure 1.9). The same data can be accessed through, for example, JDBC with SQL, ODBC with SQL, SOAP/XML, and MDX. The data virtualization server is reponsible for translating the API and language supported by the data stores to the ones needed by the data consumers.

Because multiple APIs are supported, many different tools from different vendors can exploit an open data virtualization server. The effect is that the meta data specifications entered in a data virtualization server can be shared. For example, if we define that the Northern Sales Region doesn't include the Washington State, each and every tool that accesses the data virtualization server can use that same specification, whether it's Excel, JasperSoft, or SAS Analytics. This improves the maintainability of the environment, but it also minimizes the chance that users using different tools see inconsistent results.

1.11 **Other Forms of Data Integration**

With data virtualization, data can be integrated, but it's not the only solution for integrating data from different data stores. As indicated in Section 1.4, different technical solutions exist to integrate data, including ETL, ELT, and replication. This section briefly explains those other styles. For more information, see Section 2.7.

ETL (Extract Transform Load) is a form of data integration heavily used in data warehouse environments. With ETL, integration is realized by copying data from mutiple *source data stores* and by storing the integrated and transformed result in a separate, *target data store*. The latter is needed to hold the integrated data. A target data store might be the data store that is being accessed by the data consumers (Figure 1.10). Because all the data in a target data store is somehow derived from the data in the source data stores, it's also referred to as a *derived data store*.

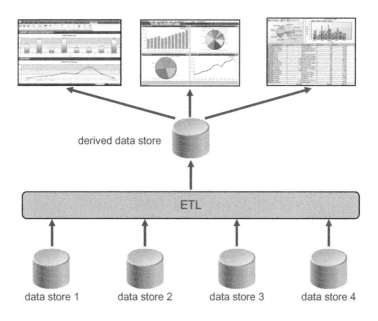

FIGURE 1.10

With an ETL solution, the result of integrating data is stored in a derived data store before the data can be used by data consumers.

During the copying process, data is joined, transformed, and cleansed. Usually, this copying process is scheduled. At certain time intervals new data is extracted from the data sources, integrated, and stored in the derived data store. If data virtualization offers on-demand integration, then ETL offers *scheduled integration*.

ELT (Extract Load Transform) is, in a way, a special version of ETL. With ELT, data is also copied to a derived data store and transformations is also scheduled. The main difference between ETL and ELT is the order in which actions take place. In ETL the data stored in the derived data store has been transformed and cleansed. In ELT extracted data is first stored in the derived data store and subsequently transformed and cleansed, leading to a second form of storage (Figure 1.11). In a way, all the data is stored twice.

The third data integration solution is called *replication*. Whereas with ETL and ELT, copy processes are scheduled and data is sent over in batches, replication is initiated when source data has been inserted or existing data has been updated or deleted. In fact, right after such a change takes place, the data is copied to a target data store. So data is not copied in batches, but more or less as individual records or small groups of records. Usually, replication only takes a few microseconds.

Because with replication, copying takes place right after the source data has been changed and because the copying process itself is very fast (only a few records), the data in the target data store has a very low latency, which is close to up to date.

Replication is usually classified as a data integration technology, but maybe this is not really correct. Although some of the data replication technologies can replicate and integrate data from

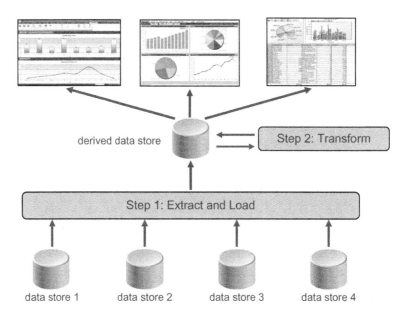

FIGURE 1.11

With an ELT solution, data is first copied to a derived data store before it is integrated.

multiple data sources, it's not their strength. In other words, replication is more a fast data copy technology with limited integration and transformation features than a data integration technology. Actually, the strengths of replication are the speed with which data can be copied and the ability to keep the data in a target data store synchronized with the source data store.

1.12 The Modules of a Data Virtualization Server

Internally, every data virtualization server has its own technical architecture, but on a conceptual level, all of them consist of at least two main modules: a design module and a runtime module. In addition, there is a dictionary for storing meta data specifications. These three are shown in Figure 1.12.

The *design module* is used by analysts, designers, and possibly users to enter virtualization specifications. This is where specifications such as concept definitions; data models; and specifications for transformation, cleansing, and integration are entered. All these specifications are stored in a dictionary.

The *runtime module* is the module used when data consumers access the virtualization layer. It's the module that handles all the incoming requests. It determines the best strategy for running the queries, knows how to access different data store technologies, knows how to integrate data, and so on. It consists of a scheduler, a storage engine, a cache manager, a query optimizer, and so on.

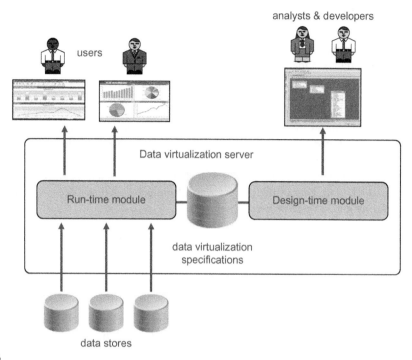

FIGURE 1.12

A data virtualization server is made up of a design module, a runtime module, and a dictionary for storing all the specifications.

1.13 **The History of Data Virtualization**

The history of the term *data virtualization* is relatively young. When exactly the term was first coined is unclear. It looks as if Eric Broughton used the term first in a paper published in 2005 (see [12]). However, the concepts, some of the products, and the research are much older.

Because data virtualization products are so rich in functionality, many technologies contributed to their development. Therefore, to present a full picture of its history, we have to include the history of distributed databases, data federation, XSLT and XQuery, and mashups as well.

Distributed databases: Technologically, one of the key features of data virtualization servers is data federation: being able to efficiently join data from a heterogeneous set of data stores. The first time data federation technology was implemented was in *distributed database servers*. In a distributed database server, multiple independent database servers can operate as one logical database. This means that a data consumer can enter a query in which multiple tables managed by different database servers are joined. It's the task of the distributed database server to make all the databases look like one big database. In order to join data from different database servers, they had to implement data federation technology.

An important aspect is that such a *distributed join* is processed as efficiently as possible. When those products were first released, networks were still slow compared to nowadays, so most of the research was focused on minimizing the amount of network traffic. In the 1980s the first commercial database servers were released that supported distributed joins, including those of Ingres, Oracle, and Sybase.

Most of the initial research in data federation was done by IBM in their famous *System R* project*, which started way back in 1979 (see [13] and [14]). Another project that contributed heavily to distributed queries was the *Ingres project*, which eventually led to the open source SQL database server called Ingres, now distributed by Actian Corporation. System R* was a follow-up project to IBM's System R project. The latter is the birthplace of SQL. Eventually, System R led to the development of most of IBM's commercial SQL database servers, including SQL/DS and DB2. The *System R* project* was started in 1979. The goal of the project was to implement a distributed database server. See [15] for more information on these projects.

In the beginning, the focus of most of the research and development was on optimizing access in a homogeneous data store environment—for example, all data stores would be DB2, Ingres, or Oracle databases. Later on, products allowed distributed joins in heterogeneous environments, where other SQL-based or SQL-like database servers were involved. So the first distributed databases were the first products to support data federation technology, and data virtualization products of today inherit strongly from that technology.

Data federation servers: The first products that can claim to be dedicated data federation servers were IBM's DataJoiner and Information Builder's EDA/SQL (Enterprise Data Access). The former was introduced in the early 1990s and the latter in 1991. Both products were not database servers but were primarily products for integrating data from different data sources. Besides being able to access most SQL database servers, these were the first products able to access non-SQL databases. Both products have matured and have undergone several name changes. After being part of IBM DB2 Information Integrator, DataJoiner is currently called IBM InfoSphere Federation Server, and EDA/SQL has been renamed to iWay Data Hub and is part of Information Builders' Enterprise Information Integration Suite.

XSLT: Due to the success of XML, more and more data in organizations and on the Internet is available in the form of XML documents. To transform the structure of XML documents, a standard language was invented in 2000 called *XSLT*. The language is managed by the W3C standardization organization. It's a powerful language for performing transformations. Through the years, XSLT has been implemented by many vendors in many products. All those implementations have made XSLT a mature technology.

Because data virtualization servers have to be able to manipulate data that is formatted with XML, a language was needed for flattening the hierarchical structures of XML documents and for assigning a hierarchical structure to relational tables. XSLT is more than suitable for that. So the history of data virtualization is also tied to the history of XSLT. Again, data virtualization benefits from all the research and development done in this area.

XQuery: In 2001, the first working draft of the *XQuery* standard was released. XQuery is a query and functional programming language for querying, inserting, updating, and deleting collections of XML documents. It enables, among many other things, to join XML documents, extract elements from documents, select documents, and to join relational data with XML data. Compared to XSLT, XQuery is a more powerful query language, one that is, with respect to functionality, more comparable to SQL. See [16] for an extensive description of XQuery.

Like XSLT, the XQuery standard is managed by the W3C organization. Noteworthy is that one of the main designers of XQuery is Donald Chamberlin, who was also one of the two main designers of SQL. Currently, most of the SQL database servers support XQuery natively. For example, IBM's DB2, Oracle, and Microsoft's SQL Server can all process XQuery statements. All the research and development that has gone into merging SQL and XQuery can be exploited by the data virtualization vendors.

Mashups: The Internet is a treasure trove of valuable data. Unfortunately, a large portion of it is not available in a structured form; most of it can't be accessed the way data in an SQL database can be accessed. Most of that data is hidden (and sometimes deeply hidden) in HTML pages. For example, the prices of flights are available on the websites of airlines, and weather-related data is available from various weather sites, but it is not easy to get it out of those pages in a programmatic way. Those pages have to be navigated to get the right data. It's not simply a matter of sending SQL or XQuery statements to those websites.

Mashups are web-based applications that access data from different sources on the Internet and combine them in one application. For example, a mashup might combine crime numbers coming from one website with maps from Google. To be able to develop this type of application, the vendors of such tools need technology to navigate websites in an efficient and robust way. These tools should be able to understand all the languages used inside these HTML pages, including scripting languages. Mashup tools do exactly that.

The vendors of dedicated tools for developing mashups have invested heavily in making this navigation process as rock-solid as possible. Data virtualization servers should be able to extract data from those websites as well, and thus can benefit from all the development and research done in this area. In fact, at least one of the data virtualization vendors has a background in mashup technology. It's how they started.

As indicated, in the early 1990s the first data virtualization products, which were still called data federation products at that time, were introduced by IBM and Information Builders. After 2000, more vendors entered the market. For example, the first versions of both Composite Data Virtualization Platform and the Denodo Platform were released in 2002. MetaMatrix, founded in 1999, was acquired by Red Hat, and they released the MetaMatrix products as open source in 2011. Around 2010, more products were released, including Informatica Data Services and Queplix Virtual Data Manager.

For a long time, data virtualization was not considered strategic technology by most organizations. It was primarily seen as a technology for solving a particular technological problem. It wasn't regarded as a technology for making information systems more agile, but purely as a technological solution without a clear business benefit. Around 2008, this all changed. Business intelligence specialists in particular started to see the potential value of data virtualization. They were looking for a new and more agile form for doing data integration besides ETL, and they found data virtualization. By now, data virtualization has become mainstream technology; it's seen as a worthy alternative for data integration. What has also helped acceptance is that the products have reached a certain maturity level.

1.14 The Sample Database: World Class Movies

Most of the examples in this book use the same sample database. It's a production database for a fictitious company called World Class Movies (WCM), which is an online retail firm offering movies for sale and rental. The database consists of a set of tables to keep track of customer information and information on sales and rentals.

This database is a subset of the one designed by Roland Bouman and Jos van Dongen for their book *Pentaho Solutions; Business Intelligence and Data Warehousing with Pentaho and MySQL* (see [1]). If you're interested in loading the database yourself, go to the website www.r20.nl, find the cover of this book, click on it, and it will bring you to a page that shows where and how you can download the data. Not all the tables in this database are used in this book, only those displayed in the data model presented in Figure 1.13.

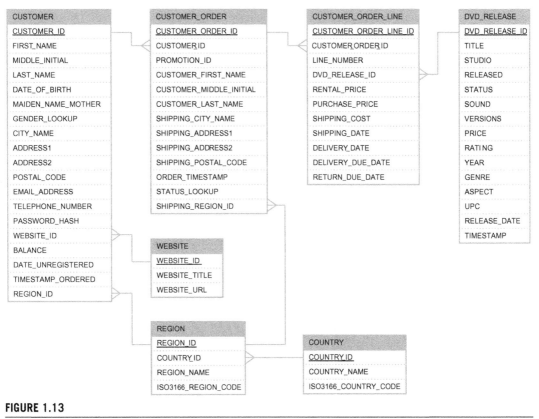

FIGURE 1.13

The data model of the sample World Class Movies database.

Here are the definitions of the tables:

The CUSTOMER table (145,373 rows):

```
CREATE TABLE CUSTOMER       (
    CUSTOMER_ID             INTEGER NOT NULL,
    FIRST_NAME              VARCHAR(30) NOT NULL,
    MIDDLE_INITIAL          CHAR(1) DEFAULT NULL,
    LAST_NAME               VARCHAR(30) NOT NULL,
    DATE_OF_BIRTH           DATE NOT NULL,
    MAIDEN_NAME_MOTHER      VARCHAR(30) NOT NULL,
    GENDER_LOOKUP           SMALLINT NOT NULL,
    CITY_NAME               VARCHAR(64) NOT NULL,
    ADDRESS1                VARCHAR(50) NOT NULL,
    ADDRESS2                VARCHAR(50) DEFAULT NULL,
    POSTAL_CODE             VARCHAR(10) NOT NULL,
    EMAIL_ADDRESS           VARCHAR(64) NOT NULL,
    TELEPHONE_NUMBER        CHAR(12) NOT NULL,
    PASSWORD_HASH           VARCHAR(41) NOT NULL,
    WEBSITE_ID              SMALLINT NOT NULL,
    BALANCE                 DECIMAL(6,2) NOT NULL DEFAULT '0.00',
    DATE_REGISTERED         DATE DEFAULT NULL,
    DATE_UNREGISTERED       DATE DEFAULT NULL,
    TIMESTAMP_CHANGED       CTIMESTAMP NOT NULL DEFAULT CURRENT_TIMESTAMP,
    REGION_ID               INTEGER NOT NULL DEFAULT '0',
    PRIMARY KEY             (CUSTOMER_ID))
```

The CUSTOMER_ORDER table (588,974 rows):

```
CREATE TABLE CUSTOMER_ORDER     (
    CUSTOMER_ORDER_ID           INTEGER NOT NULL,
    CUSTOMER_ID                 INTEGER NOT NULL,
    PROMOTION_ID                SMALLINT DEFAULT NULL,
    CUSTOMER_FIRST_NAME         VARCHAR(30) NOT NULL,
    CUSTOMER_MIDDLE_INITIAL     CHAR(1) DEFAULT NULL,
    CUSTOMER_LAST_NAME          VARCHAR(30) NOT NULL,
    SHIPPING_CITY_NAME          VARCHAR(64) NOT NULL,
    SHIPPING_ADDRESS1           VARCHAR(50) NOT NULL,
    SHIPPING_ADDRESS2           VARCHAR(50) DEFAULT NULL,
    SHIPPING_POSTAL_CODE        VARCHAR(10) NOT NULL,
    ORDER_TIMESTAMP             TIMESTAMP NOT NULL DEFAULT CURRENT_TIMESTAMP,
    STATUS_LOOKUP               SMALLINT NOT NULL,
    SHIPPING_REGION_ID          INTEGER NOT NULL DEFAULT '0',
    PRIMARY KEY                 (CUSTOMER_ORDER_ID))
```

The CUSTOMER_ORDER_LINE table (1,359,291 rows):

```
CREATE TABLE CUSTOMER_ORDER_LINE  (
    CUSTOMER_ORDER_LINE_ID          INTEGER NOT NULL,
    CUSTOMER_ORDER_ID               INTEGER NOT NULL,
    LINE_NUMBER                     SMALLINT NOT NULL,
    DVD_RELEASE_ID                  INTEGER NOT NULL,
    RENTAL_PRICE                    DECIMAL(6,2) DEFAULT NULL,
    PURCHASE_PRICE                  DECIMAL(6,2) DEFAULT NULL,
    SHIPPING_COST                   DECIMAL(6,2) DEFAULT NULL,
    SHIPPING_DATE                   DATE DEFAULT NULL,
    DELIVERY_DATE                   DATE DEFAULT NULL,
    DELIVERY_DUE_DATE               DATE DEFAULT NULL,
    RETURN_DUE_DATE                 DATE DEFAULT NULL,
    PRIMARY KEY                     (CUSTOMER_ORDER_LINE_ID),
    UNIQUE                          (CUSTOMER_ORDER_ID, LINE_NUMBER),
    UNIQUE                          (CUSTOMER_ORDER_ID, DVD_RELEASE_ID))
```

The DVD_RELEASE table (149,709 rows):

```
CREATE TABLE DVD_RELEASE            (
    DVD_RELEASE_ID                  INTEGER NOT NULL,
    TITLE                           VARCHAR(255) DEFAULT NULL,
    STUDIO                          VARCHAR(50) NOT NULL,
    RELEASED                        DATE DEFAULT NULL,
    STATUS                          VARCHAR(50) NOT NULL,
    SOUND                           VARCHAR(20) NOT NULL,
    VERSIONS                        VARCHAR(20) NOT NULL,
    PRICE                           DECIMAL(5,2) NOT NULL,
    RATING                          VARCHAR(10) NOT NULL,
    YEAR                            DATE DEFAULT NULL,
    GENRE                           VARCHAR(20) NOT NULL,
    ASPECT                          VARCHAR(10) NOT NULL,
    UPC                             CHAR(13) DEFAULT NULL,
    RELEASE_DATE                    DATE DEFAULT NULL,
    TIMESTAMP                       TIMESTAMP NOT NULL,
    PRIMARY KEY (DVD_RELEASE_ID))
```

The REGION table (75 rows):

```
CREATE TABLE REGION             (
    REGION_ID                   INTEGER NOT NULL,
    COUNTRY_ID                  SMALLINT NOT NULL,
    REGION_NAME                 VARCHAR(50) NOT NULL,
    ISO3166_REGION_CODE         CHAR(2) NOT NULL,
    PRIMARY KEY                 (REGION_ID))
```

The COUNTRY table (239 rows):

```
CREATE TABLE COUNTRY          (
    COUNTRY_ID                SMALLINT NOT NULL,
    COUNTRY_NAME              VARCHAR(50) NOT NULL,
    ISO3166_COUNTRY_CODE      CHAR(2) NOT NULL,
    PRIMARY KEY               (COUNTRY_ID),
    UNIQUE                    (COUNTRY_NAME),
    UNIQUE                    (ISO3166_COUNTRY_CODE))
```

The WEBSITE table (5 rows):

```
CREATE TABLE WEBSITE     (
    WEBSITE_ID           SMALLINT NOT NULL,
    WEBSITE_TITLE        VARCHAR(50) NOT NULL,
    WEBSITE_URI          VARCHAR(60) NOT NULL,
    PRIMARY KEY          (WEBSITE_ID),
    UNIQUE               (WEBSITE_TITLE),
    UNIQUE               (WEBSITE_URI))
```

1.15 **Structure of This Book**

Chapter 2 describes business intelligence and data warehousing. It explains the building blocks that make up most classic business intelligence systems, such as staging areas, operational data stores, data marts, and ETL tools. This chapter ends with a summary of the limitations of business intelligence systems with classic architectures. Chapters 3, 4, 5, and 6 describe how data virtualization products work under the hood—how they operate. These chapters will give readers a better understanding of what those products can and cannot do. Chapter 3 describes the concepts used by data virtualization servers, such as virtual tables, mappings, and nesting of virtual tables. Chapter 4 focuses on management and security aspects of data virtualization. Chapter 5 deals with optimization of queries. Chapter 6 focuses on caching of data. Query optimization and caching are both important internal concepts for data virtualization servers because they determine the performance, availability, and scalability of these products.

Chapter 7 describes in detail what the impact is of applying data virtualization in a business intelligence system. In detail it explains how data virtualization can simplify the entire architecture and how this will lead to a more agile architecture. This more agile architecture fits the changing world of business intelligence better, where decisions have to be made faster. In addition, business intelligence systems based on data virtualization are more suited to support forms of reporting and analytics that need access to operational data.

What if the data coming from data stores is not 100 percent correct, or what if some values are missing? How do we handle these and similar issues when data virtualization is applied in a business intelligence system? Chapter 8 addresses some of these standard design issues by presenting a set of design guidelines.

Service-oriented architectures (SOA) is another area that can benefit strongly from data virtualization. Chapter 9 explains what those benefits can be. It also touches on developing so-called data services and composite services.

The objective of master data management (MDM) is to ensure consistency of data and control of that same data in an organization. In real life, MDM is a set of processes and tools for guaranteeing data consistency and for enforcing this control. Data virtualization can be a powerful instrument for MDM. The relationship between MDM and data virtualization is described in Chapter 10.

Data virtualization servers offer various features to manage and control data. Regardless of how many features they offer, an organization still has to keep control over the quality and trustworthiness of data. This is the domain of information management. Chapter 11 describes how data virtualization will affect and enrich the following aspects of information management: database design, data governance, data cleansing, and data profiling.

In 2009, I introduced a new business intelligence architecture called *the data delivery platform*. This architecture for designing agile business intelligence systems is based on data virtualization. Chapter 12 explains what this architecture looks like, how data virtualization is applied, and its advantages and disadvantages.

Although data virtualization and its predecessors have been around for some time, we are still at the start of its evolution and commercial success. In the coming years, we will see the release of newer versions of existing data virtualization products and the introduction of new products. As to be expected, with every new version and product, new features will be added and the products will become more powerful, faster, and scalable. With every new version and product, the future of data virtualization will slowly reveal itself. Chapter 13 lists what the future has in store for data virtualization. In addition, the CTOs of three data virtualization vendors present their views on the future.

Business Intelligence and Data Warehousing

2.1 Introduction

Data virtualization can be deployed usefully in many application areas, including service-oriented architectures, master data management, Internet-based applications, and business intelligence, just to name a few. This book primarily focuses on how to exploit data virtualization in business intelligence systems. It discusses how it will make these systems more agile.

To clearly explain the difference between a business intelligence system that does deploy data virtualization and one that doesn't, this chapter describes the concepts and building blocks of classic business intelligence systems, such as central data warehouse, data mart, operational store, ETL, and replication. It also lists the limitations of those classic systems in regard to the support of modern-day user requirements. In addition the reasons why some of these data stores were introduced are being reinvestigated. This is necessarry for explaining why data virtualization can be beneficial.

Chapter 7 is a follow-up chapter for this one. After describing in the coming chapters how data virtualization products work, Chapter 7 explains what business intelligence systems look like when data virtualization is being applied.

Note: Readers who are familiar with business intelligence and data warehousing can skip this chapter. For those who need a more extensive introduction on business intelligence, see [17] and for data warehousing, see [18].

2.2 What Is Business Intelligence?

The success of most organizations is highly dependent on the quality of their decision making. Without a doubt, aspects such as the quality and price of the products and services delivered by an organization have a major impact on whether they are successful as well. For example, releasing a faulty car model on the market can lead to bankruptcy of a car manufacturer, or services that are priced too high can make an organization go out of business. But even if the quality is perfect and the price is acceptable, it's still not a guarantee for success. The reason is that one incorrect decision can destroy a product—and even a whole organization. For example, marketing a product incorrectly or distributing products inefficiently can lead to business disasters.

The field of *business intelligence* focuses on supporting and possibly improving the decision-making process of organizations. This is done by supplying an organization with the right data at the right time and in the right form. Note that business intelligence is not about making decisions but about supporting the process of making decisions.

Many definitions of business intelligence exist. In this book, we use the definition introduced by Boris Evelson of Forrester Research (see [19]):

Business intelligence is a set of methodologies, processes, architectures, and technologies that transform raw data into meaningful and useful information used to enable more effective strategic, tactical, and operational insights and decision making.

From this definition we can derive that business intelligence is not just a tool or some design technique but is everything needed to transform and present the right data in such a form that it will improve the decision-making process.

The term *business intelligence* was first coined in 1958 by Hans Peter Luhn in an article written for an IBM publication (see [20]). He defined business intelligence as "the ability to apprehend the interrelationships of presented facts in such a way as to guide action toward a desired goal." For a long time the term wasn't used until Howard Dresner, an analyst with Gartner, reintroduced it in 1989 (see [21]). The way Dresner defined it is very much in line with how we define it today. Since 1989, the term has caught on and has become widely accepted.

Before the term *business intelligence* became popular, the term *decision support* was used. It's unclear why the name changed, because this latter term conveys the meaning quite well. Nevertheless, to stay in line with other literature available on this topic, we use the term *business intelligence* throughout this book.

2.3 Management Levels and Decision Making

The topic of decision making is directly related to management and to the various management levels found in an organization. A popular way to identify different management levels is through the *management pyramid* (Figure 2.1).

The focus of *strategic management* is on the performance of the entire organization. Most of the decisions made on this level concern the entire organization. Some examples are: Should we acquire a new organization? Should we enter new markets? Should the organization be flattened? Should we outsource all IT? Decisions made by strategic management have long-term consequences and objectives.

FIGURE 2.1

In the classic management pyramid, three management levels are identified.

Tactical management is concerned with planning for and controlling the units in an organization, such as marketing, sales, and production. Normally their decision making has an impact on the short or medium term.

Operational management deals with the day-to-day operations of the organization. Examples of decisions made on this management level are: How many pallets of soda should be delivered at a particular store the next day? Are there enough drivers scheduled for all the parcels to be delivered? What measures should be taken now that an incoming airplane with many passengers who have to make connecting flights has been seriously delayed?

2.4 **Business Intelligence Systems**

A *business intelligence system* is defined as follows:

> *A business intelligence system is a solution developed to support and improve the decision-making process of an organization.*

A wide range of tools is available that is designed specifically to support this decision-making process. All those different tools can be classified in two main categories: *reporting tools* and *analytical tools*. Reporting tools allow users to study, filter, aggregate, summarize data and so on. In most cases, what is presented to the users is what *has* happened in the organization. Analytical tools are based on statistics, data mining, and operations research, and they support algorithms for forecasting, predictive analysis and optimization. Most organizations apply only reporting and haven't really discovered what analytics can mean for them. This is somewhat unfortunate, because it's a fact that applying analytics can improve the performance of organizations. Thomas Davenport summarized it as follows: "[There is] a striking relationship between the use of analytics and business performance. . . . High performers were 50 percent more likely to use analytics strategically . . . and five times as likely as low performers" (see [22]). To summarize, reporting tools show what has happened (looking backward), whereas analytical tools show what will possibly happen and how processes can be improved (looking forward).

Both categories of tools consist of multiple subcategories. Table 2.1 lists a number of those subcategories. Note that commercially available products don't always exactly fall into one of these categories. More and more, products offer sufficient functionality to belong to multiple categories.

Table 2.1 The Main Categories and Subcategories of Tools to Support Business Intelligence

Reporting Tools	Analytical Tools
Executive Reporting Tools	Predictive Modeling Tools
OLAP Tools	Forecasting Tools
Spreadsheets	Optimization Tools (Operations Research)
BAM/KPI/Dashboarding Tools	Statistical Analysis Tools
Data Visualization Tools	Data Mining Tools
Geo Visualization Tools	
Data Discovery/Exploitation Tools	

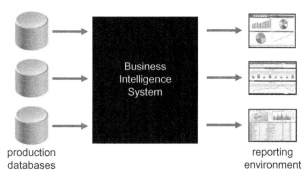

FIGURE 2.2

To users, a business intelligence system is, and should be, a black box.

What most users see of a business intelligence system is the user interface of their reporting or analytical tool, which is the way it should be. For users, what's behind the glass is and should be a black box (Figure 2.2). Users know that the data they need for their decision making is gathered in production systems, such as the invoice management system, the sales system, and the finance system. But how that data gets to the reports is not relevant for them. As long as they have access to the right data, as long as it is accurate (and trustworthy), as long as it has the right quality level, and as long as the performance of the tool is fast enough, they are satisfied. This is comparable to cell phones. If you call someone, you don't care how the connection is made—whether landlines or satellites are used—as long as the quality of the connection is good and there are no delays.

But to create those reports, a complex architecture has to be designed and developed to get the right data in the right form and at the right time from the production systems to the reports. It's the responsibility of the IT department to develop an architecture that can do that. Such an architecture consists of many components, tools, and data stores. All these components are described in the following sections.

2.5 The Data Stores of a Business Intelligence System

The following types of data stores can be found in business intelligence systems:

- Data warehouse
- Data mart
- Data staging area
- Operational data store
- Personal data store

2.5.1 The Data Warehouse

Just like engines need gas to run, reporting and analytical tools need data to operate. Without data, these products have no value. So somehow these tools need access to the data gathered in production databases, because that's where most of the available data needed by the users resides. Technically, it's possible to connect those reporting tools directly to the production databases (Figure 2.3). This

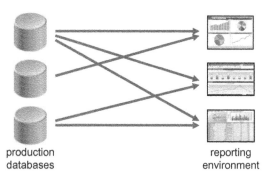

FIGURE 2.3

The reporting tools are connected directly to the production databases.

production databases

reporting environment

approach, although it seems attractive because of its simplicity, will not work in most organizations, for several reasons. The following are the most important ones:

- *Data integration:* Data needed by reports might be stored in multiple production databases. For example, all the data related to a customer might be spread out over multiple systems. This would mean that the reporting tool needs access to all those systems and is responsible for integrating all the data. This whole integration process makes report development more complex, and integration logic is repeated in many reports. It can possibly lead to inconsistent results.
- *Defective data:* Data stored in production systems might be faulty or missing. If reports are written directly on these data stores, they will have to deal with handling that defective data. This will be hard, because most of those tools don't support the right features for that. In addition, if it would be possible, how do we guarantee that all the different reports (possibly developed with different tools) transform the defective data to correct data in the same way?
- *Data consistency:* If different reporting tools use different technical solutions for integrating data from multiple production databases, how do we guarantee that the same integration logic is applied? In other words, how do we guarantee consistency of reports? It could well be that in two reports slightly different transformation rules are applied.
- *Historical data:* Not all production databases keep track of history. For example, in many systems, if, for example, the address of a customer is changed, the old address is overwritten. For certain reports and forms of analytics, historical data is needed. For example, you need historical data to be able to do regression analysis to get some sales predictions. So if production systems do not keep track of historical data, an additional data store is required to make reporting and analytics on historical data possible.
- *Interference:* The queries executed by the reporting tools on the production databases might cause too much interference on the production systems. A query might be so I/O intensive that users entering new data in the production environment feel a performance degradation. In other words, the business users will be blocking the users of the production systems and thus interfering with the production itself. This is unacceptable for every production environment.
- *Query performance:* Production databases are primarily designed and optimized to support production applications. The queries executed by the reporting tools can be quite complex. Running them on those production databases can lead to very poor performance. In fact, the performance can be so poor that users have to wait for hours before they see the results. In the meantime, that query creates a lot of interference.

- *External data:* In this type of solution there is not really room for analyzing external data. Imagine that a report wants to analyze the influence of weather conditions on the sales of particular products. For most organizations, weather-related data is external data and not stored in production databases. It has to be acquired from an external source. But where is it stored within the solution depicted in Figure 2.3?

To overcome most of those issues, business intelligence systems are usually developed around a *data warehouse*. A data warehouse is a separate data store designed specifically for reporting and analytics. Data is periodically copied from production databases to such a data warehouse (Figure 2.4). In most cases, an ETL-based solution is chosen to implement the integration process, which means that data in the data warehouse is periodically refreshed.

If we reconsider the disadvantages of reporting straight on the production databases, a data warehouse–based solution overcomes them as follows:

- *Data integration:* Data coming from different systems is integrated once and the data is stored in an integrated fashion. Reporting tools, therefore, don't have to deal with integration of data.
- *Defective data:* With an ETL script, defective data can be cleansed, which leads to a data warehouse containing less nondefective data. The consequence is that reports don't have to handle the defective data, and all of the reports share the result of the same cleansing operations.
- *Data consistency:* Because all reports extract data from the data warehouse in which data has been integrated, fewer problems will occur with the consistency of reports.
- *Historical data:* Even if production databases don't keep track of history, the data warehouse can be designed in such a way that it does. The data warehouse becomes the place to store all the "old" data.
- *Interference:* The queries generated by reporting and analytical tools will not run on production databases directly, causing no interference. However, periodically, data must be copied from the production databases to the data warehouse, which is like a complex query. But this can be done at night or over the weekend when there is no or limited usage of the production systems.
- *Query performance:* The data warehouse can be designed and optimized specifically for the reporting queries only. This will improve query performance.
- *External data:* If external data is needed for reporting, it can be stored in the data warehouse and becomes as easy to access as internal data.

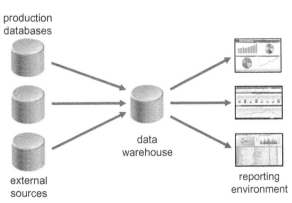

production
databases

data
warehouse

external
sources

reporting
environment

FIGURE 2.4

The data warehouse is a special data store designed specifically to support business intelligence.

Several definitions of data warehouse exist. We use Bill Inmon's definition because of its widespread usage in the industry. This definition was introduced in one of his popular books on data warehousing entitled *Building the Data Warehouse*, which was published in the 1990s (see [23]):

A data warehouse is a subject-oriented, integrated, time-variant, nonvolatile collection of data in support of management's decision-making process.

Note: In his more recent book, *DW 2.0—The Architecture for the Next Generation of Data Warehousing*, he updated the end of the definition slightly so "management's decision-making process" became "management's decision" (see [24]). But this modification has not changed the general meaning of the definition, so we continue to use his original one.

This definition uses four important concepts. *Subject-oriented* means that all the data related to specific subjects is stored together. For example, all the customer data is stored together and all the product data is stored together. The opposite of subject-oriented is *application-oriented*, in which a database contains data that is relevant only for a particular application. This leads to a situation where customer data is spread out over multiple databases. This seriously complicates reporting because data for a particular report has to be retrieved from multiple databases. *Integrated* means a consistent encoding of data so data can be retrieved and combined in an integrated fashion.

A data warehouse is a *nonvolatile* database. When a database is primarily used to generate reports, it's inconvenient for users when the data in the reports changes constantly. Imagine that two users have to attend the same meeting, and to prepare for it, they both need to query the database to get the sales records for a particular region. Imagine that there are ten minutes between these two queries. Within those ten minutes the database might have changed, so at the meeting, the users will have inconsistent data. To prevent this, a data warehouse is updated periodically, not continuously. New data elements are added each evening or during the weekend.

Note that this notion of nonvolatility makes sense for those decisions that don't need access to operational data. But as indicated in Section 1.2, the need for accessing operational data is growing. We will come back to this issue in various sections of the book.

Time variance is another important aspect of a data warehouse. Normally, a production database is kept as small as possible because the smaller the database, the faster the queries. A common way to keep databases small is to delete old data. Old data can be stored on magnetic tape or DVD for future use. However, users of data warehouses expect to be able to access historical data. They want to find out, for example, whether the total number of boat tickets to London has changed in the last ten years. Alternatively, they would like to know in what way the weather affects the sales of beer, and for that purpose they want to use the data of the last five years. This means that considerable amounts of historical data has to be included and that almost all the data is time variant. This is one of the reasons why some data warehouses are colossal.

If we develop a system that adheres to the above definition of the term *data warehouse*, that system is not a complete solution, so it's not a complete business intelligence system. A data warehouse by itself does not supply users with the right data at the right time and in the right form to improve their decision making. We need extra modules, such as analytical and reporting tools, ETL tools, a staging area, and data marts, to develop a working business intelligence system. In other words, to develop a business intelligence system, we need more than just a data warehouse. But although the data warehouse is just one of the modules, it might be a crucial one: it's the spider in the web.

This definition of data warehouse also contains the term *collection of data*. What does that mean? Does it signify that the data in the data warehouse should be physically stored as one collection, or is it enough when the data is presented as a collection? Based on the definition itself, it's hard to say. But if we read others books and articles written by Bill Inmon, we have to conclude that he strongly favors a stored collection of data. In addition, according to The Free Dictionary (www.thefreedictionary.com), the definition of the term *warehouse* (not data warehouse) is "a place in which goods or merchandise are stored; a storehouse." This definition also associates the term *storing* with warehouse. Therefore, in this book we assume that a data warehouse is a *stored* collection of data.

The definition ends with "in support of management's decision making process." This is to emphasize why a data warehouse is developed. The reason it's developed is not for keeping track of historical data and not for supporting production systems, but it's an instrument to support the decision-making process of the organization. It can keep track of historical data and so on, but those are not the primary goals for developing a data warehouse.

Occasionally, one encounters the term *enterprise data warehouse*. The reason why the term *enterprise* is added is to emphasize that the data warehouse is a data store that is not designed for only one or two departments or divisions but for the entire enterprise. In this book, we treat both terms as synonyms.

2.5.2 The Data Marts

If a data warehouse is really one large data store, all the reporting and analytical tools access that one data store, which can lead to a query workload that's too intense for the database server managing the data warehouse. For this reason, many organizations have developed *data marts* to offload the query workload (other reasons might apply as well) (Figure 2.5). Data marts were popularized by Ralph Kimball in his book (see [25]).

Each data mart is developed for a specific group of users, normally all users with comparable data needs. This means that a data mart contains a subset of all the data from the data warehouse. And quite often, whereas a data warehouse contains the lowest level of data, a data mart contains a slightly aggregated version of all that data. If data marts are in place, most reports run on one of those data marts instead of on the data warehouse, thus offloading the query workload.

production
databases

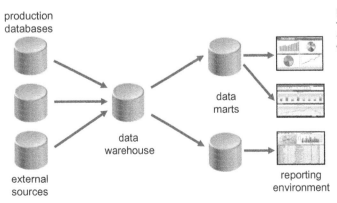

data
marts

data
warehouse

external
sources

reporting
environment

FIGURE 2.5

A business intelligence system extended with data marts.

Another reason for deploying data marts is that it allows storage technology and a storage structure to be used that are geared toward the reports and the reporting tools. For example, for certain reports, query performance might be much better if the data is stored in a multidimensional database server where data is stored in a cube-like form.

If an organization needs data marts, it's not necessary to have a data warehouse as well (Figure 2.6). In this situation, there is not just one database that holds all the data, but the data is distributed over a set of data marts. If users need to run reports on data distributed over multiple data marts, the reporting tools themselves have to integrate those data marts.

The main advantage of using a data mart–only architecture is development speed. When an organization starts from scratch, developing a data mart for a small group of users requires less time than when a data warehouse is developed for a large group of users.

There are some disadvantages to this architecture. First, some of the disadvantages of the solution displayed in Figure 2.3 apply here as well, such as data integration, defective data, and data consistency. Secondly, it's difficult to guarantee that the ETL scripts that refresh the data marts transform the same data the same way to present it consistently.

2.5.3 **The Data Staging Area**

For technical and conceptual reasons, in some situations copying data from production systems straight to a data warehouse might be too complex. Therefore, in many business intelligence systems, data is first copied into a *data staging area* before it reaches the data warehouse (Figure 2.7). If a data staging area is developed, it acts like nothing more than a landing area. Data that has been inserted, changed, or deleted in the production systems is as quickly as possible, copied to this area. During the copying process, as few changes should be made to the contents and structure of the data. In an ideal situation, the structure of the tables in the staging area is identical to that of the tables in the production systems, meaning no changes are required; it will be a one-to-one copying of data. All the transformations and cleansing operations would be applied in the second copying step: from the data staging area to the data warehouse.

After data has been copied to the data warehouse, it can be removed from the staging area. So the size of a staging area is usually small compared to that of the production databases and the data

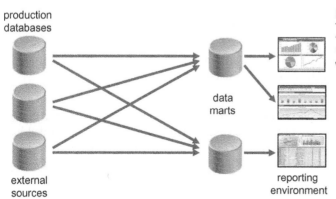

production
databases

data
marts

external
sources

reporting
environment

FIGURE 2.6

A business intelligence system using multiple data marts but no data warehouse.

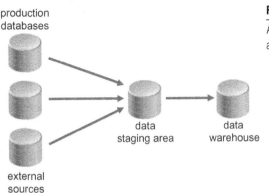

production
databases

data
staging area

data
warehouse

external
sources

FIGURE 2.7

A business intelligence system using a data staging area.

warehouse. It should only contain the extracted data that hasn't been processed for the data warehouse yet. We use the following definition:

> *The data staging area is a temporary and intermediate data store loaded with data from the production systems.*

There are various reasons for extending a business intelligence system with a staging area:

- Normally, data from production systems has to undergo a lot of processing before it's in a form suitable for storage in a data warehouse; incorrect values have to be transformed, missing data values have to be found, and so on. If data is copied straight from the production systems to the data warehouse, all this processing can lead to serious interference of these systems. It's a good idea to disturb the production systems as little as possible and just take a one-to-one snapshot of the data and do all the processing afterward.
- If certain tables in the data warehouse are only refreshed once a week or once a month, data might get lost. For example, imagine that some data in a production system has changed twice in the period between two refreshes, or that data have been inserted and deleted between two refreshes. In this case, when the data warehouse is refreshed, the older value of the first insert and the data deleted is missed. To ensure that no inserts, no deletes, and no updates get lost, all data changes are copied to the data staging area.
- The data staging area can also be used to keep track of data that may not be needed in the data warehouse. It might be that we want to keep track of the data, but we don't know yet how we will use it in the data warehouse environment. In other words, the only thing we know is that we would like to do something with this data in the future, but we don't know what yet. By copying all the data to the staging area, we have safeguarded that this data won't get lost.

When the data in the staging area has been transformed and copied to a warehouse, it can be deleted. But there might be reasons to keep it. In that case, it's usually referred to as a *persistent staging area*. By keeping all that data, the staging area can be used when the data has to be reloaded into the data warehouse. Note that a data staging area might also be relevant to a business intelligence system using no data warehouse but data marts only. In this case, the data marts are fed with new data coming from the data staging area.

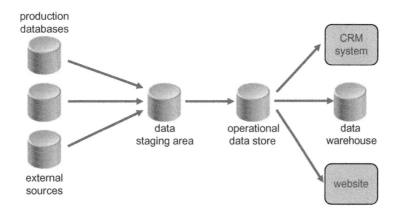

FIGURE 2.8

A business intelligence system using an operational data store (ODS) that is also used by some other systems.

2.5.4 **The Operational Data Store**

Whether data is coming from production systems or from a data staging area, it has to be processed (integrated, transformed, cleansed) before it can be loaded into the data warehouse (or data marts). But there might be other IT systems interested in this integrated, transformed, and cleansed version of the data. For example, the organization's website might want to access the data in an integrated fashion, and the same might apply for a master data management system and a customer relationship system.

When the need for integrated data exists throughout the IT systems, it can be useful to introduce an *operational data store* (ODS) (Figure 2.8). An ODS presents an integrated view of the operational data as it's currently available in the production systems.

Bill Inmon defines the ODS as follows (see [26]):

> *The operational data store is an architectural construct where collective integrated operational data is stored.*

An ODS is subject-oriented; data that logically belongs together is stored together. For example, if customer data is stored in multiple systems, it's brought together in the ODS. An ODS is integrated; all the transformations are applied to make the data fit together. An ODS is volatile; when data is added to a production database, or when it's deleted and updated, this fact is reflected as quickly as possible in the ODS. So the ODS should be able to present a relatively up-to-date state of the operational data. An ODS is not time-variant like a data warehouse. Normally, no history is kept in an ODS.

An ODS can be loaded with data from the production systems or, if available, from the data staging area. In some systems the data staging area and the operational data store are merged. In most cases that means that the ODS takes over the role of the data staging area.

The advantage for the data warehouse of having an ODS in place is that much of the data integration and data transformation have already taken place, thereby simplifying the work to be done to get the data into the data warehouse.

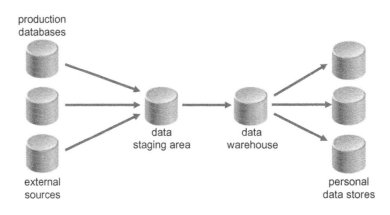

FIGURE 2.9

A business intelligence system using personal data stores.

2.5.5 **The Personal Data Stores**

All the data stores described so far are developed for a group of users. In some business intelligence systems, data stores are developed for personal use. A *personal data store* (PDS) is designed specifically for the needs of one individual user (Figure 2.9). A PDS can be a simple spreadsheet developed by a user to store descriptions of codes used in some tables or to store predicted sales values not available in the data warehouse. A PDS can also be a simple file containing data from an external organization. In most cases the users want to analyze this data, or they want to combine it with internal data. Some reporting and analytical tools create a small database on the machine of the user. This can also be seen as a PDS.

Sometimes a PDS is created for performance reasons. Another reason can be that the user is disconnected from the rest of the system, and if the PDS is stored on that user's computer, the PDS allows for reporting even when disconnected.

Although this type of data store has been deployed in many business intelligence systems, there is no generally accepted term for it. Some refer to it as a "personal data warehouse" or simply a "cube." This latter term stems from the storage technology deployed by some tools, which is based on so-called multidimensional cubes. In this book we call it a "personal data store."

2.5.6 **A Comparison of the Different Types of Data Stores**

Table 2.2 compares all the different types of data stores described in the previous sections. The following are the meanings of each type of data:

- Volatile data indicates whether the data in a data store is constantly updated. The state of the data is in sync with the source data or close to in sync.
- Detailed data means whether the data store contains only the lowest level of detail.
- Integrated data indicates whether data that logically belongs together is stored together.
- Time-variant or historical data refers to whether the data store also contains history, meaning the older versions of the data.

	Volatile Data	Detailed Data	Integrated Data	Time-Variant/ Historical Data	Summarized, Aggregated, and Derived Data	Enterprisewide Data
Production database	✓	✓				
Data staging area	✓	✓				
Operational data store	✓	✓	✓			✓
Data warehouse		✓	✓	✓	✓	✓
Data mart		✓	✓	✓	✓	
Personal data store			✓	✓	✓	

Table 2.2 Comparison of the Different Data Stores in a Business Intelligence Architecture

- Summarized, aggregated, and derived data means that data is not stored at the lowest level of detail but has somehow been derived from original source data by applying aggregations.
- Enterprisewide data means that a data store is developed for a large part of the organization. The opposite is a data store developed for a small group of users.

Note: In the figures in the previous sections, a separate database symbol (⬤) is used for each data store. By introducing all these symbols and by assigning names to them, it might appear that technically these different data stores have to be different databases managed by different database servers. This, however, is not the case. It is possible to store all the tables of the staging area, the data warehouse, and the data marts in one big database managed by one database server. Whether or not this is done is purely a technical issue determined by performance, scalability, availability, and security considerations.

2.6 Normalized Schemas, Star Schemas, and Snowflake Schemas

Each data store has a *schema*. The definitions of all the tables with their columns, primary keys, and foreign keys form such a schema. For example, the schema of the sample WCM database consists of the definitions of tables such as CUSTOMER, CUSTOMER_ORDER, and DVD_RELEASE.

Certain schema forms have become so popular that they have been given names. Because we refer to them throughout this book, the four most well-known ones are:

- Normalized schema
- Denormalized schema
- Star schema
- Snowflake schema

This section should be considered a refresher course on schema forms. For more in-depth descriptions, see [27] and [25]. Additionally, this is not an exhaustive list of schema forms. Other schema forms, such as data vault (see [28]), are worth mentioning, but we leave these to the more specialized books.

2.6.1 Normalized Schemas

The *normalized schema* is the oldest of the four. The first articles written on normalized schemas were published at the beginning of the 1970s (see, for example, [29] and [30]). In normalization, columns are assigned to tables in such a way that each business fact is stored only once, or in other words, a table should not contain duplicate data. William Kent once summarized it this way: In a normalized table, each column that is not part of the primary key should be dependent on the key, the whole key, and nothing but the key (see [31]). Informally, this means that between two nonprimary key columns, there may not exist a one-to-one or a one-to-many relationship.

The goal of normalized schemas is to avoid storage of duplicate data so that stored data can't become inconsistent. Because tables with a normalized schema don't contain duplicate data, they are highly suitable for supporting transactions in which data is inserted, updated, and deleted. The reason is that because there is no duplicate data, each insert, update, and delete involves only one row. Therefore, it has long been the preferred schema form for developing production databases.

2.6.2 Denormalized Schemas

A *denormalized schema* is, as the name suggests, the opposite of a normalized schema. When tables do not adhere to the above rules and contain duplicate data, they have a denormalized schema. For example, if the column WEBSITE_TITLE would also be added to the CUSTOMER table, the latter would contain duplicate data. The following table shows a subset of the columns and rows of that extended version of the CUSTOMER table:

```
CUSTOMER_ID   FIRST_NAME   LAST_NAME   WEBSITE_ID   WEBSITE_TITLE
-----------   ----------   ---------   ----------   -------------
2             Virginia     Lee              1       World Class Movies
4             Catherine    Davis            1       World Class Movies
8             Daniel       Redd             1       World Class Movies
12            George       Handy            1       World Class Movies
15            Aaron        Moore            1       World Class Movies
16            Jeff         Cox              1       World Class Movies
20            Naomi        Tickle           1       World Class Movies
:             :            :                :       :
```

It's evident that for each customer, a website ID and website title are stored. But because customers share websites, the fact that a particular website ID belongs to a particular website title is repeated over and over again. This table shows this very clearly. For example, the combination of the website ID 1 and title World Class Movies would be stored 58,014 times in this denormalized version of the CUSTOMER table. The reason is that the nonprimary key columns WEBSITE_ID and WEBSITE_TITLE have a one-to-one relationship and therefore contain duplicate data. Or, in William Kent's words, the column WEBSITE_TITLE is dependent on a column which is not part of the primary key—namely, WEBSITE_ID.

For a long period of time, normalized schemas were preferred for designing the tables of databases. With the coming of data warehouses and data marts, other schema forms became popular; star schema and snowflake schema are the two most well-known ones. Ralph Kimball contributed considerably to these newer schema forms.

2.6.3 **Star Schemas**

Figure 2.10 shows a database design with a *star schema*; it represents some of the data from the sample database (see Figure 1.13). In a star schema the tables are classified as *dimension tables* (or *dimensional tables*) and *fact tables*. Here, CUSTOMER, DVD_RELEASE, and DATE form the dimension tables and TRANSACTION forms a fact table. Star schema owes its name to its graphical representation where the fact table forms the center and the dimension tables are drawn as rays originating from that center, together forming a star.

Every dimension table features a primary key of one column and a set of attributes describing the dimension. The CUSTOMER table is a typical example of a dimension table. Each row in a dimension table represents some business object—in this case, each row represents a customer. All the nonprimary key columns of a dimension table contain data describing that business object. Dimension tables don't have relationships with one another, only relationships with fact tables.

Fact tables are the central tables in a star schema. Every fact table contains a primary key that consists of all the primary keys of the dimension tables it refers to. A row in a fact table usually

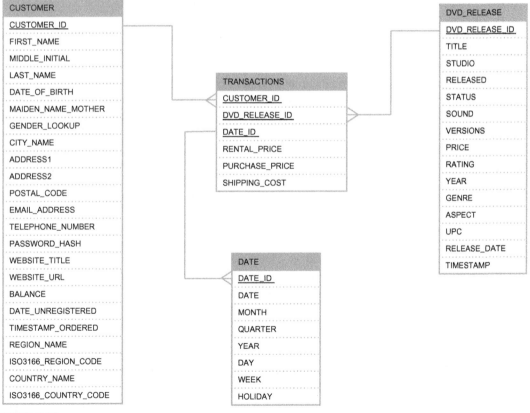

FIGURE 2.10

A star schema representation of a subset of the data in the WCM sample database.

represents a *business event*. Examples of potential fact tables are money withdrawals from a bank account, a booking for a flight, and a payment at a counter.

In Figure 2.10, TRANSACTION is the fact table. It refers to three other tables—the CUSTOMER table, the DVD_RELEASE table, and the DATES table—and therefore its primary key consists of the primary keys of those three tables. This implies that one row in the TRANSACTION table represents how much a customer paid to purchase and/or rent a particular DVD release on a particular date. The nonprimary key columns of a fact table are all measures. Usually, measures are numeric values that are additive numbers, such as the rental price, the purchase price, and the shipping costs. Fact tables don't have relationships with one another, only relationships with dimension tables (usually with more than one).

Because of this particular primary key structure, the relationship of a fact table with each dimension table is always one-to-many. Thus, each row in the TRANSACTION table belongs to at minimum and at maximum one customer, one DVD release, and also one date, and for each customer, for each DVD release, and for each date, there can be many transactions.

The key columns in dimension and fact tables of star schemas are filled with *surrogate key values*. These are values with no meaning to the business users. Therefore, they are sometimes called *meaningless key values*. In most cases these are just plain numbers. All the primary key columns of the CUSTOMER, DVD_RELEASE, and DATE tables contain surrogate, meaningless keys. An example of a *meaningful key* (the opposite) would be if real date/time values were used as the primary key values of the DATE table. Surrogate keys are used to obtain never-changing key values that forever represent business objects (dimensions) or business events (facts). These key values used to identify the objects and events are necessary because there have to be some values that never change.

Noteworthy is that a fact table has a normalized schema, whereas a dimension table is denormalized. For example, the columns WEBSITE_TITLE and COUNTRY_NAME in the CUSTOMER table are denormalized because they're both nonprimary keys and a one-to-many relationship exists between them. When there are multiple customers living in the same country, they all have the same country name and the same iso3166 country code. This is duplicate data and therefore the table is denormalized.

Almost every star schema contains a date dimension. This is not surprising, because a fact table captures some business event. Since such an event takes place somewhere in time, the moment that the event occurred is a necessary part of its description. Most of the data in this table, such as the month and the week, is derived data. These columns are added to improve the performance of queries, but there are columns that don't contain derived data, such as holiday.

The primary goal of arranging tables as a star schema is to limit the number of tables that have to be accessed and joined when a query is processed. The often-cited advantage of avoiding table joins is improved query performance. Another advantage is that it becomes much easier to write queries and to present the end user with a set of options from which a tool can generate a query. The fact that duplicate data increases the amount of required storage is not considered important. Also, the fact that duplicate data can lead to inconsistent data is not considered a significant disadvantage either, which makes sense in a data warehouse environment where all the inserts and updates are executed in a very controlled fashion.

A data store can contain many fact tables and thus many star schemas. If fact tables share the same dimension tables, these dimension tables are called *conformed dimension tables*. This is only possible if those fact tables have been designed in such a way that they can use the same dimension tables.

2.6.4 **Snowflake Schemas**

In a way, a *snowflake schema* resembles a star schema. Both organize the tables around a central fact table and use surrogate keys. The essential difference is that the dimension tables in a snowflake schema are normalized (Figure 2.11). As Figure 2.11 shows, some columns are removed from the CUSTOMER table and are placed in three extra tables.

A fact table in a snowflake schema has only relationships with dimension tables, just as in a star schema. Dimension tables, on the other hand, can have relationships with one another, and the relationships that exist are all one-to-many relationships. For example, for each region there are many customers, and each customer belongs to only one region. In a way, these dimension tables form a hierarchy. For example, in Figure 2.11, the CUSTOMER table falls hierarchically under the REGION table, which falls under the COUNTRY table. In other words, the data in the REGION table has a lower granularity level than that of the CUSTOMER table. In fact, in both snowflake schemas and star schemas, no many-to-many relationships are used.

The advantage of a snowflake schema is that less duplicate data is stored than in an equivalent star schema. In addition, a snowflake schema can support queries on the dimension tables on a lower granularity level. For the query, in order to get the URL of a website title, only a very small table has to be queried. With respect to the keys of fact and dimension tables of snowflake schemas, they are also filled with surrogate key values, just like the keys in star schemas.

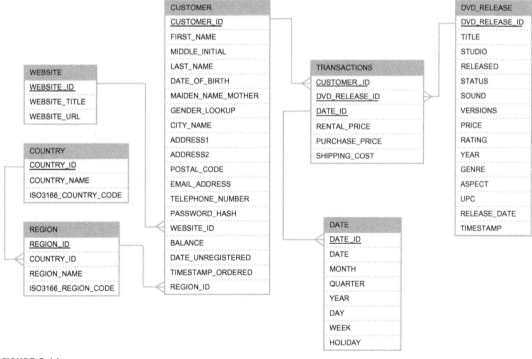

FIGURE 2.11

A snowflake schema representation of a subset of the data in the WCM sample database.

2.7 **Data Transformation with Extract Transform Load, Extract Load Transform, and Replication**

To get data from the production databases to the various data stores, data must be copied. For example, data must be copied from the production databases to the data staging area or the ODS, from the ODS to the data warehouse, from the data warehouse to the data marts, and so on. However, the format and contents of the data stored in the production databases is quite different from how users want to see the data in their reporting and analytical tools. For example, in production systems, customer data might be spread out over multiple databases, while users want to have an integrated view; data in the production systems might be heavily coded, while users want to see meaningful values; historical data might be missing from the source systems, while users need it for trend analysis; or the values of data elements in source systems might be incorrect (defective data), while users want to work with correct data. To summarize, source data have to be "massaged" before users can use it. This whole process is sometimes referred to as *data transformation*. So when data moves from production databases via a data staging area to a data warehouse, it has to be transformed.

Organizations can develop homemade applications for all the required transformations, but it's recommended to use dedicated tools. This will improve productivity and maintenance. In Section 1.2, the three popular technologies for copying data in business intelligence systems—ETL, ELT, and replication—have been introduced briefly. In this section they are explained in more detail.

Note: Data virtualization is also a form of data transformation. How and when that technology can be deployed in business intelligence systems are discussed extensively in Chapter 7.

2.7.1 **Extract Transform Load**

Extract Transform Load (ETL) is one of the most popular technologies for copying and transforming data. With ETL tools, data is retrieved from one or more source data stores. The data is then transformed, cleansed, and integrated, and finally stored in a target data store (Figure 2.12). In many business intelligence systems, production databases and data staging areas typically act as the source data stores, whereas data marts and PDSs are examples of target data stores.

All the required operations that have to be applied when processing data is specified in an ETL script. Each ETL tool offers a wide range of operations to process the data, ranging from the simplest

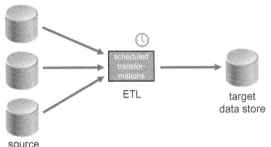

source
data stores

ETL

target
data store

FIGURE 2.12

With an ETL solution, data is periodically copied from a set of source data stores to a target data store using scheduled transformations.

transformations, such as the concatenation of two strings, to highly complex transformations, such as the deduplication of rows. Data can also be aggregated, summarized, and cleansed. Most ETL tools support some flow-like language to specify those operations. Figure 2.13 contains a screenshot depicting an example of such a flow specification. Each icon in this flow represents an operation.

ETL tools have been designed to copy data in a batch-oriented style. So every time an ETL script is run, it handles a whole batch of data. For example, all the new data inserted to, updated in, and deleted from the CUSTOMER table in the last week is copied to a target data store. In other words, periodically data in the target data store is *refreshed*. ETL scripts are usually scheduled—for example, they run every Sunday at 2 p.m., every evening at 11 p.m., or every two hours. In this book we call this form of transformation a *scheduled transformation*. Most of ETL support lineage and impact analysis capabilities as well, so designers can study the relationships between table structures and ETL specifications.

2.7.2 **Extract Load Transform**

Extract Load Transform (ELT) differs from ETL in the order in which operations are executed. With ETL, after data has been extracted from a source data store, it's transformed, and the transformed data is then stored (loaded) in a target data store (Figure 2.14). ELT also starts with an extract operation but stores the data in a target data store in a nontransformed form; in the last step, the data is transformed and stored again. At the end, ELT and ETL lead to the same end result: transformed data in a target data store.

Note: ELTL would have been a better name for ELT because it starts with an Extract, which is followed by a Load, then a Transform, and finally the transformed data is Loaded again.

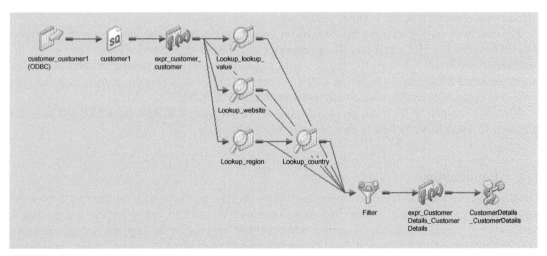

FIGURE 2.13

An example of transformation using a flow-like language.

Reprinted with permission of Informatica Corporation.

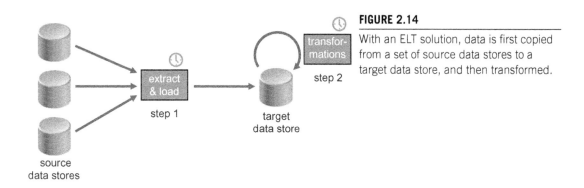

FIGURE 2.14

With an ELT solution, data is first copied from a set of source data stores to a target data store, and then transformed.

Besides the difference in the order in which operations are executed, there is also a difference in how ETL and ELT solutions work together with database servers. With ETL, the tools do most of the heavy lifting. They process all the complex transformation operations and use the database servers simply for retrieving the source data and for inserting the new, transformed data. In a way, with ETL the full capabilities of a database server are not used.

ELT tools try to exploit the power of the database servers more. Many of the transformations and integration operations can be processed by a database server. So what ELT tools do is delegate as much of the operations to the database servers. It's almost as if the ELT tool becomes like a puppeteer and the database servers the puppets. It tells the database servers to retrieve, transform, and load the data. The effect is that after the data is loaded into a set of tables, the same data is retrieved, transformed, aggregated, filtered, and copied to another table. These types of operations can be easily done by a database server itself using so-called INSERT-SELECT statements. Sometimes this delegation of operations to a database server is called *pushdown*.

The benefit of staying within a database server is that there is little to no time lost with data transmission between the ELT server and the database server. Most of the operations are processed by the database server itself. This way, the full power of a database server is exploited. Another advantage is that the target database now holds the original, nontransformed data plus the transformed data. For some data consumers, having access to the original data can be useful.

Note: With respect to the tools, more and more of them support ETL as well as ELT. It's up to the designers to determine which form they prefer in which situation.

2.7.3 Replication

The third form of copying is called *replication*. Like with ETL and ELT, with replication, data is also copied from one data store to another. However, whereas ETL and ELT are optimized to copy data in batches (large groups of records are copied together), with replication the copying is done record by record or transaction by transaction. Replication is normally used when the insert, update, or deletion of data also has to be applied in another data store and as quickly as possible, preferably in microseconds. In addition, we want these replicators to minimize the interference they create on the source data stores. The primary objective of replication is speed, so its integration and transformation capabilities are limited compared to ETL solutions.

Replication technology is very well suited for copying data from production databases to a data staging area or an ODS, and not so much for copying to data marts and PDSs. Usually, these two don't have to be refreshed continuously. Using replication to keep them up to date would not make a lot of sense.

To minimize interference on the source systems, some replication tools are able to extract data from the log files instead of from the database files in which the data is changed. This means that the replicator constantly reads these log files to inspect whether a transaction has been committed. If that's the case, relevant data is copied from the log files to the target system. This reading of log files is sometimes referred to as *change data capture* (CDC).

2.8 **Overview of Business Intelligence Architectures**

As indicated in the previous sections, there are many different ways to develop a business intelligence system. One organization might base its solution on a data warehouse, extended with an operational data store, and a number of PDSs, whereas another might decide to use a staging area and a number of data marts, and yet another could choose to develop its whole business intelligence system straight on their production systems. But whatever they select, their solution is based on an architecture. In this book we call this type of architecture a *business intelligence architecture*, and we use the following definition:

> *A business intelligence architecture is a set of design guidelines, descriptions, and prescriptions for integrating various modules, such as data warehouses, data marts, operational data stores, staging areas, ETL tools, and analytical and reporting tools to form an effective and efficient business intelligence system.*

Every organization can invent its own business intelligence architecture. An organization can also select a predefined and well-known architecture. The advantage of picking a well-known one is that most of them have been thought through, are based on experiences, and have been tested and used over and over again. By choosing them, the developers "inherit" all those experiences.

The following are some of the more popular ones:

- The data mart is central to Ralph Kimball's *data warehouse bus architecture* (DWBA), described in his book *The Data Warehouse Lifecycle Toolkit* (see [25]). A business intelligence system based on the DWBA consists of possibly a persistent staging area and a number of data marts. Sometimes this architecture is referred to as the *data mart bus architecture*.
- Bill Inmon, together with Claudia Imhoff and Ryan Sousa, introduced the *corporate information factory* (CIF) architecture in [32]. A CIF-based system is minimally made up of an ODS, a data warehouse (which is logical, since Bill Inmon is one of the founders of the data warehouse concept), and, if needed, a set of data marts. An alternative name for this architecture is the *hub and spoke architecture*.
- Another architecture is the *centralized data warehouse architecture*. In this architecture, no data marts or PDSs are used. Most reports are run on one central data warehouse that is probably loaded with data from an ODS or a data staging area.
- In the *federated architecture,* all the reporting and analytical tools are linked to some data federation layer, which by itself retrieves its data from all kinds of sources, including production databases, data warehouses, and data marts.

- One of the newer business intelligence architectures is called the *data delivery platform* (DDP). This new and agile architecture is based on data virtualization and is described separately and extensively in Chapter 12.

According to [33], the first two architectures in this list were the two most popular ones in 2006.

Note: In this book, we use the term *business intelligence architecture* instead of the more frequently used term *data warehouse architecture* because some of these predefined architectures, such as the DWBA, are not based on a data warehouse whatsoever. It would be awkward to call something a data warehouse architecture if it's not based on a data warehouse at all. It would be like calling a plane that can't carry any cargo a cargo plane. We prefer the term *business intelligence architecture*, because it reflects the purpose of the architecture better: business intelligence. Additionally, it doesn't refer to one of the modules on which an architecture can be based.

2.9 New Forms of Reporting and Analytics

In 1964, Bob Dylan wrote the song "The Times They Are A-Changin'." Most likely, he was never a business intelligence expert (although with Dylan you never know). But this text is very much true for the current world of business intelligence. In the beginning, users were satisfied with simple tabular reports that showed what had happened. This was followed by the wish to show the data more graphically. Next, users wanted to have more dynamic capabilities: They wanted to play with the data in the report, and they wanted to be able to do so-called drill-downs and roll-ups. And the new demands kept coming, and it hasn't stopped yet. Their wish list keeps changing. They request new types of reporting and analytical capabilities. So the big question is, can classic business intelligence systems support the new forms of reporting and analytics? Some of the new forms of reporting and analytics are described in the next section. When the need exists to implement them, each of these will undoubtedly have a serious impact on how business intelligence systems should be designed and developed.

2.9.1 Operational Reporting and Analytics

Operational reporting and analytics refer to forms of reporting and analytics applied by operational management. In most cases, the analytical needs of operational management require access to almost 100 percent up-to-date data or, in other words, (near) real-time data. We use the term *operational data* to refer to 100 percent up-to-date data.

Many examples of cases where operational analytics are needed exist. For example, a retail company might want to know whether a truck that is already en route to deliver goods to a specific store should be redirected to another store that has a more urgent need for those products. It would not make sense to execute this analysis with yesterday's data. Another application area is credit card fraud detection. A classic form of credit card fraud is when stolen card data are used to purchase products. Each new purchase has to be analyzed to see if it fits the buying pattern of the card owner and whether the purchase makes sense. One of the checks can be whether two purchases in different cities occurred within a short period of time of each other. For example, if a new purchase is made in Boston and a purchase was made in San Francisco just a few seconds earlier, the odds are that this is a case of fraud. But this form of analysis only makes sense when executed on operational data.

For operational reporting and analytics, business users must have at least access to operational data. A challenge is that most data warehouses offer refresh rates of once-a-day or once-a-week, so they don't contain operational data. Another challenge is that in classic business intelligence systems, the reports are "far away" from that operational data. For the new data, the road from the source system to the report, is a long one.

2.9.2 Deep and Big Data Analytics

For many reports and forms of analytics, storing detailed data is not necessary; aggregated data or slightly aggregated data is sufficient. For example, to determine the total sales per region, there is no need to store and analyze all the individual sales records. Aggregating the data on, for example, customer number is probably adequate. But for some forms of analytics, detailed data is a necessity. This is called *deep analytics*. When an organization wants to analyze whether trucks should be rerouted, or when it wants to determine which online ad to present, detailed data has to be analyzed. The most well-known area that requires detailed data is *time-series analytics*. But detailed data means that the data store holding the data will grow enormously, potentially leading to serious problems with query performance.

A new form of analytics that resembles deep analytics is called, quite rightly so, *big data analytics*. Many traditional information systems exist that store and manage large numbers of records. More recently, new systems have been built that store an amount of data magnitudes larger than those in the more traditional systems. For example, click-stream applications, sensor-based applications, and image processing applications all generate massive numbers of records per day. The amount of records here is not measured in millions but sometimes in trillions. Analyzing this amount of data is a challenge.

For both deep analytics and big data analytics, comparable solutions should be developed just as for operational analytics. Users should be given direct access to the production systems or the staging area. The sheer size of this data and the amount of new data coming in make it close to impossible to continuously refresh the data warehouse with all this data.

2.9.3 Self-Service Reporting and Analytics

Before users can invoke their reports, the IT department has to set up a whole environment. *Self-service reporting and analytics* allow users to develop their own reports with a minimal setup required by the IT department. Self-service analytics is useful when a report has to be developed quickly and there is no time to prepare a complete environment. For example, an airline wants to know how many passengers will be affected by a particular strike tomorrow. Additionally, when a requested report will only be used once, self-service analytics can be helpful as well. In both cases, it would not make sense to develop a data store first, such as a data mart or PDS, that contains aggregated data before running the reports. For the first example, creating such a data store would take too long, and for the second example, it's not worth the effort.

Self-service is probably the most important new form of analytics and reporting. The study by the Aberdeen Group in March 2011 shows that more than 60 percent of the respondents see enabling business users to be more self-sufficient as their primary strategy for delivering agile business intelligence (see [2]). (See Section 7.6.9 for more on self-service.)

Self-service analytics might also be called *unplanned analytics* because the data warehouse administrators have no idea which queries will be executed and when. This means it's impossible to optimize and tune the data warehouse on forehand for these queries.

2.9.4 Unrestricted Ad-Hoc Analysis

Besides classic forms of reporting and analytics, operational management has needs that are not typical for higher levels of management. In an operational environment, situations might arise that require a direct response. Imagine that a truck owned by a retail company was supposed to deliver 15 pallets of a particular type of soda at a store in Boston before opening time. Unfortunately, the truck has engine troubles and has been parked on the side of the road. The challenge for the manager on duty is to find an alternative way of getting the soda to the store. One alternative is to send an empty truck to the stranded truck, load the pallets, and bring them to the store. But are there empty trucks available in the area? Another alternative might be to check whether there is another store in the area from which soda can be retrieved. Or is it better to just send a new shipment? Whatever the solution, this manager needs access to up-to-date data. It would be useless to give him access to yesterday's data because that won't tell him where the trucks are *right now*.

In addition, because the solution can be anything, a manager must have access to a system that can point him to the various solutions. He should be able to freely query the available data. For example, he should be able to enter a query that includes the key words *soda*, *Boston*, and *trucks*. The result should show him everything the system knows about those keywords, and hopefully somewhere in that answer he will find the best solution.

Although most data warehouse environments don't support this form of analysis, many organizations would benefit from it. Think about a hospital environment where a patient is brought in who urgently needs a particular type of operation. However, all the operation rooms are occupied. So what should be done? Find another hospital? When will an operating room be available? Another example is an airport that has to close temporarily because of heavy fog conditions. What do you do with the airplanes that are supposed to land there? Or what do you do when the cargo doors of a recently landed airplane won't open? What do you do with the luggage? In both situations, users should be able to freely navigate all available data.

What's special about these examples is that the analysis is triggered by an incident. Something unexpected happens and the organization has to react, and it has to react fast. Classic reports work well for reoccurring problems, but not for unique cases. In a classic data warehouse environment, letting users query along nondefined relationships would involve quite a lot of work. Existing tables have to be extended with new data, ETL scripts have to be adapted, and so on. But because this is an incident, there is no time to do this.

In the preceding situations, what's needed is a new form of analysis—a form where users can freely analyze data (with almost no restrictions) without the IT department having to predefine tables and relationships. Users should also have access to operational data. We call this form of analysis *unrestricted ad-hoc analysis*. The adjective "unrestricted" is added to distinguish it from the more traditional form of ad-hoc analysis. With traditional ad-hoc analysis, users can also enter any query, but only predefined tables and relationships can be used. If certain relationships don't exist, the user can't use them for analysis. So although the traditional form is ad-hoc analysis, it's still restricted.

Unrestricted ad-hoc analysis is hard to implement with a classic business intelligence system because users should have access to the data when they ask for it and whatever the source is. There will be no time to prepare data marts and PDSs for them. These users need the opportunity to access any data store.

2.9.5 360-Degree Reporting

Customers of an insurance company regularly call the company's call center with questions related to their insurance. For a call center operator, it might be useful to see not only the data directly related to that insurance but be able to get a 360-degree view of this customer—in other words, a complete picture. This 360-degree view might include whether the customer has other insurance plans, whether he has been complaining via email, whether he tweeted negatively about the company, how often he called, and how many of the calls were about the same issue. The more data the call center operator has available, the better the operator's understanding of that customer, and the better equipped he is to make the customer happy.

What the operator needs is a 360-degree view of the customer. Data from the production systems and/or data warehouse won't provide such a view because it probably only contains structured data coming from the production systems. What is needed is data from all kinds of data sources and combined, ranging from data coming from unstructured to structured sources and coming from internal to external sources. Being able to show a full picture of a specific concept is called *360-degree reporting*.

In most cases, 360-degree reporting is done on the lowest level of detail. It's done on an individual customer, an individual bank account, or a single product. Most current data warehouses have been designed to show aggregated data and primarily structured data coming from production databases. For 360-degree reporting, access to the lowest level of detail is needed and access to unstructured data sources is as important as access to structured data sources.

Data marts in many classic business intelligence systems don't contain enough data for 360-degree reporting. In most cases, they contain that subset of data required for the current reports. Neither do data warehouses give access to all the available data from all the information systems. Emails, text belonging to scanned contracts, weather-related data from external sources, and so on, could all be examples of data not loaded. But this might be the data the user needs to solve his problem.

2.9.6 Exploratory Analysis

Imagine that the manager of a group of retail stores in the Boston area finds out that sales of all brands of soft drinks in those stores have been very low. Obviously, he'd want to find out why this is happening. The reason might not be that evident, and there could be many reasons. One reason might be that lately, deliveries to the Boston stores have been seriously delayed, so these products often are not available. It could also be that many of the employees have been home sick with the flu. This would probably mean that the stores aren't stocking the shelves regularly, which can impact sales negatively. There could also be an external reason, such as customers not shopping due to bad weather conditions. Another external reason could be that a competitor has started a special promotion where those brands of soft drinks are on sale for half price.

Classic reporting won't help to determine the source of the problem. Reports created with those tools will show, for example, that the sales are behind, but not why. They are restricted to showing predefined reports, and if no report has been developed to answer this question, the manager won't find the underlying problem.

Analytical tools offer the manager features to view data from all angles and at each possible level of detail. However, he can only discover relationships between data elements via links, relations, keys, and dimensions that have been predefined in the database. If, in a multidimensional cube, sales data is not related to delivery data or employee sickness, it won't be able to show that delivery issues are causing the problems.

Statistical and data mining tools won't help either, because these tools, although very powerful, can only create models on the data supplied. In a way, we have to guide these tools. If the manager thinks delivery is causing the problem, we can use tools to determine statistically that this is indeed the case. But that's not the manager's problem. He doesn't know yet whether delivery is the problem, so he is still looking for the reason. And, as indicated, the reason can be anything.

In other words, those products are very useful when we have some idea of the reason for a problem. What this manager needs is a tool with which he can find the problem himself. When found, he can switch to the reporting and analytical tools to study the problem in more detail.

What is needed is a tool that allows the manager to query, navigate, browse, and analyze data without any restrictions. It should allow the manager to relate data elements for which no relationships or tables have been predefined. He should be able to ask questions such as "What's happening in Boston?" or "Anything special during the week of May 13, 2012?" And when an answer is returned, he should be able to continue along that path. This is what we call *exploratory analysis* or investigative analysis.

The key difference between unrestricted ad-hoc analysis and exploratory analysis is that the former is used when an incident happens and a solution has to be found right away. Exploratory analysis might be useful for these urgent issues as well, but also for those issues where a fast response is not essential.

Implementing exploratory analysis on a classic business intelligence system will have the same issues as unrestricted ad-hoc and text analysis. This form also requires access to a wide range of data sources and to unstructured data sources.

2.9.7 **Text-Based Analysis**

On May 4, 2011, *USA Today* reported that Wall Street traders mine tweets for investment clues. They monitor and decode the words, opinions, rants, and even keyboard-generated smiley faces posted on social media sites. In other words, they're analyzing text.

Many examples exist where analyzing text can improve the decision-making process of an organization. For example, an insurance company might want to analyze all contracts (textual documents) to find out how many of them will expire within one year. An electronics company might be interested in analyzing all the messages on Twitter to find out if their products are mentioned and whether those messages are positive or not. Consider all the information in emails sent and received by an organization, all the information on the web, and in social media networks. This form of analysis, in which unstructured data are analyzed, is referred to as *text-based analysis*.

Most current business intelligence systems allow users to analyze data coming from structured data sources—that is, production databases—but they don't allow users to exploit unstructured data (text) for reporting and analysis. This is a seriously missed opportunity, because the amount of unstructured data is enormous, and there is a wealth of information hidden in it. The Wall Street scenario is a perfect example of why organizations would want to analyze unstructured data (in this example, tweets) for decision making. So the big questions are: How can these currently untapped sources of unstructured data be used for reporting and analytics? How can unstructured data be integrated with the structured data stored in current data warehouses? How can we enrich classic business intelligence systems to the benefit of the organization?

2.10 **Disadvantages of Classic Business Intelligence Systems**

For many years, business intelligence systems have been developed based on the concepts outlined in this chapter. As indicated, many of those systems are based around a chain of data stores and transformation processes, and, in addition, many data stores contain derived data. Figure 2.15 shows an example of a common business intelligence system based on such an architecture, which consists of a data staging area, an ODS, a data warehouse, a number of data marts, and a few PDSs. In this system, data is copied from one data store to another until it's stored in one that is accessed by a reporting tool. Because of all the copying, the data warehouse, the data marts, and the PDSs do contain a considerable amount of derived data. In fact, in such an architecture, all the data in, for example, a data mart is derived from the data warehouse.

We call systems with this type of architecture *classic business intelligence systems*. The reason why so many of them have been developed in this way has to do with the state of software and hardware of the last 20 years. These technologies had their limitations with respect to performance and scalability, and therefore, on one hand, the reporting and analytical workload had to be distributed over multiple data stores, and on the other, the transformation and cleansing processes had to be broken down into multiple steps.

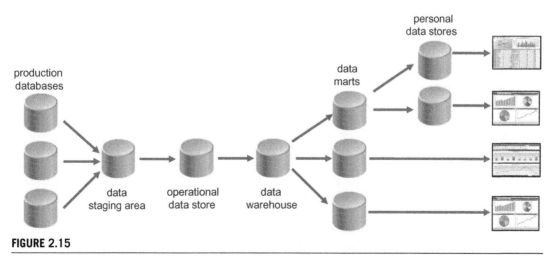

FIGURE 2.15

Many business intelligence systems consist of a chain of data stores linked with ETL, ELT, and replication jobs.

But as always with technologies and solutions, regardless of how valuable they were when introduced, they have an expiration date. It's like with these powerful old three-mast ships that were used successfully hundreds of years ago to discover new lands. Regardless of how good and effective they were in those days, eventually they were replaced by steamships. It's the same with the horse and carriages that were eventually replaced by cars, and many more examples can be given.

Some of the disadvantages of these classic systems are becoming clear:

Disadvantage 1—Duplication of Data: The first disadvantage relates to the huge amount of duplicate data stored in these systems. Most of the data stores contain data derived from the other data stores. For example, if the contents of a data mart are derived from that of the data warehouse, 100 percent of the data in the data mart is redundant. The same applies to the PDSs that might be packed with redundant data. Even a data staging area and a data warehouse will contain masses of overlapping data. Additionally, inside a data store, a lot of duplicate data might be stored. Most of that duplicate data is stored to improve the performance of queries, reports, and ETL scripts. This duplicate data is hidden in indexes, materialized query tables, columns and tables with aggregated data, staging areas, and so on.

Data warehouses take up huge amounts of storage—in fact, terabytes, and sometimes even petabytes of storage. But how much original data is there really? An extensive study done by UK-based analyst Nigel Pendse shows that the actual reported volume of accessible net data in the largest business intelligence applications is approximately 5 gigabytes of original data (see [34]). This is the median value. This number sounds realistic, but how does it match the results of many other studies indicating that the average data warehouse is 10 (or more) terabytes large? If this would all be original data, according to the study of Pendse, 2,000 different business intelligence applications would be needed with no overlapping data elements to get to 10 terabytes, and that is highly unlikely. It is known that data warehouses do sometimes include data not accessible for business intelligence applications, such as raw detailed data, indexes, and so on, but there isn't enough of this to explain the huge data space occupied. Therefore, these numbers show clearly that the amount of duplicate stored data is phenomenal.

Obviously, there is a reason for storing all this duplicate data, and the reason is performance. To speed up queries, we need those indexes, materialized query tables, columns with aggregated data, derived data stores, and so on.

Storage is not that expensive anymore, so what's the issue? The issue is agility. The more duplicate data that is stored, the less flexible the architecture is. Every change made requires an extra change on the duplicate data. There will be costs involved in keeping duplicate data synchronized. Storing duplicate data might also lead to data inconsistencies. Business intelligence systems can be simplified considerably by removing most of the duplicate data.

Disadvantage 2—Nonshared Meta Data Specifications: The second disadvantage of the classic systems can be described with the term *nonshared meta data specifications*. Many reporting and analytical tools allow us to include specifications to make report definitions more data source independent. For example, in the Universe concept of SAP's Business Objects, we can define specific terms and relationships between tables. This is perfect for all the reports created with that tool, but what if we want to develop other reports—for example, with Excel or with the IBM/Cognos tools? It means these meta data specifications have to be replicated in those tools.

To summarize, many specifications entered in tools are not being shared. Organizations tend to set up heterogeneous environments in which different tools are used for different tasks, so this need for shared specifications does exist. This example of nonshared specifications relates to reporting and analytical tools, but examples of other nonshared specifications exist within ETL tools and database servers as well. Nonshared meta data specifications decrease flexibility, are hard to manage, and can lead to inconsistent reporting results.

Disadvantage 3—Limited Flexibility: An important disadvantage relates to flexibility. The field of software engineering has taught us that if we design a system, we have to separate the storage structure from the application structure because if we separate them cleanly, changes on the storage structure do not always require changes to the application structure, or vice versa. This is good for maintenance and flexibility. As indicated in Section 1.5.1, David L. Parnas was one of the first to recognize the importance of the concepts of information hiding (alias encapsulation) and abstraction. Later on, these concepts became the basis for other concepts such as object orientation, component-based development, and service-oriented architectures.

Every software engineer regards abstraction and encapsulation as very fundamental concepts, but it looks as if the business intelligence specialists don't. Most business intelligence systems are not at all based on those two concepts. Almost all the reports are tied to a particular database server technology. Let's use a simple example: Imagine we are using a reporting tool in which we can write our own SQL statements to access the database, and we are using all the proprietary bells and whistles of that database server to get optimal performance. What happens if we want to replace that database server by another—one that supports a slightly different SQL dialect? Or we want to switch to an MDX-based database server, or maybe we want to access an external database that does not return a table but an XML document? In probably all those situations, we have to dramatically change the report definitions.

It's important that the concepts of abstraction and encapsulation are adopted in business intelligence systems to improve their flexibility and to make it easier to implement changes and adopt new emerging technologies.

Disadvantage 4—Decrease of Data Quality: When multiple copies of the same data exist, there is always a risk that the data becomes inconsistent. In other words, storing duplicate data, which, as indicated, is done extensively in classic business intelligence systems, involves a data quality risk. David Loshin formulates it as follows (see [35]):

> *Each time data is copied, it is also subjected to any number of data transformations, each of which provides an opportunity for the introduction of data errors. Each subsequent copy resembles the original data source less. Copying data can only lead to entropy and inconsistency.*

In every business intelligence system, one of the goals should be to minimize duplication of data to minimize data quality risks.

Disadvantage 5—Limited Support for Operational Reporting: Another disadvantage relates to operational reporting and analytics. More and more organizations show interest in supporting this new challenging form of business intelligence. With operational business intelligence, the reports that the decision makers use have to include more up-to-date data. Refreshing the source data once a day is not enough for them. Decision makers who are quite close to the business processes, such as operational managers, especially need 100 percent up-to-date data. But how is this done? One doesn't have to be a technological wizard to understand that if data has to be copied four or five times from one data store to another in order to get from the production databases to the reports, doing this in just a few microseconds is close to impossible. Most business intelligence systems are not designed in such a way that the operational reports are linked to the operational data. We have to simplify the architecture to support operational business intelligence. Bottom line, the architecture has to be simplified by removing data stores and minimizing the number of copy steps.

Disadvantage 6—Limited Support for Reporting on Unstructured and External Data: The growing interest for analytics and reporting on unstructured and external data brings us to the last disadvantage. Most data warehouses are loaded with structured data coming from production databases, but rarely ever do we find unstructured and external data in there. To allow reporting on these new data sources, many specialists propose to handle these two data sources in the same way internal production data has always been handled: if it's not structured, make it structured and copy it into the data warehouse so that it becomes available for analytics and reporting. In other words, the proposals are based on copying data. They want to shape these data sources so they fit in a classic business intelligence architecture.

But why not run the analytics straight on the unstructured data source itself and straight on the external data source? In a way, that would be the Internet-style solution. If we search something on the Internet, we don't first copy all the pages needed to one of our own databases. No, the data stays where it is. Likewise, more and more of the document management systems do allow us to analyze their databases straight on, thereby reducing the need to copy their data to a data warehouse first. Unfortunately, many business intelligence tools don't support access to those systems. With respect to external data, doing business intelligence over the Internet on external data can be done today in a very sophisticated way with mashup tools (see Section 1.13).

Note: We would like to emphasize that the disadvantages mentioned in this section relate to business intelligence systems and *not* to business intelligence architectures per se. For example, many business intelligence systems based on the CIF (corporate information factory) have been developed in which data marts are implemented as physical data stores. The CIF does not dictate this, but because of the available hardware and software technologies, many organizations went for that implementation. Data virtualization makes it possible to develop virtual data marts (see Sections 7.5.2 and 7.6.2). A business intelligence system developed that way can still be qualified as supporting the CIF.

2.11 Summary

This chapter gives an overview of the various components a business intelligence system is composed of, such as a data warehouse, a data mart, a data staging area, ETL scripts, and so on. In addition, the different styles of data transformation are explained with which data is copied from one data store to another.

Most existing business intelligence systems have a classic architecture consisting of a chain of databases and transformation processes. These classic business intelligence systems have supported us well, and for many organizations they will still be the right solution for a few more years to come. But because of various reasons, it's time for a new architecture. First of all, the challenge for those organizations is to support the following new reporting and analytical needs with such an architecture:

- Data consumers need access to data at the lowest level of detail.
- Data consumers need access to operational data.
- Data consumers need access to new data stores quickly.

- Data consumers need access to data stores containing so much data that copying it to a data warehouse or data mart would take too much time and would be too costly.
- Data consumers need access to unstructured and external data sources, probably without having to copy all that data first.

In addition, a new architecture is needed because business intelligence systems have to be more flexible (see Section 1.2) and because of all the new technology that has become available and that organizations want to exploit. In many situations, existing business intelligence systems have to be redesigned dramatically to be able to support these needs. Deploying data virtualization in a business intelligence system makes it easier. But before we dive into this topic, the coming chapters explain how data virtualization works.

Data Virtualization Server: The Building Blocks

3

3.1 Introduction

In this and the following three chapters we're opening up the hood of a data virtualization server and taking a peek at the internal technology and the building blocks. Topics addressed include the following:

- Importing existing tables and nonrelational data sources
- Defining virtual tables, wrappers, and mappings
- Combining data from multiple data stores
- Publishing virtual tables through APIs, such as SQL and SOAP
- Defining security rules
- Management of a data virtualization server
- Caching of virtual tables
- Query optimization techniques

This chapter deals with the first four items on this list.

3.2 The High-Level Architecture of a Data Virtualization Server

The high-level architecture of a data virtualization server is simple (Figure 3.1). To the data consumers, accessing data in a data virtualization server feels like accessing data in a database server. Data consumers can send queries to the data virtualization server, and the results are returned. They have no idea where or how the data is stored. Whether it's stored in an SQL database, stored in a spreadsheet, extracted from a website, or received from a web service, it is hidden for them.

The objects that the data consumers see have different names in different products, such as *derived view*, *view*, and *logical data object*. In this book we call them *virtual tables*. The names the products assign to the data being accessed are also different. Examples of names in use are *physical data object* and *base view*. In this book we use the term *source table*.

A source table can be, for example, a table in an SQL database, external data coming from a website, a spreadsheet, the result of invoking a web service, an HTML page, or a sequential file. Source tables are defined and managed outside the control of the data virtualization server. Although some of these sources are not actually tables at all, we will still refer to them as source tables because in reality most of the data stores accessed are SQL databases and because this book is aimed at business intelligence systems in which most data consumers use SQL.

59

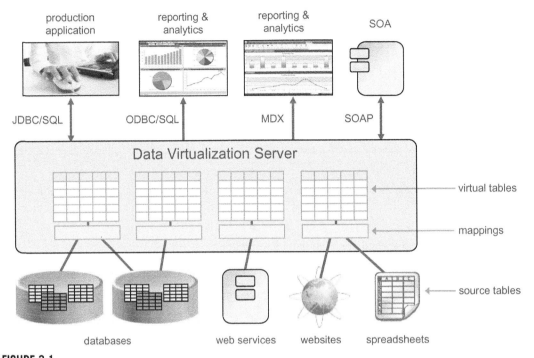

FIGURE 3.1

The architecture of a data virtualization server. The data virtualization server hides where and how data is stored.

How the data of source tables is transformed to a virtual table is defined in a *mapping*. In other words, a virtual table receives a content by linking it to source tables through a mapping. Virtual tables, mappings, and source tables are the main building blocks of a data virtualization server. All three will be discussed extensively in this chapter.

Each data virtualization server offers various APIs for accessing those tables. One data consumer can access the virtual tables through, for example, a classic JDBC/SQL interface, whereas another can access that same table using MDX, and a third through a SOAP-based interface. The first data consumer will see the data as ordinary tables; the MDX application will see multidimensional cubes; and through the SOAP-based interface, the returned data will have an XML form. Regardless of the form, all data consumers will see the same data, but none of them has any idea where or how the data in those tables is stored.

3.3 Importing Source Tables and Defining Wrappers

Before a source table can act as a source for a virtual table, it has to be *imported*. Importing a source table means that it's made known to the data virtualization server. The importing process is relatively simple when a source table is a table stored in an SQL database. The developer logs on to the data virtualization server, and from the data virtualization server a connection is made with the database server that holds the source table. When a connection is established, the data virtualization server

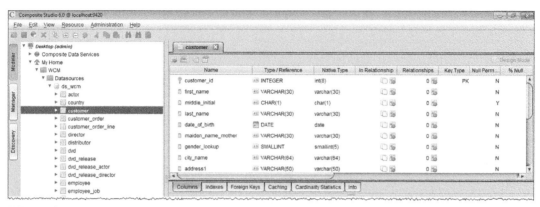

FIGURE 3.2

The data types of the columns of the CUSTOMER table are transformed to a standard data type.

Reprinted with permission of Composite Software.

accesses the *catalog* of the database. The catalog is a set of tables in which descriptions of all the tables and columns of the database are stored. The tables from the database are then presented to the developer. For example, on the left-hand side of Figure 3.2, the list of tables in the WCM database is presented. Next, the developer picks the required table, and the data virtualization server extracts all the meta data available on that table and stores it in its own dictionary.

When a source table has been selected for import, the data virtualization server determines whether some values have to be transformed to a more standardized form. The reason is that different database servers store values of particular data types differently. For example, database servers might store floating point values differently. To be able to compare values managed by different database servers correctly, the values have to be transformed to a standard form. In other words, for each and every column, a data virtualization server has to check whether a transformation is required to transform the values to a more standardized form to make comparisons possible. This means that data virtualization servers have to understand for each different data source how specific data types are handled. Figure 3.2 shows how the native data types of the columns of the source table CUSTOMER are transformed to a standard data type (column called Type/Reference). For example, the data type int(8) of the first column called customer_id is transformed to INTEGER. All this transformation work is done automatically and behind the scenes.

When a source table has been imported, the data virtualization server has created a *wrapper table*, or *wrapper* for short. Some of the products use other names, such as *base view* and *view*. Quite a bit of meta data is extracted during the import process and stored by the data virtualization server in its dictionary. All this meta data is assigned to the definition of the wrapper table. The meta data might include the following:

- The network location of the server where the source table resides
- Information on the database connection to be able to log on to the database server so that the data virtualization server knows where it is and how it can be accessed
- The name, owner, and date created of the source table
- The structure of the source table, including the columns and their names
- For each column of the source table, the data type and the not null specification

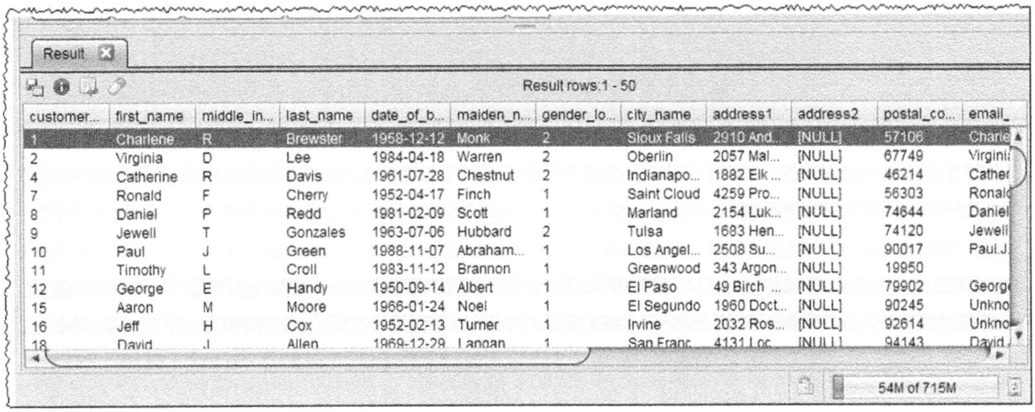

customer...	first_name	middle_in...	last_name	date_of_b...	maiden_n...	gender_lo...	city_name	address1	address2	postal_co...	email_
1	Charlene	R	Brewster	1958-12-12	Monk	2	Sioux Falls	2910 And...	[NULL]	57106	Charle
2	Virginia	D	Lee	1984-04-18	Warren	2	Oberlin	2057 Mal...	[NULL]	67749	Virgini
4	Catherine	R	Davis	1961-07-28	Chestnut	2	Indianapo...	1882 Elk...	[NULL]	46214	Cather
7	Ronald	F	Cherry	1952-04-17	Finch	1	Saint Cloud	4259 Pro...	[NULL]	56303	Ronal
8	Daniel	P	Redd	1981-02-09	Scott	1	Marland	2154 Luk...	[NULL]	74644	Daniel
9	Jewell	T	Gonzales	1963-07-06	Hubbard	2	Tulsa	1683 Hen...	[NULL]	74120	Jewell
10	Paul	J	Green	1988-11-07	Abraham...	1	Los Angel...	2508 Su...	[NULL]	90017	Paul.J
11	Timothy	L	Croll	1983-11-12	Brannon	1	Greenwood	343 Argon...	[NULL]	19950	
12	George	E	Handy	1950-09-14	Albert	1	El Paso	49 Birch ...	[NULL]	79902	George
15	Aaron	M	Moore	1966-01-24	Noel	1	El Segundo	1960 Doct...	[NULL]	90245	Unkno
16	Jeff	H	Cox	1952-02-13	Turner	1	Irvine	2032 Ros...	[NULL]	92614	Unkno
18	David	J	Allen	1969-12-29	Langan	1	San Franc	4131 Loc	[NULL]	94143	David

Result rows:1 - 50

54M of 715M

FIGURE 3.3

The virtual contents of the wrapper called CUSTOMER can be displayed right after it has been defined.

Reprinted with permission of Composite Software.

- Available primary and foreign keys defined on the source table
- The number of rows in the source table and the distribution of values for each column; this type of information is extracted for query optimization purposes

In most data virtualization servers, when a wrapper table has been defined on a source table, it can be queried right away by the data consumers. The virtual contents of this wrapper table is 100 percent identical to that of the source table. To illustrate this, Figure 3.3 shows the contents of a new wrapper defined on the CUSTOMER source table. No changes are made to the data, except that, as indicated, column values of particular data types are transformed to a standard data type. By enabling direct access to the data via wrappers, developers can study the contents of the source tables. This can be useful to determine whether the data is according to expectations and whether or not it needs to be transformed.

A wrapper table behaves like any table in an SQL database. It can be queried and, if the underlying database servers allow it, data in the virtual contents of a wrapper can be inserted, updated, and deleted as well. The relationship between wrappers and source tables is a many-to-one. One or more wrappers can be defined for a source table, and a wrapper is always defined on at maximum one source table.

Some data virtualization servers allow a wrapper to be decoupled from the underlying source table. This is called an *unbound wrapper table*. This means that a wrapper table can be defined with no source table. It's also possible to decouple a wrapper table from its existing source table and later bind it to another source table (rebind). However, this can only be done if that second source table has the same structure as the first one. This can be useful, for example, to redirect a wrapper from a source table with test data to one containing the real data. This can be done without having to change the wrapper itself. The advantage is that data consumers and other virtual tables don't have to be changed.

Note: Importing non-SQL tables, which is slightly more difficult, is addressed in detail in Section 3.8.

3.4 Defining Virtual Tables and Mappings

As indicated, a wrapper table shows the full contents of a source table. Also, a wrapper has the same structure as the source table it's bound to. Maybe not all the data consumers want to see that contents.

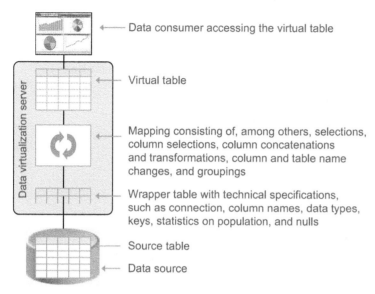

Data consumer accessing the virtual table

Virtual table

Mapping consisting of, among others, selections, column selections, column concatenations and transformations, column and table name changes, and groupings

Wrapper table with technical specifications, such as connection, column names, data types, keys, statistics on population, and nulls

Source table

Data source

FIGURE 3.4

The relationships among virtual tables, mappings, wrappers, and source tables.

Some might not want to see all the rows, others not all the columns, still others who want to see the data in an aggregated style, and some who want to see a few source tables joined as one large table. In this case, we have to define *virtual tables* on top of the wrappers.

Defining a virtual table means defining a *mapping*. The mapping defines the structure of a virtual table and how the data from a source table (or set of source tables) should be transformed to become the contents of the virtual table. The mapping can be called the definition of a virtual table. A mapping usually consists of operations such as row selections, column selections, column concatenations and transformations, column and table name changes, and groupings. Without a mapping, a virtual table has no contents and can't be queried or updated.

Figure 3.4 shows the relationships among the concepts virtual table, mapping, wrapper, and source table. In that same figure, a notation technique is introduced that we will use throughout this book. The table with the dotted lines represents a virtual table, the box with the two bend arrows represents a mapping, the table without a line at the bottom represents a wrapper table, and the table inside the database icon represents a source table.

To avoid the diagrams becoming overly complex and too layered, in most of them we combine the icons for wrapper and source table, and we combine the icons for mapping and virtual table (see Figure 3.5). The disk icon inside the source table icon indicates that the source data is stored in a table in an SQL database. Unless it's important to make the distinction, we use these combined icons.

In a way, a virtual table is very much like the view concept in SQL database servers. Basically, the definition of an SQL view is made up of a name, a structure (a set of columns with their respective data types), and a query definition. The contents of the view is virtual and is derived from underlying tables and views. A virtual table of a data virtualization server also has a name, a structure (a set of columns with their respective data types), and a query definition (the mapping), and the contents of a virtual table is also virtual and is derived from underlying data sources, such as source tables.

Different languages are used by the data virtualization servers for defining a mapping. Languages in use are SQL, ETL-like flow languages, extended SQL, XML-related languages such as XSLT and XQuery, procedural programming languages, and sometimes a combination of these. We'll look at a few examples.

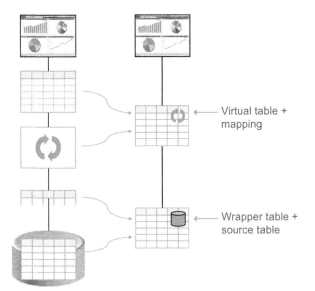

FIGURE 3.5

Combined icons for, on one hand, the virtual table and its mapping and, on the other hand, for the wrapper and the source table.

Virtual table + mapping

Wrapper table + source table

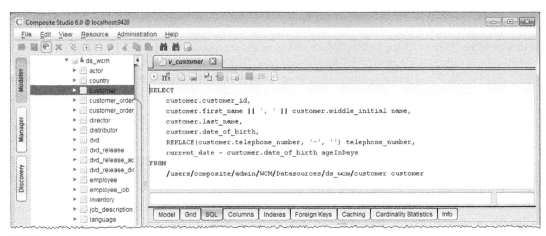

FIGURE 3.6

In this example, SQL is used to define a virtual table.

Reprinted with permission of Composite Software.

Figure 3.6 shows the mapping of a virtual table called V_CUSTOMER using an SQL language. The mapping is defined on the wrapper for the CUSTOMER table. This virtual table holds for each customer the CUSTOMER_ID, the FIRST_NAME concatenated with the MIDDLE_INITIAL, the LAST_NAME, the DATE_OF_BIRTH, the TELEPHONE_NUMBER from which dashes have been removed, and the customer's age in days. As an alternative, Figure 3.7 shows the definition of that same virtual table using a grid-like language. The top right-hand side of the figure contains the mapping.

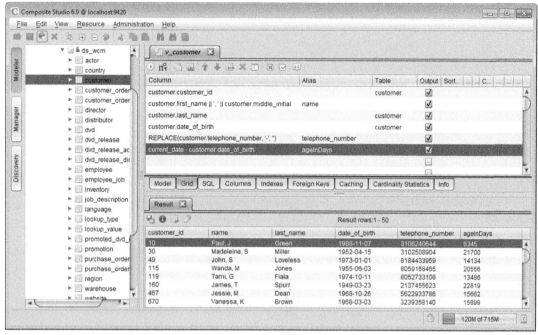

FIGURE 3.7

In this example, a grid-like language is used to define a virtual table.

Reprinted with permission of Composite Software.

Figure 3.8 shows a third alternative with a comparable mapping developed with a flow-like language. It consists of multiple operations (each symbol representing a transformation). The first symbol (🖾) indicates the source table that is queried—in this case, the RealCUSTOMERS table. The second symbol (🍸) indicates a filter that is used to select a number of rows. The third one (🗗) indicates that the values of a column are transformed. And finally, the fourth symbol (📁) represents a grouping of rows that leads to aggregation of data.

When a virtual table has been created, its virtual contents can be viewed. For example, on the bottom right-hand side in Figure 3.7, the contents of the V_CUSTOMER virtual table is presented. This makes it possible for developers to check those contents and see if the data is coming through correctly.

The complexity of a mapping can range from simple to very complex. For example, data from multiple source tables can be joined together, data can be aggregated, or particular column values can be transformed. In other words, transformation operations can be specified. Here are some of the transformation operations supported by many data virtualization server products:

- Filters can be specified to select a subset of all the rows from the source table.
- Data from multiple tables can be joined together.
- Columns in the source table can be removed from the virtual table.
- Values can be transformed by applying a long list of string manipulation functions.

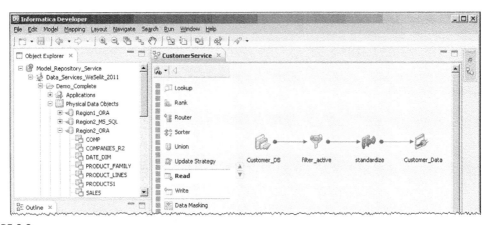

FIGURE 3.8

An example of a mapping using a flow-like language.

Reprinted with permission of Informatica Corporation.

- Columns in the source table can be concatenated.
- Names of the columns in the source table and the name itself can be changed.
- New virtual and derivable columns can be added.
- Group-by operations can be specified to aggregate data.
- Statistical functions can be applied.
- Rows can be deduplicated.
- Sentiment analysis can be applied to text.
- Fuzzy joins can be used to compare textual data.
- Incorrect data values can be cleansed.
- Rows can be sorted.
- Rank numbers can be assigned to rows.

Final remark: The differences between a wrapper table and a virtual table are minimal. Both can be accessed by data consumers, and they both look like regular tables. The difference is that a wrapper is defined on a source table (it wraps a source table), whereas a virtual table is defined on wrappers and other virtual tables. Virtual tables need wrappers, while wrapper tables don't need virtual tables.

3.5 Examples of Virtual Tables and Mappings

This section contains some examples of mappings to give a better understanding of what's possible when defining virtual tables. We use SQL for defining the mappings, but all these examples can also be specified using other mapping languages. In general, when examples of mappings are shown in this book, we primarily use SQL. The reason is that SQL is familiar to most developers.

Note: We assume that for each source table in the sample database, a wrapper table is defined that shows the full contents of that source table. Names of the wrappers are identical to the source tables they are bound to.

The transformations applied in Example 3.1 are quite simple. Complex ones can be added as well, as Example 3.2 shows.

EXAMPLE 3.1

Define a virtual table on the CUSTOMER wrapper that contains the CUSTOMER_ID, the DATE_OF_BIRTH, the POSTAL_CODE, the EMAIL_ADDRESS for all those customers with a postal code equal to 90017, 19108, or 48075, and who registered after 2006. The mapping in SQL looks like this:

```
DEFINE      V_CUSTOMER AS
SELECT      CUSTOMER_ID,
            FIRST_NAME || ', ' || MIDDLE_INITIAL || '' LAST_NAME AS FULLNAME,
            DATE_OF_BIRTH, POSTAL_CODE, EMAIL_ADDRESS
FROM        CUSTOMER
WHERE       POSTAL_CODE IN ('90017', '19108', '48075')
AND         YEAR(DATE_REGISTERED) > 2006
```

Virtual contents of V_CUSTOMER consisting of 199,336 rows (we show only the first four rows):

CUSTOMER_ ID	FULLNAME	DATE_OF_ BIRTH	POSTAL_ CODE	EMAIL_ADDRESS
10	Paul J, Green	1988-11-07	90017	Paul.J.Green@mailinator.com
691	Roseanne C, Hubble	1985-01-06	90017	Roseanne.C.Hubble@spambob.com
729	Thomas L, Chase	1965-05-12	48075	Thomas.L.Chase@dodgit.com
1390	Michele K, Hicks	1946-05-12	19108	Michele.K.Hicks@trashymail.com
: :		:	:	:

Explanation

In this mapping, the columns of the virtual table—CUSTOMER_ID, DATE_OF_BIRTH, POSTAL_CODE, and EMAIL_ADDRESS—are copied unmodified from the source table columns. A new virtual column is defined by concatenating the first name, middle initial, and the last name of a customer. This mapping also contains two filters. With the first filter, only customers from the specified postal codes are selected, and with the second filter, only customers registered after the year 2006 are selected. In this example, SQL is used for specifying the mapping. Some products help to create mappings by using a wizard that guides the developer in creating the code (Figure 3.9).

FIGURE 3.9

Some data virtualization servers support wizards to guide developers when developing mappings.

Reprinted with permission of Denodo Technologies.

EXAMPLE 3.2

Define a virtual table that contains for each DVD release the release_id, the title, and a category code (1–4) that is derived from the genre; each genre belongs to one category.

```
DEFINE    V_RELEASE AS
SELECT    DVD_RELEASE_ID, TITLE,
          CASE
            WHEN GENRE IN ('Action/Adventure','Action/Comedy','Animation','Anime',
                'Ballet','Comedy','Comedy/Drama','Dance/Ballet','Documentary')
              THEN 1
            WHEN GENRE IN ('Drama','Drama/Silent','Exercise','Family','Fantasy',
                'Foreign','Games','Genres','Horror','Karaoke','Late Night')
              THEN 2
            WHEN GENRE IN ('Music','Musical','Mystery/Suspense','Opera','Rap',
                'Satire','SciFi','Silent','Software','Special Interest')
              THEN 3
            WHEN GENRE IN ('Sports','Suspense/Thriller','Thriller','TV Classics',
                'VAR','War','Western')
              THEN 4
            ELSE NULL END AS CATEGORY
FROM      DVD_RELEASE
```

(continued)

Virtual contents of V_RELEASE (we show only the first four rows):

```
DVD_RELEASE_ID  TITLE                         CATEGORY
--------------  -----                         --------
            6   101 Dalmatians (1961)              1
            8   10th Kingdom (Old Version)         3
            2   10                                 1
            7   101 Dalmatians (1996)              2
            :   :                                  :
```

Explanation

A complex case expression is used to derive a new category from the genre. In a mapping, data from multiple tables can also be joined to form one virtual table.

EXAMPLE 3.3

Define a virtual table that shows for each customer the customer_id, the name of the region and the name of the country where the customer is located, and the title of the website of the customer (if available).

```
DEFINE   V_CUSTOMER_DATA AS
SELECT   C.CUSTOMER_ID, R.REGION_NAME, CY.COUNTRY_NAME, W.WEBSITE_TITLE
FROM     CUSTOMER AS C, REGION AS R, COUNTRY AS CY, WEBSITE AS W
WHERE    C.REGION_ID = R.REGION_ID
AND      R.COUNTRY_ID = CY.COUNTRY_ID
AND      C.WEBSITE_ID = W.WEBSITE_ID
```

Virtual contents of V_CUSTOMER_DATA consisting of 145,373 rows (we show only the first four rows):

```
CUSTOMER_ID  REGION_NAME  COUNTRY_NAME  WEBSITE_TITLE
-----------  -----------  ------------  -------------
     200031  Alberta      Canada        World Class Movies
     200127  Alberta      Canada        World Class Movies
     200148  Alberta      Canada        World Class Movies
     200212  Alberta      Canada        World Class Movies
          :  :            :             :
```

Explanation

Because the region name, country name, and website title are not stored in the CUSTOMER table, joins with the source tables REGION, COUNTRY, and WEBSITE are needed to retrieve that data. It's as if the codes stored in the CUSTOMER table are replaced by their respective names.

Some users might be interested in overviews—in other words, in aggregated data. Mappings can be used to summarize detailed data into aggregated data.

EXAMPLE 3.4

For each year, get the total rental price and the total purchase price.

```
DEFINE    V_PRICES_BY_YEAR AS
SELECT    YEAR(CO.ORDER_TIMESTAMP) AS YEAR,
          SUM(COL.RENTAL_PRICE) AS SUM_RENTAL_PRICE,
          SUM(COL.PURCHASE_PRICE) AS SUM_PURCHASE_PRICE
FROM      CUSTOMER_ORDER_LINE AS COL, CUSTOMER_ORDER AS CO
WHERE     COL.CUSTOMER_ORDER_ID = CO.CUSTOMER_ORDER_ID
GROUP BY  YEAR(CO.ORDER_TIMESTAMP)
```

Virtual contents of **V_PRICES_BY_YEAR** consisting of nine rows:

```
YEAR   SUM_RENTAL_PRICE   SUM_PURCHASE_PRICE
----   ----------------   ------------------
2000            2380.00              6364.31
2001           19090.00             51337.11
2002           53905.00            143218.77
2003           98155.00            273041.17
2004          210220.00            615026.88
2005          343010.00            959619.26
2006          576235.00           1587859.72
2007         1137685.00           3472137.39
2008         5574265.00          20142485.06
```

Explanation

In this mapping, data from the CUSTOMER_ORDER_LINE table is joined with data from the CUSTOMER_ORDER table. Next, the rows are grouped based on the year part of the order timestamp.

As indicated, some products use flow languages to develop comparable logic (Figure 3.10). Each box in this diagram represents an operation of the process. For example, in the box called Joiner, the two tables are joined, and in the Aggregator box, rows with the same year are grouped together. Developers can also decide to study a mapping with less details (Figure 3.11).

Virtual tables can also be defined to implement certain business objects. Imagine that the concept "a top ten customer" is defined as a customer who belongs to the top ten customers with the highest total value for rentals plus purchases. This is illustrated in Example 3.5.

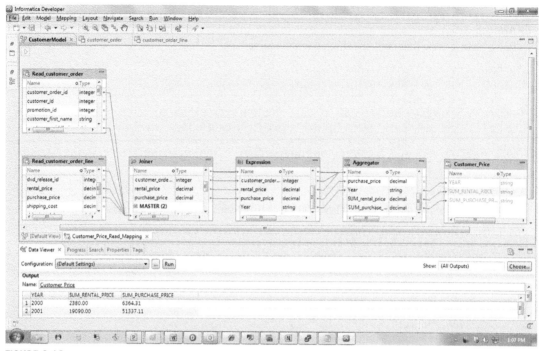

FIGURE 3.10

The detailed mapping of Example 3.4 using a flow language.

Reprinted with permission of Informatica Corporation.

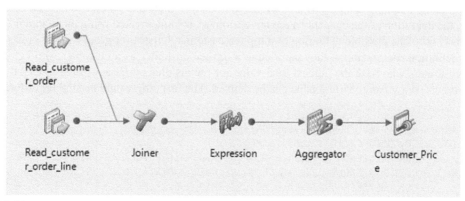

FIGURE 3.11

The high-level mapping of Example 3.4 using a flow language.

Reprinted with permission of Informatica Corporation.

EXAMPLE 3.5

Define a virtual table that contains the top ten customers.

```
DEFINE    V_TOP_TEN_CUSTOMER AS
SELECT    CO.CUSTOMER_ID, C.LAST_NAME,
          SUM(COL.RENTAL_PRICE) + SUM(COL.PURCHASE_PRICE) AS PRICE
FROM      CUSTOMER_ORDER_LINE AS COL, CUSTOMER_ORDER AS CO, CUSTOMER AS C
WHERE     COL.CUSTOMER_ORDER_ID = CO.CUSTOMER_ORDER_ID
AND       CO.CUSTOMER_ID = C.CUSTOMER_ID
GROUP BY  CO.CUSTOMER_ID, C.LAST_NAME
ORDER BY  PRICE DESC
LIMIT     10
```

Virtual contents of the V_TOP_TEN_CUSTOMERS virtual table consisting of ten rows:

```
CUSTOMER_ID  LAST_NAME  PRICE
-----------  ---------  -----
     180346  Somers     3147.59
      30975  Thies      2917.73
      80660  Jenkins    2847.87
      82339  Baca       2747.88
     191530  Rush       2729.84
     223906  Scates     2677.88
     188612  Innes      2614.86
       1112  Tyson      2599.87
      90101  Soto       2588.45
     209248  Rodriquez  2572.94
```

Explanation

The join in the mapping is added to look up the amount of rentals and purchases of each customer. In fact, the definition of the concept "a top ten customer" is implemented using the mapping.

This is only one possible definition of a top ten customer. Other user groups might prefer a different definition. For example, they can define a top ten customer as a customer who belongs to those customers who have the highest total value for rentals plus purchases in the last 12 months. For those users, a separate virtual table can be defined. The mapping would be slightly different:

```
DEFINE    V_TOP_TEN_CUSTOMER_VERSION2 AS
SELECT    CO.CUSTOMER_ID, C.LAST_NAME,
          SUM(COL.RENTAL_PRICE) + SUM(COL.PURCHASE_PRICE) AS PRICE
FROM      CUSTOMER_ORDER_LINE AS COL, CUSTOMER_ORDER AS CO, CUSTOMER AS C
WHERE     COL.CUSTOMER_ORDER_ID = CO.CUSTOMER_ORDER_ID
AND       CO.CUSTOMER_ID = C.CUSTOMER_ID
AND       DATE(ORDER_TIMESTAMP) > DATE('2008-12-26') - INTERVAL 1 YEAR
GROUP BY  CO.CUSTOMER_ID, C.LAST_NAME
ORDER BY  PRICE DESC
LIMIT     10
```

Virtual contents of the V_TOP_TEN_CUSTOMERS_VERSION2 virtual table consisting of ten rows:

```
CUSTOMER_ID   LAST_NAME   PRICE
- - - - - - -  - - - - -   - - - -
     82339    Baca        2747.88
     80660    Jenkins     2587.92
    209248    Rodriquez   2572.94
    191530    Rush        2557.90
     77162    Roberts     2517.88
     84248    Patrick     2477.89
    106157    Hill        2454.35
      1112    Tyson       2427.93
    128844    Carr        2327.93
    206543    Mckean      2287.92
```

Explanation

The customers Somers, Thies, Scates, Innes, and Soto, who are in the virtual contents of the first virtual table, are not in the contents of the second, while Roberts, Patrick, Hill, Tyson, Carr, and McKean have been added. So different definitions lead to different answers.

Both definitions can live next to each other: one virtual table for one user group and the other for a second group. Let's look at Example 3.6, which involves a more complex definition.

EXAMPLE 3.6

Define a virtual table that contains all the active customers. Active customers are defined as those who rented or bought at least one movie in each of the last four months.

```
DEFINE       V_ACTIVE_CUSTOMER AS
SELECT       C.CUSTOMER_ID, LAST_NAME
FROM         CUSTOMER AS C
WHERE        NOT EXISTS
            (SELECT  *
             FROM (SELECT 2008 AS YEAR, 1 AS MONTH
                   UNION SELECT 2008, 2
                   UNION SELECT 2008, 3
                   UNION SELECT 2008, 4) AS YM
             WHERE  NOT EXISTS
                   (SELECT *
                    FROM    CUSTOMER_ORDER AS CO
                    WHERE   CO.CUSTOMER_ID = C.CUSTOMER_ID
                    AND     YEAR(CO.ORDER_TIMESTAMP) = YM.YEAR
                    AND     MONTH(CO.ORDER_TIMESTAMP) = YM.MONTH))
ORDER BY 1
```

Explanation

The contents of this virtual table contains just two customers: Foster (83060) and Rogers (119377). In reality, the middle query would not contain the year 2008 four times and would not contain the specification of four months. Expressions such as YEAR(CURRENT_DATE) would be used to look at the most recent orders and dates. However, because the sample database was created some time ago, in this example, we have to check for a fixed year and particular months. The benefit of implementing the definitions of business objects inside the mappings of virtual tables is that all data consumers use those definitions. And if definitions (read mappings) have to be changed, there is a direct impact on all reports.

So far, the transformation operations used in the examples in this section are all common to the standard SQL language. In data virtualization it's sometimes necessary to apply more powerful operations, such as deduplication, fuzzy join, and sentiment analysis. For all three, we show how well these complex operations have been integrated in the data virtualization servers.

Deduplication means that rows with a set of equal values are considered to represent the same business object. For example, if two rows in the CUSTOMER table are identical with respect to their first name, last name, and date of birth, they are considered the same customer. Most data virtualization products support deduplication functions.

EXAMPLE 3.7

Define a virtual table that contains all the customers but with deduplication applied.

```
DEFINE      V_DEDUPLICATED_CUSTOMER AS
SELECT      *
FROM        DEDUPLICATION(CUSTOMER
                ON FIRST_NAME, INITIALS, LAST_NAME, DATE_OF_BIRTH
                WHEN > 99)
```

Explanation

The data virtualization server accesses the CUSTOMER table and determines whether duplicate rows exist. Some products use statistical algorithms to calculate the chance that rows do represent the same business object. The result of that calculation is a percentage; the higher the percentage, the higher the chance that the objects are identical. The value 99 in this example indicates that we only want rows to be merged together when the data virtualization server is at least 99 percent sure they're the same.

With a *fuzzy join*, tables are joined based on whether data looks alike. In most cases this is used to compare textual data. Imagine, for example, that we want to join the CUSTOMER table with an external file containing customer address data as well. We want to check whether our customers in the CUSTOMER table appear in that external file. Because different keys are used in that external file, we can't do a simple join. A join on the address columns won't help either, because names might be spelled differently or incorrectly. A fuzzy join helps here. A fuzzy join checks whether the addresses of our customers resemble the addresses in the external customer file. Such a join operation has been trained to deal with misspellings and errors (see Example 3.8).

EXAMPLE 3.8

Define a virtual table that shows which customers appear in the external file.

```
DEFINE    V_FUZZY_JOIN AS
SELECT    C.CUSTOMER_ID, CE.KEY, FUZZY()
FROM      CUSTOMER AS C, CUSTOMER_EXTERNAL AS CE
WHERE     (C.LAST_NAME, C.CITY, C.ADDRESS1, C.ADDRESS2, C.POSTAL_CODE) ~
          (CE.NAME, CE.CITY_NAME, CE.STREET, CE.EXTRA, CE.ZIP_CODE)
```

Explanation

The operator ~ indicates the fuzzy join. In this example the fuzzy join is executed on five columns of the CUSTOMER table with five fields of the external file. The result of the fuzzy join contains all the rows where, very likely, two customers are identical. The fuzzy join takes into account slightly different spellings and so on. The function FUZZY returns a percentage indicating how sure the fussy join is about whether these two addresses are really identical.

Text can be analyzed using an operation called *sentiment analysis*. This operation assigns a value to the text indicating whether the text has a positive or a negative ring to it. Using the operation is easy, but the internals are quite complex. Sentiment analysis requires some understanding of words and grammar. Somehow it has to be able to understand the semantics of the text. In fact, before such a function can be invoked, it probably has to be trained somewhat. It probably has to be told what positive words and what negative words are.

EXAMPLE 3.9

Assume that a wrapper table exists called CUSTOMER_TWEET that contains tweets that customers have written about WCM. Define a virtual table that shows a sentiment value for each of these tweets.

```
DEFINE    V_TWEET AS
SELECT    TWEET_ID, CUSTOMER_ID, SENTIMENT(TWEET_TEXT)
FROM      CUSTOMER_TWEET
```

Explanation

Depending on the sentiment analysis operation in use, the result is a simple value indicating whether the text is positive, negative, or unknown, or the result is a relative value on a scale of 0 to 100 indicating how positive the tweet is (100 being extremely positive, 50 unknown, and 0 very negative). The complexity of the function is completely hidden to the developers.

Finally, some data virtualization servers allow any external function to be invoked from within the mapping. Such a function can be a simple piece of code written in Java, but it can also be an external web service. For example, it can be a function that invokes the Google web service that determines the geographic coordinates of an address. This would allow us to retrieve those coordinates for all the

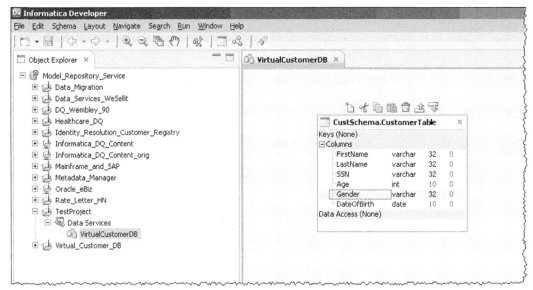

FIGURE 3.12

Defining a new virtual table called CustomerTable without a mapping.

Reprinted with permission of Informatica Corporation.

customers in the sample database. Only once does the web service have to be defined as a function within the data virtualization server, and afterward, it can be invoked like any other function.

To summarize, mappings are not limited to the straightforward operations usually supported by a standard SQL language. Most data virtualization servers support a rich set of operations and even allow developers to extend that list with self-made or external functions.

3.6 Virtual Tables and Data Modeling

Some data virtualization servers allow *unbound virtual tables* to be defined. These are virtual tables without mappings, without links to source tables. To the designers it will feel as if they're working in a design environment. Afterward, when the structure of a virtual table has been defined, a mapping can be added.

In these data virtualization servers, defining the structure of a virtual table is relatively simple: it's purely a matter of defining column names, data types, and so on. As an example, Figure 3.12 shows the definition of a virtual table called CustomerTable with six columns. The process of defining such a virtual table is not much different from defining a real table in an SQL database server. For obvious reasons, because such a virtual table is unbound (it doesn't have a mapping), it can't be accessed.

Allowing designers to develop unbound virtual tables offers a number of advantages. One advantage of separating a virtual table definition from a mapping (and thus source tables) is that the designers don't have to concern themselves initially with the existing structure of the source table. They can focus entirely on what they want the virtual tables to look like or what the data consumers need. Especially if the structures of the source tables are not very well structured, it may be better to first design the required structures of the virtual tables. This approach is usually referred to as *top-down design* or *outside-in design*.

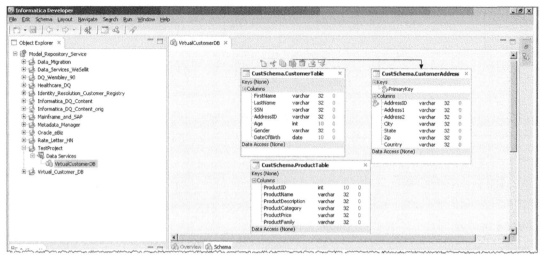

FIGURE 3.13

Defining a data model consisting of three virtual tables and their relationships.

Reprinted with permission of Informatica Corporation.

Another advantage is that this approach allows virtual tables to be "moved" to other wrappers over time: *rebinding* virtual tables. For example, when the real data is migrated to another database, only the mapping of the virtual table has to be redirected. This can also be useful when a virtual table has to be redirected from a source table in a testing environment to one in a production environment.

Some data virtualization servers offer a full-blown modeling interface to design the structure of the virtual tables and their interrelationships. Figure 3.13 shows an example where a data model is developed consisting of three virtual tables and their interrelationships.

3.7 Nesting Virtual Tables and Shared Specifications

Just as views in an SQL database can be nested (or stacked), so can virtual tables in a data virtualization. In other words, a virtual table can be defined on top of other virtual tables. A virtual table defined this way is sometimes referred to as a *nested virtual table*. A nested virtual table is also defined with a mapping, but one where data is retrieved from other virtual tables. Figure 3.14 shows a nested virtual table defined on a nonnested one. Virtual tables can be nested indefinitely.

The biggest benefit of being able to nest virtual tables is that it allows for meta data specifications to be shared. Let's illustrate this with the example depicted in Figure 3.15. Here, two nested virtual tables are defined on a third. Let's assume that the data requirements of the two data consumers are partially identical and partially different. The advantage of this layered approach is that the specifications to be shared by both data consumers are defined in virtual table V_1, and the specifications unique to the data consumers are implemented in virtual tables V_2 and V_3. This means that the applications share common specifications: the ones defined in the mapping of V_1. If we change those common specifications, that change will automatically apply to V_2 as to V_3. Let's illustrate this with Example 3.10.

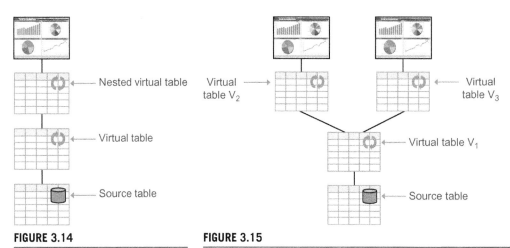

FIGURE 3.14

A nested virtual table is defined on other virtual tables.

FIGURE 3.15

Shared specifications in virtual table V_1.

EXAMPLE 3.10

On the virtual table V_CUSTOMER defined in Example 3.1, we can define the following two virtual tables with their respective mappings:

```
DEFINE    V_POSTAL_CODE AS
SELECT    POSTAL_CODE, SUM(BALANCE), COUNT(CUSTOMER_ID)
FROM      V_CUSTOMER
GROUP BY  POSTAL_CODE

DEFINE    V_CUSTOMER_SUBSET AS
SELECT    *
FROM      V_CUSTOMER
WHERE     POSTAL_CODE = 19108
AND       CUSTOMER_ID IN
          (SELECT   CO.CUSTOMER_ID
           FROM     CUSTOMER_ORDER AS CO
           WHERE    CO.CUSTOMER_ID = VT_CUSTOMER.CUSTOMER_ID
           AND      YEAR(CO.ORDER_TIMESTAMP) = 2008)
```

Explanation

These two mappings share the specifications that make up the mapping of V_CUSTOMER—for example, FULLNAME is a concatenation of the columns FIRST_NAME, MIDDLE_INITIAL, and LAST_NAME, and the two filters. In addition, both have their own specifications. In the first virtual table called V_POSTAL_CODE, customer data is aggregated per postal code, and in the second one, only customers from postal code 19108 who have ordered something in 2008 are included. If we make a change to the mapping of V_CUSTOMER, both virtual tables inherit the change.

Shared specifications don't have to be repeated anymore inside reporting and analytical tools. This allows those tools to focus on their strengths, such as analytics, visualization, reporting, and drill-downs. Shared specifications also improve the consistency of reporting results, the speed of development, and ease of maintenance: specifications have to be updated only once.

3.8 Importing Nonrelational Data

In the previous sections, we assumed that all the source tables are SQL tables. But not all data needed for analytics and reporting is stored in SQL tables. It might be stored in all kinds of data stores and formats, such as XML documents, NoSQL databases, websites, and spreadsheets. Importing SQL tables is quite straightforward, but importing other forms of data can be somewhat more complex. This section describes how data stored in the following nonrelational tables can be imported:

* XML and JSON Documents
* Web Services
* Spreadsheets
* NoSQL Databases
* Multi-Dimensional Cubes and MDX
* Semistructured Data
* Unstructured Data

In this section we restrict ourselves to importing some of the more popular nonrelational data stores. Some data virtualization servers do support other types of data stores, such as the following:

* Hierarchical and network database servers such as Bull IDS II, Computer Associates Datacom and IDMS, IBM IMS, Model 204, Software AG Adabas, and Unisys DMS
* SPARQL and triplestores
* Sequential and index-sequential files, such as C-ISAM, ISAM, and VSAM
* Comma-delimited files

3.8.1 XML and JSON Documents

An unimaginably large amount of valuable data is available in XML and JSON (JavaScript Object Notation) documents. It can be data inside documents available on the Internet or documents inside our own organization. It can be simple, such as an invoice, but it can also be complex and large, such as an XML document containing a full list of all the commercial organizations of a country that is periodically passed from one government organization to another. Obviously, there is a need to query that data and to join it with data coming from other data stores. We will initially show how this works with XML and then with JSON.

There are three characteristics of XML documents that make them different from the rows in SQL tables. First, each XML document contains data as well as meta data; second, an XML document might contain *hierarchical structures*; and third, it might contain *repeating groups*. With respect to the meta data, the structure of the document is within the document itself; see Example 3.11.

EXAMPLE 3.11

An XML document that holds for customer 6 the last name, the initials, and the address.

```
<customer>
    <customer_id>6</customer_id>
    <name>
        <lastname>Parmenter</lastname>
        <initials>R</initials>
    </name>
    <address>
        <street>Haseltine Lane</street>
        <houseno>80</houseno>
        <postcode>1234KK</postcode>
        <city>Stratford</city>
    </address>
</customer>
```

This document contains data values such as 6, Parmenter, and Stratford, plus it contains the meta data describing that, for example, 6 is the customer_id, that Parmenter is the last name of the customer, and that Stratford is the city where the customer is located.

As indicated, an XML document might also have a hierarchical structure. In the previous example, the element "lastname" belongs hierarchically to the name element which belongs hierarchically to the customer element. This means, for example, that Stratford is the city belonging to the address belonging to customer 6. In addition, XML documents might contain repeating groups. A repeating group is a set of values of the same type; see Example 3.12.

EXAMPLE 3.12

An XML document that holds for two customers their last names, their initials, and their lists of orders:

```
<customerlist>
    <customer>
        <id>6</id>
        <name>
            <lastname>Parmenter</lastname>
            <initials>R</initials>
        </name>
        <orderlist>
            <order>
```

(continued)

```
                    <id>123</id>
                </order>
                <order>
                    <id>124</id>
                </order>
                <order>
                    <id>125</id>
                </order>
            </orderlist>
        </customer>
        <customer>
            <id>7</id>
            <name>
                <lastname>Jones</lastname>
                <initials>P</initials>
            </name>
            <orderlist>
                <order>
                    <id>128</id>
                </order>
                <order>
                    <id>129</id>
                </order>
            </orderlist>
        </customer>
    </customerlist>
```

This document contains two repeating groups: customerlist and orderlist. Customerlist contains two customers (6 and 7), and both customers have a list of orders; customer 6 has three orders and customer 7 has two orders.

Concepts such as hierarchy and repeating group have no equivalent in SQL tables. Therefore, to be able to use XML documents as source tables, inside the wrappers they have to be flattened to tables consisting of columns and records.

Removing hierarchies is accomplished by removing the intermediate layers. For example, the document in Example 3.11 looks like this after flattening:

CUSTOMER_ID	LASTNAME	INITIALS	STREET	HOUSENO	POSTCODE	CITY
6	Parmenter	R	Haseltine Lane	80	1234KK	Stratford

Flattening a repeating group is somewhat more difficult. Generally, there are two ways to transform a hierarchical structure to a flat table structure. First, a table can be developed in which each row represents one customer with his set of orders. This table can look like this:

CUSTOMER_ID	LASTNAME	INITIALS	ORDER_ID1	ORDER_ID2	ORDER_ID3
6	Parmenter	R	123	124	125
7	Jones	P	128	129	

The structure of this table can lead to numerous practical problems when defining and querying virtual tables. In addition, how many columns should we reserve for orders in this table? We went for 3 here, but shouldn't it be 10 or even 100? In an XML document, this number is unlimited, but we can't define a variable number of columns in a table. This would mean we have to introduce a maximum of orders per customers, which in this example is set to 3.

A more practical solution is to create a table where each row represents an order placed by a customer. This removes both repeating groups from the table. This table can look like this (note that this table has a denormalized schema):

ORDER_ID	CUSTOMER_ID	LASTNAME	INITIALS
123	6	Parmenter	R
124	6	Parmenter	R
125	6	Parmenter	R
128	7	Jones	P
129	7	Jones	P

In most data virtualization servers, this flattening of the XML structure is defined in the wrapper. Special tools and languages are supported to create them. For example, Figure 3.16 shows a wrapper for an XML document in which some elements from an XML document are flattened to become a wrapper called Employee with four columns: CompanyName, DeptName, EmpName, and EmpAge. In this figure, the field Operation Output contains the structure of the XML document, and the field called Transformation Output contains the required wrapper structure. A transformation is specified by linking elements from the XML document to columns in the data source (curly lines). The lines indicate how the hierarchical structure of the XML document should be mapped to a table with columns.

Behind the scenes, the language used in the wrapper for specifying this transformation is usually XSLT or XQuery; for both, see Section 1.13. Both are standardized languages that are used for executing the transformation. The graphical presentation of XSLT or XQuery offers only limited functionality. If developers want to, they can use the full power of XSLT or XQuery by coding by hand.

When a wrapper table is defined, it can be used like any other wrapper, so virtual tables can be defined on it. Using the standard set of icons, this would look like Figure 3.17. This wrapper table on top of an XML document can be used by any virtual table. This makes it possible, for example, to join data stored in XML documents with data stored in SQL tables (Figure 3.18). The developer who creates the virtual table doesn't see that one wrapper is bound to an SQL table and the other to an XML document.

When defining wrappers on XML documents, the question is always: How much of the transformation is placed in the wrapper and how much in the mapping of the virtual table? One factor that plays an important role here is performance. Is the module running the wrapper code faster than the module running the mapping? This question is hard to answer. The topic is discussed extensively in Chapter 6.

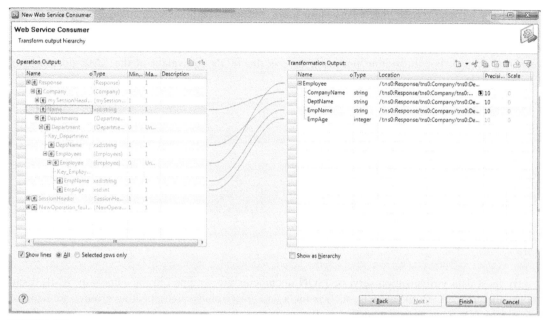

FIGURE 3.16

Transforming a hierarchical XML structure to a flat table.

Reprinted with permission of Informatica Corporation.

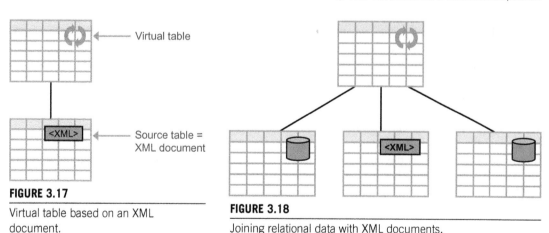

FIGURE 3.17

Virtual table based on an XML document.

FIGURE 3.18

Joining relational data with XML documents.

Note: An XML structure doesn't always have to be flattened before it becomes usable. It depends on what the data consumer needs. For example, if the data consumer wants to use standard SQL to query the data, the data has to be flattened, since SQL does not support queries that manipulate hierarchical data structures. However, if the data consumer is a web service, it can handle hierarchical structures. Therefore, it's probably recommended to go through the entire process without flattening the XML structure or hierarchy. More on this topic in Section 3.10.

Another document type that is becoming more and more popular is *JavaScript Object Notation* (JSON). JSON owes its popularity to the fact that it's more lightweight than XML and can be parsed faster. JSON shares some characteristics with XML, such as data plus meta data, hierarchies, and repeating groups. For illustration purposes, here is the JSON equivalent of the XML document in Example 3.11:

```
{ "customer": {
   "id": 6,
   "name": {
        "lastname": "Parmenter",
        "initials": "R" }
   "address": {
        "street": "Haseltine Lane",
        "houseno": "80",
        "postcode": "1234KK",
        "city": "Stratford"}
}
```

By most data virtualization servers, JSON documents are wrapped in the same way XML documents are wrapped. All the aspects, such as meta data, hierarchies, and repeating groups, are handled comparably. Data has to be flattened as well.

3.8.2 Web Services

Another valuable type of data store is a web service. A web service might give access to external data, such as demographic data, weather-related data, or price information of competitive products. It might also be that data stored inside a packaged application can only be accessed through a web service that has been predefined by the vendor. More and more, internal and external information is accessible through web services only. For example, websites such as http://www.infochimps.com, https://datamarket.azure.com/, and http://www.data.gov/ offer access to all kinds of commercial and noncommercial data. Therefore, a data virtualization server should make it possible to make web services accessible to every data consumer.

Informally, a web service represents some functionality and has a technical interface. This section focuses on SOAP as the interface because it's still the most popular interface, although others do exist. If a web service has a SOAP interface, it means that the returned data is formatted as an XML document. This implies that much of what has been described in the previous section also applies to SOAP. The only difference is that when a service is invoked, input parameters might have to be specified. But besides that difference, developing a data source for a SOAP service is comparable to developing one for an XML document. Figure 3.19 shows the icon used for wrappers defined on web services.

Figures 3.20 and 3.21 show how a wrapper is defined on an external, public web service called TopMovies. It's a simple web service that, when invoked, returns a list of the top ten movies. In both figures the window at the top right-hand side contains the specification to flatten the result. At the bottom right-hand side, the result is presented, which is a table with ten rows, each consisting of one value representing the title of a movie.

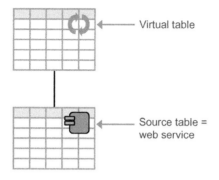

FIGURE 3.19

Virtual table defined on a SOAP-based web service.

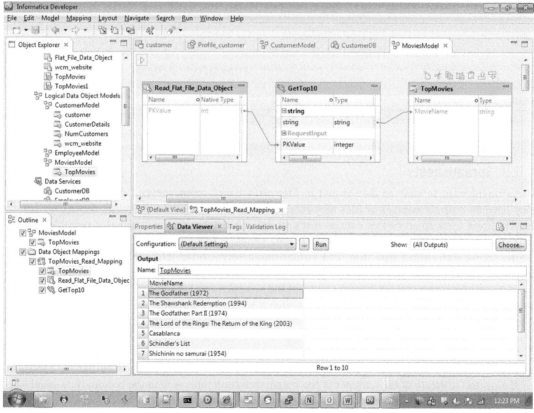

FIGURE 3.20

Developing a wrapper on an external web service called TopMovies.

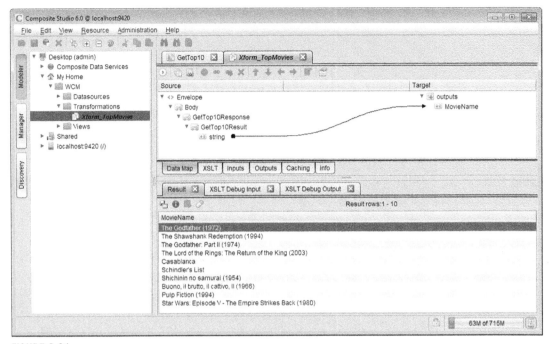

FIGURE 3.21

Developing a wrapper on an external web service called TopMovies.

Reprinted with permission of Composite Software.

3.8.3 Spreadsheets

Users might want to analyze data stored in Microsoft Excel spreadsheets. This can be private data they have built up themselves or files they received in the form of spreadsheets. A data virtualization server allows users to acces that data as if it's stored in a database, plus it makes it possible to combine spreadsheet data with data stored in other data stores.

To access spreadsheet data in a data virtualization server or to join spreadsheet data with other data stores, a wrapper has to be defined for the spreadsheet (Figure 3.22). When defining the wrapper table, rows of the spreadsheet become rows in the wrapper and columns of the spreadsheet become columns in the wrapper table. When defining such a wrapper, the developer has to do some guiding. The main reason is that a spreadsheet doesn't contain enough meta data, which means it's hard for a data virtualization server to derive the table structure from the spreadsheet cells automatically.

As an example, Figure 3.23 shows a spreadsheet containing a small set of website_ids, the website title, and the URL. Figure 3.24 shows that a wrapper is defined for a spreadsheet; at the top right-hand side, the structure of the wrapper is presented: three columns. And at the bottom right-hand side, the contents of the wrapper is displayed.

3.8.4 NoSQL Databases

At the end of the 2000s, a new generation of database servers was introduced, consisting of products such as Apache *Cassandra* (see [36]) and Apache *Hadoop* (see [37]), 10Gen *MongoDB* (see [38]),

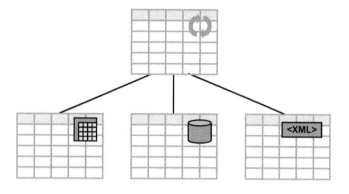

FIGURE 3.22

Joining spreadsheet data with relational data and XML documents.

	A	B	C	D
1	website_id	website_title	website_uri	
2	1	World Class Movies	http://www.worldclassmovies.com/	
3	2	Cool movies as Hot as they get	http://cool.worldclassmovies.com/	
4	3	Premium World Class Movies	http://premium.worldclassmovies.com/	
5	4	Really cheap movies	http://cheap.worldclassmovies.com/	
6	5	Exclusive World Class Movies	http://exclusive.worldclassmovies.com/	
7				
8				

FIGURE 3.23

Spreadsheet with data on websites.

CouchDB (see [39]), *Terrastore*, *Oracle NoSQL Database*, *HyperTable*, and *InfiniteGraph*. Because some of them are open source database servers, multiple distributions are commercially available. For example, Hadoop is also available from Cloudera, HortonWorks, IBM, MapR Technologies, and Oracle, and Cassandra is also available from DataStax.

What binds all these database servers is the fact that they don't support SQL or that SQL is not their primary database language. That's why the catchy name *NoSQL* is used to refer to them. In the beginning, NoSQL stood for *No SQL*, implying that the data managed by these database servers is not accessible using SQL. They supported their own database language(s) and API(s). Nowadays, NoSQL stands for *Not Only SQL*. Most of these products still don't offer SQL as their primary language, but a minimal form of SQL support has been added by some.

This heterogeneous group of database servers can be subcategorized in document stores, key-value stores, wide-column stores, multivalue stores, and graph data stores. Some of these database servers have been designed to handle larger quantities of transactions or more data than traditional SQL database servers can.

Traditional SQL database servers are generic by nature. They have been designed to support all types of applications, ranging from high-end transactional to straightforward batch reporting

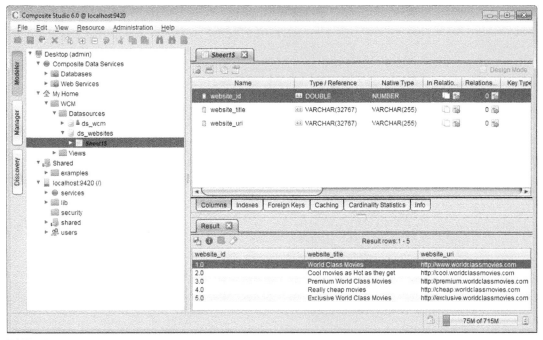

FIGURE 3.24

Developing a wrapper on a spreadsheet.

Reprinted with permission of Composite Software.

applications. Therefore, they support functionality for all those applications. However, this is not true for NoSQL database servers. Most of them are designed for a limited set of application types—for example, for querying immensely large databases or for processing massive numbers of transactions concurrently. They accomplish this by *not* implementing the functionality needed by the other application types and only including the functionality needed by that same set. Compared to the traditional database servers, they can be viewed as stripped database servers (Figure 3.25).

Due to their increasing popularity, more and more organizations have data stored in these NoSQL products. Unfortunately, most reporting and analytical tools aren't able to access NoSQL database servers, because most of them need an SQL or comparable interface. There are two ways to solve this problem. First, relevant data can be copied from a NoSQL database to an SQL database. However, in those situations in which a NoSQL solution is selected, the amount of data is probably massive. Copying all that data can be time-consuming, and storing all that data twice can be costly.

Another solution is to use a data virtualization server on top of a NoSQL database server and to wrap the NoSQL database to offer an SQL interface. The responsibility of the data virtualization server is to translate the incoming SQL statements to the API or to the SQL dialect of the NoSQL database server. Because the interfaces of these database servers are proprietary, the vendors of the data virtualization servers have to develop a dedicated wrapper technology for each of them.

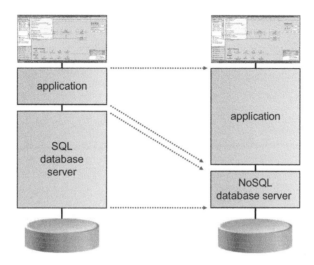

FIGURE 3.25

NoSQL database servers try to offer more query performance or higher transaction levels by not implementing all the features of a traditional SQL database server. The size of each rectangular box represents the amount of functionality offered.

Some NoSQL databases store data in a hierarchical style and some use repeating groups. So the wrapper of a data virtualization server should be able to flatten data coming from a NoSQL database. This flattening is similar to that for XML and web services. Nevertheless, by placing a data virtualization server on top of a NoSQL database, the data is opened up for almost any reporting and analytical tool, and data can be joined with other data sources.

Another feature of some of the NoSQL databases is that they are schema-less. Simply put, this means when a new row is inserted to a table with a set of predefined columns, column values can be added for which no columns have been predefined. The effect is that each row in a table can have a slightly different set of columns. The key benefit of schema-less databases is flexibility. If new data has to be stored, no redesign of the table structures and no data migration is required. The new values are just added. The way data virtualization servers handle this feature is that in the wrapper table the columns are defined that are retrieved. New columns wil only be retrieved when introduced in the definition of the wrapper.

The icon used for NoSQL databases is shown in Figure 3.26. The icon represents a set of databases or, in other words, a large amount of data.

Note: Some of the NoSQL database servers are used for storing semistructured data. How that type of data is handled by wrappers is discussed in Section 3.8.6.

3.8.5 Multidimensional Cubes and MDX

A very popular database technology used in business intelligence systems is multidimensional cubes. This database technology is not based on tables and columns, but on *dimensions, facts,* and *hierarchies*. It's designed and optimized specifically for analytical queries. Often, database servers that support multidimensional cubes offer great query performance.

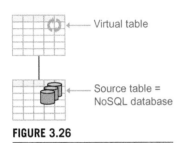

FIGURE 3.26

Data stored in NoSQL databases can also be wrapped.

FIGURE 3.27

Selecting the dimensions and measures of a cube to include in the flattened table.

Reprinted with permission of Denodo Technologies.

Most of the products using cubes support the database language *MDX* (MultiDimensional Expressions) designed by Microsoft. Microsoft's MDX was first introduced as part of its *OLE DB for OLAP* specification in 1997 and has quite some support in the market. The specification was quickly followed by a commercial release of Microsoft OLAP Services 7.0 in 1998 and later by Microsoft Analysis Services. Many vendors have currently implemented the language, including IBM, Microstrategy, Mondrian, Oracle, SAP, and SAS.

MDX is a powerful language for querying cubes, but it has a few limitations. For example, it can't join SQL tables with cubes, nor can data in different cubes be joined. With a data virtualization server, cubes can be wrapped. The approach to create a wrapper table on a cube is comparable to creating one on an XML document, except that XSLT or XQuery is not used internally but MDX. Defining the wrapper table is primarily a matter of selecting the relevant dimensions and measures of a cube (Figure 3.27). The data virtualization server does the rest. Figure 3.28 shows the icon used for MDX databases.

Being able to access multidimensional cubes as tables offers several practical advantages:

- Data stored in the cubes can be joined with any type of data store technology, such as SQL tables, XML documents, web services, and other cubes.
- If data is stored in cubes, it can only be accessed by tools supporting MDX (or a comparable language). By creating a wrapper table, the data is opened up to any reporting tool using SQL,

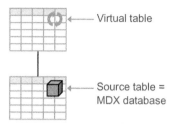

FIGURE 3.28

With a wrapper table an SQL interface can be presented for the data stored in MDX databases; additional virtual tables can be defined on top of such a wrapper table to transform the data in a form required for the data consumers.

Company code	Currency	Fiscal year	Cumulative Balance (SAP Demo)	Sales for the Period (SAP DEMO)	Total Credit Postings (SAP Demo)	Total Debit Postings (SAP Demo)
IDES AG Germany	Euro	Calendar year, 4 spec. periods 2001	-155.126,00 EUR	37.178.640,00 EUR	37.178.640,00 EUR	37.023.513,00 EUR
IDES UK	Pounds sterling	Calendar year, 4 spec. periods 2001	£ -564.375,00	£ 21.821.364,00	£ 21.821.364,00	£ 21.256.989,00
IDES France	Euro	Calendar year, 4 spec. periods 2001	-222.957,00 EUR	22.536.827,00 EUR	22.536.827,00 EUR	22.313.871,00 EUR
IDES US Inc.	US Dollar	Calendar year, 4 spec. periods 2001	$ -409.985,00	$ 30.423.505,00	$ 30.423.505,00	$ 30.076.172,00
IDES Canada	Canadian Dollar	Calendar year, 4 spec. periods 2001	-314.222,00 CAD	61.273.376,00 CAD	61.273.376,00 CAD	60.959.154,00 CAD

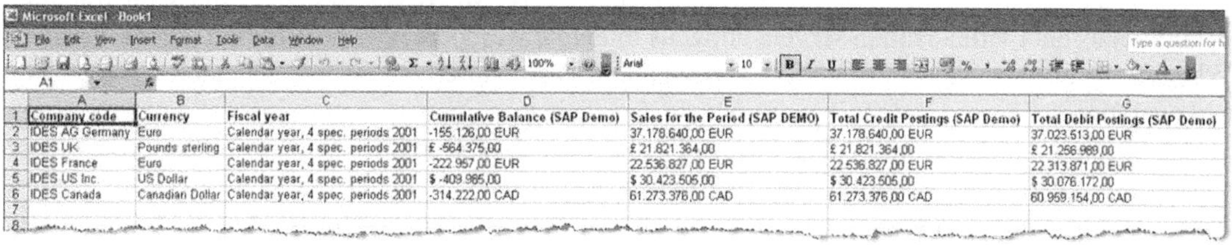

FIGURE 3.29

The flattened view of a cube.

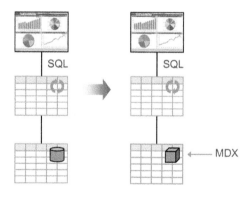

FIGURE 3.30

Seamlessly migrating from SQL to MDX.

or, in other words, it can be accessed by almost any reporting tool available on the market. For example, data stored in a cube can be accessed by Excel; the result might look like Figure 3.29.

- Migration to MDX becomes easier. If particular SQL queries on a set of source tables are slow, and if we expect that running similar queries on an MDX implementation will be faster, the data can be moved to a cube, and the data virtualization server will hide the fact that cubes and MDX are used (Figure 3.30). No rewrite of the report is required in this situation.

3.8.6 **Semistructured Data**

In the previous section we assume that all the data in the data sources is structured data. This section covers wrapping sources that contain *semistructured data*. The next section deals with unstructured data. What's special about semistructured data is that it does have structure, but seeing and using that structure is sometimes a technological challenge; applications have to work hard to discover that structure. An example of semistructured data is the data "hidden" in HTML pages. For example, weather-related data, the member data of social media networks, and the movie data on the IMDB website are all probably semistructured. An enormous amount of semistructured data is available in HMTL format on the Internet.

Another well-known example of semistructured data can be found in the weblogs: the long and complex URLs. Extracting measures such as average page hits by user or the total view time is not always that straightforward. These weblogs are mostly stored in files, but more and more websites have switched to NoSQL databases for their scalability.

Let's first describe how to define a wrapper table on HTML pages to extract the semistructured data. Various data virtualization servers allow us to define wrappers on top of HTML-based websites. When ready, all that "hidden" data becomes available as structured data in a virtual table for reporting and analytics.

Developing a wrapper on HTML pages is not always easy. Code has to be developed that understands how to navigate a website and that knows which data elements to extract from the HTML pages. This process of extracting data from HTML pages is sometimes referred to as *HTML scraping*.

Imagine we want to extract from the IMDB website (www.imdb.com) a list with all the movies in which actor Russell Crowe performed. The result of such a query returns an HTML page that looks like the one in Figure 3.31. To start the navigation, a wrapper has to understand in which field the

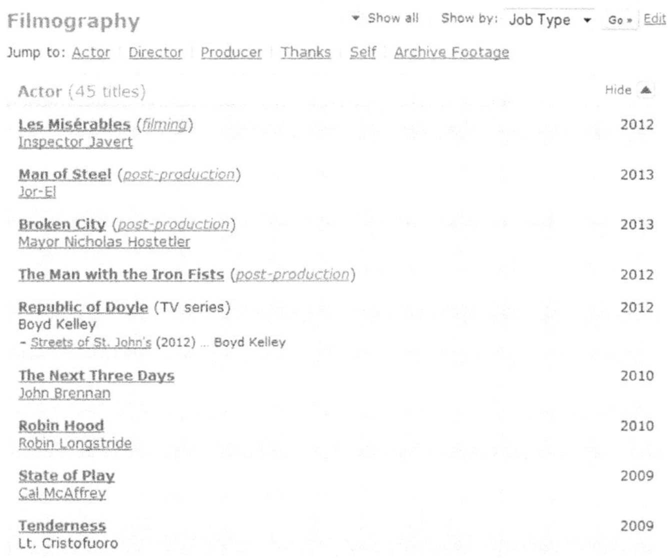

FIGURE 3.31

This HTML page shows the first of all the movies in which Russell Crowe performed.

value Russell Crowe has to be entered. It has to know which button to click to start the search for all the movies he played in. Next, the wrapper has to understand the structure of the returned page, the meaning of all the data elements on the page that the page contains a list of items, and that each line contains the title, the role, and the year in which the movie was released. In fact, the list for Russell Crowe is so long that the wrapper has to be able to detect that there are more movies on the next page. So it has to know how to jump to that next page. As indicated, developing a wrapper on an HTML page requires quite some work and is clearly not as easy as defining one for an SQL table.

Figure 3.32 contains a part of the wrapper code used to extract the list of Russell Crowe's movies. It's a high-level and graphical language. Operations in this language are, for example, CompleteFormandSearch (which means enter the text "Russell Crowe" and hit the Search button), ExtractMovies (this is a loop construct to get all the movies one by one), and CreateMovieRecord (add a row with data to the result). Do note that the languages used for wrapping web pages are all proprietary languages.

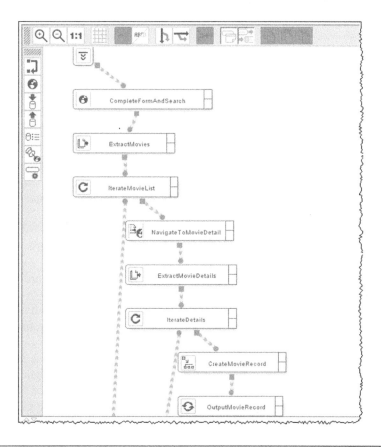

FIGURE 3.32

The wrapper code to extract from a set of HTML pages the movies Russell Crowe played in.

Reprinted with permission of Denodo Technologies.

VQL Shell					

Command log

SELECT * FROM imdb where actor='Russell Crowe'

| Execute | Stop | Load | View execution trace | ☑ Limit rows | 150 |

TITLE	ROLE	YEAR	METASCORE	OPENINGWEEKENDBOXOFFICE	ACTOR
The Next Three Days	John Brennan	2010	52/100	$6,542,779	Russell Crowe
Robin Hood	Robin Longstride	2010	53/100	$36,063,385	Russell Crowe
State of Play	Cal McAffrey	2009	64/100	$14,071,280	Russell Crowe
Body of Lies	Ed Hoffman	2008	57/100	$12,884,416	Russell Crowe
American Gangster	Richie Roberts	2007	76/100	$43,565,135	Russell Crowe
3:10 to Yuma	Ben Wade	2007	76/100	$14,035,033	Russell Crowe
Cinderella Man	Jim Braddock	2005	69/100	$18,320,205	Russell Crowe
A Beautiful Mind	John Nash	2001	72/100	$2,501,096	Russell Crowe
Proof of Life	Terry Thorne	2000	45/100	$10,207,869	Russell Crowe
Gladiator	Maximus	2000	64/100	$34,819,017	Russell Crowe
The Insider	Jeffrey Wigand	1999	84/100	$6,712,361	Russell Crowe
Mystery, Alaska	John Biebe	1999	49/100	$3,102,191	Russell Crowe
L.A. Confidential	Wendell 'Bud' White	1997	90/100	$5,211,198	Russell Crowe

FIGURE 3.33

The virtual contents of the wrapper that extracts data from a set of HTML pages.

Reprinted with permission of Denodo Technologies.

When the wrapper has been developed—meaning it understands how it can scrape the HTML pages—the virtual contents of the wrapper can be presented (Figure 3.33). This figure clearly shows that the following simple, standard SQL statement can be used to analyze the data:

```
SELECT   *
FROM     IMDB
WHERE    ACTOR = 'Russell Crowe'
```

Again, with data virtualization, a data source that doesn't have a clear structure suddenly becomes a structured data source for reporting and analytics.

This result also includes columns such as Metascore and Openingweekendboxoffice. These are columns not derived from the HTML page shown in Figure 3.31, but by navigating, for each movie found, to a separate page that contains these details.

For the analysis of weblogs, special functions are required. In fact, logic is needed that understands the structure of these weblog entries and that understands that there might be dialogs hidden in there. Dedicated weblog analysis servers have been developed specifically for this job. Data virtualization servers need to have comparable logic on board to analyze these weblogs and transform the semistructured data to structured data in tabular form that can be analyzed by more standard reporting and analytical tools.

To summarize, for each particular form of semistructured data, a dedicated solution has to be developed that unravels the structure and transforms it to a structured form. When that functionality is available, it's completely encapsulated and abstracted. It's hidden underneath the wrapper tables. This semistructured data becomes available for reporting and analytics like any other type of data.

3.8.7 **Unstructured Data**

The term *structured data* refers to data consisting of concise values, names, dates, and codes that can be interpreted in only one way. For example, POSTAL_CODE in the table CUSTOMER contains structured data. Customer 30's postal code value is 90017, and there is only one way to interpret this value, whoever reads this, whenever he reads it, and wherever he reads this. The same applies to the value 18.50 in the column PURCHASE_PRICE in the table DVD_RELEASE; it's the price for which a DVD is being sold. It might be that some values are incorrect, but that's beside the point. For a structured data value, clear rules exist on how to interpret the values.

Besides all the structured data, every organization builds up a massive amount of *unstructured data*. Unstructured data is all the data that is not concise and no specific way exists to interpret the values—in other words, it might be interpreted differently by different readers and at different times. In fact, unstructured data can't be analyzed without any form of preparation. For example, all the received emails of an organization or all the Word documents written by the employees of an organization are examples of unstructured data. The text in those emails and documents is not concise. The same sentence can be interpreted in different ways by different readers.

Most unstructured data is stored in non-SQL database servers, such as email systems; document management systems; directories with Word, Excel, and PowerPoint files; call center messages; contracts; and so on. A lot of the unstructured data is external—created by others and stored outside the organization. For example, social media websites such as LinkedIn, Facebook, and Twitter, and news sites contain a wealth of unstructured data. Most of these data stores require dedicated interfaces for retrieving data.

In most business intelligence systems, only structured data is made available for reporting and analytics. Users of most business intelligence systems are not able to exploit the unstructured data for reporting. This is a seriously missed opportunity, because there is a wealth of information hidden in unstructured data. Making unstructured data available enriches a business intelligence system and can improve the decision-making process.

Some data virtualization servers have implemented technology to work with these unstructured data sources. The effect is that a wrapper can be defined to access those unstructured sources, allowing classic reporting and analytical tools to process unstructured data and allowing unstructured data to be integrated with structured data.

As an example, Figure 3.34 shows the contents of a wrapper that retrieves from the Twitter website all the tweets that contain the strings @russellcrowe, Robin, and Hood. As can also be seen in this figure, when the wrapper has been defined, a standard SQL statement can be used to query the data:

```
SELECT    *
FROM      TWITTER_SEARCH_MESSAGES
WHERE     SEARCH = '@russellcrowe Robin Hood'
```

A wrapper defined on unstructured data can be used like any other wrapper. They can be queried, they can be joined with other virtual tables, and a virtual table can be defined that joins it with

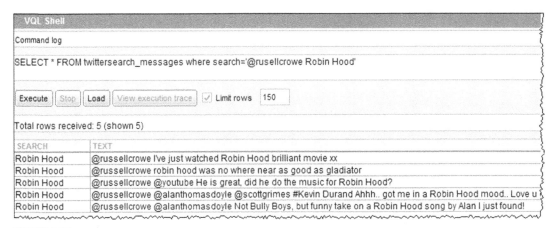

FIGURE 3.34

Wrapping a data store containing unstructured data.

Reprinted with permission of Denodo Technologies.

another wrapper. As an example, Figure 3.35 shows the result of a query on a virtual table that joins the wrapper on Twitter with the wrapper on the IMDB website defined in Section 3.8.6. The nested virtual table is called IMDB_COMBINING_TWITTER. It shows that once wrappers are defined, the internal complexity is completely hidden.

3.9 Publishing Virtual Tables

When virtual tables have been defined, they need to be *published*, which is sometimes called *exposing* virtual tables. This means that the virtual tables become available for data consumers through one or more languages and programmatic interfaces. For example, one data consumer wants to access a virtual table using the language SQL and through the API JDBC, whereas another prefers to access the same virtual table as a web service using SOAP and HTTP.

Most data virtualization servers support a wide range of interfaces and languages. Here is a list of some of the more popular ones:

- SQL with ODBC
- SQL with JDBC
- SQL with ADO.NET
- SOAP/XML via HTTP
- ReST (Representational State Transfer) with JSON (JavaScript Object Notation)
- ReST with XML
- ReST with HTML
- JCA (Java Connector Architecture)
- JMS (Java Messaging Service)
- Java (POJO)

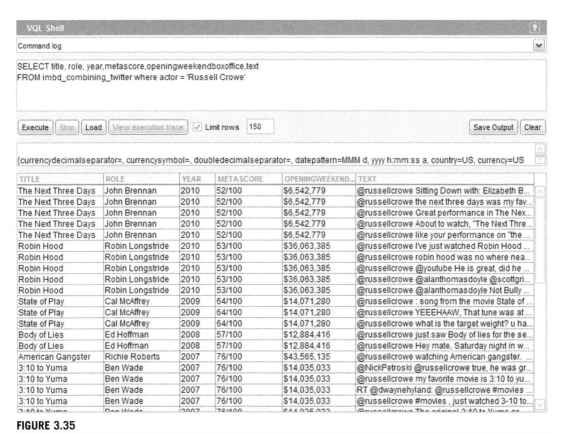

FIGURE 3.35

Query on a virtual table that joins a wrapper on semistructured data with one on unstructured data.

Reprinted with permission of Denodo Technologies.

- RSS (RDF Site Summary or Really Simple Syndication)
- SPARQL

Publishing a virtual table is usually very easy, especially if the interface is SQL-like. In that case, all an administrator has to do is switch it on (Figure 3.36). It's primarily a matter of ticking a field. When an interface has been published for a virtual table, applications and tools can access its data. For example, Figure 3.37 shows the SQL query tool WinSQL accessing the published CUSTOMER virtual table.

For each virtual table, one or many interfaces can be enabled, allowing a virtual table to be accessed via one data consumer—for example, JDBC/SQL—and the other via SOAP. This makes it possible for many applications to share the same virtual table and still use their own preferred interface.

Now, most tools used in business intelligence systems use SQL to access the data. The advantage of having other interfaces is that nonbusiness intelligence consumers, such as Internet applications, service-oriented architectures, and more classic data entry applications, can also access the same data

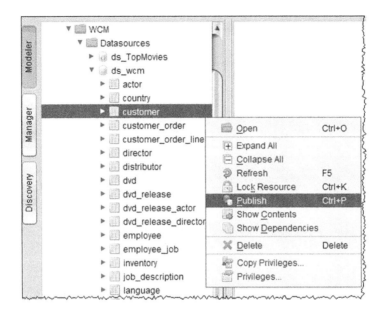

FIGURE 3.36

Enabling an ODBC/SQL or JDBC/SQL interface for a virtual table is purely a matter of switching it on.

Reprinted with permission of Composite Software.

made available to the business intelligence environment (Figure 3.38). They will share the same specifications, which will have the effect that data usage will be consistent across business intelligence and other systems.

As indicated, publishing a virtual table through SQL is easy, because the concepts used in a virtual table, such as columns and records, are identical to those of SQL. However, some of the other interfaces support other concepts. For example, some of the web service and Java-related interfaces support the concepts of parameters, hierarchy, and repeating groups. Let's discuss these three.

If a SOAP interface is created, it might be necessary to define an *input parameter*. For example, a web service might have a customer_id as input parameter and returns the customer's address. Figure 3.39 shows how such a parameter is defined. The top part of this figure contains the specification of the tables being accessed. Here, the table Input represents the input parameter, the one on the right is the result, and the one in the middle creates the connection. What a developer sees is shown at the bottom. This allows him to test the interface. The second window in the middle of the bottom displays how to supply the input parameter. Finally, the window next to it, at the bottom right-hand side, contains the result. As can be seen, the data consumer has to supply the number of a customer to invoke this web service. Defining such an interface is somewhat more difficult than with an SQL-like interface, but it's still relatively easy; in fact, most of it is generated automatically by the data virtualization server.

Returned data might have to be organized hierarchically, and it might have to contain some repeating groups. In the previous example, the structure of the returned XML document is flat—in other words, each column becomes an element in the document. To introduce some hierarchy, the output

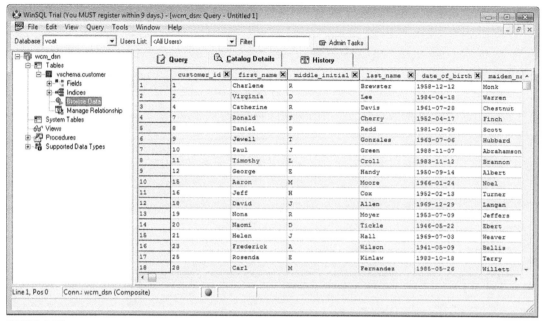

FIGURE 3.37

Accessing the data in the published CUSTOMER virtual table using an ODBC/SQL interface.

Reprinted with permission of Synametrics Technologies.

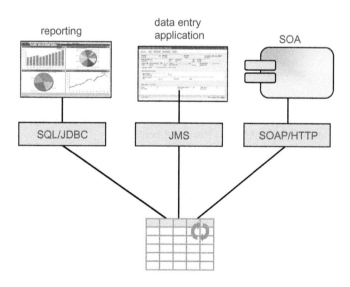

FIGURE 3.38

Reports and applications share the same virtual table definitions and can all have their preferred interface.

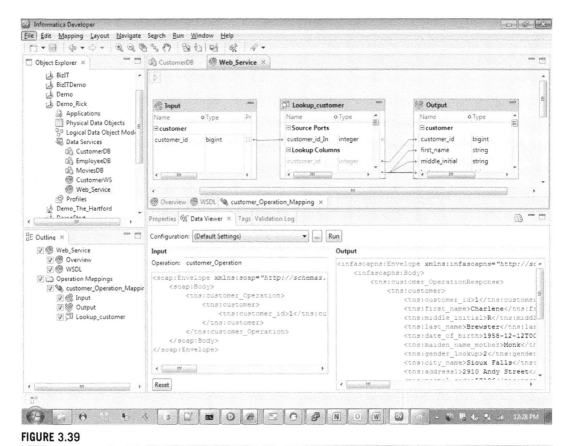

FIGURE 3.39

Defining a web service interface for a virtual table with one input parameter called customer_id.

Reprinted with permission of Informatica Corporation.

result has to be unflattened (Figure 3.40). In this example, the result has a hierarchical structure consisting of seven elements, of which Address has six subelements.

Another example is shown in Figure 3.41. The document returned by this web service consists of a region plus the list of customers based in that region. Note that in this case of creating a web service interface, defining a transformation is not mandatory. When a web service with a flat XML structure has to be developed, most data virtualization servers can automatically derive a flat XML structure from that flat virtual table's structure. However, if we want to bring some hierarchy to the structure and make it look like a real XML structure, we have to define a transformation.

To make it possible to access a web service, an XML schema has to be generated (Figure 3.42). In addition, a WSDL document has to be generated. When both have been generated, the web service is ready to be accessed.

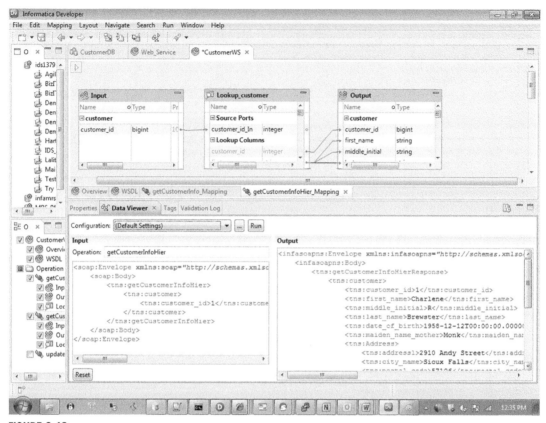

FIGURE 3.40

Defining a web service interface for a virtual table where the result has a more hierarchical structure.

Reprinted with permission of Informatica Corporation.

3.10 The Internal Data Model

So far in this chapter we assume that the virtual tables of a data virtualization server resemble the tables of SQL database servers. This means that the data model used internally is a relational one in which data is organized in tables, columns, and rows. In a relational model, for each column of a table, a row holds one value. In other words, a *cell* (which is where a column and row meet) can hold only one value such as a number, string, or date. As an example, Figure 3.43 shows a few rows of the CUSTOMER and the CUSTOMER_ORDER tables. In each of these tables, each cell contains only one value, such as 132171, Bruce, and 103819. Sometimes simple values such as these are referred to as *atomic values*, because they can't be decomposed in smaller pieces of data without losing their meaning. Some data virtualization servers use a different data model. In this section, we briefly discuss the extended relational model and the object model.

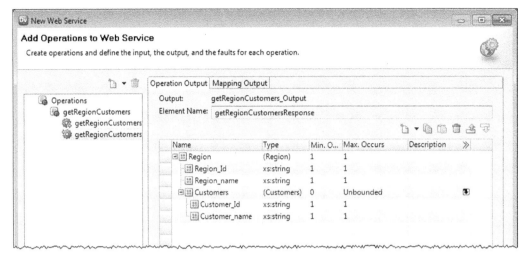

FIGURE 3.41

Defining a web service interface for a virtual table where the result contains repetition; it returns a list of customers for each region.

Reprinted with permission of Informatica Corporation.

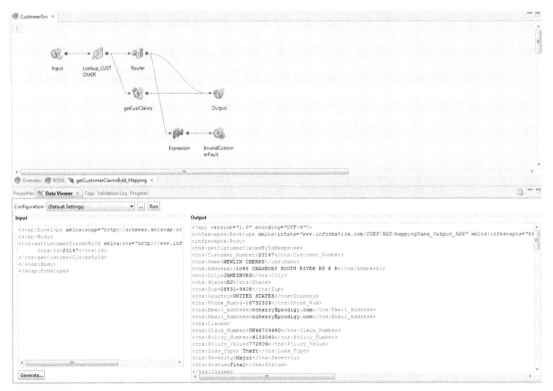

FIGURE 3.42

The generated XML schema of a web service.

Reprinted with permission of Informatica Corporation.

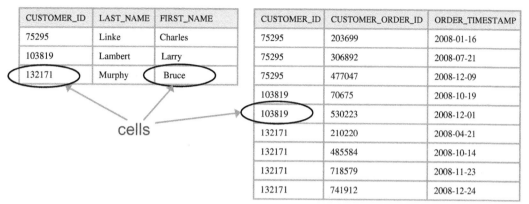

FIGURE 3.43

Virtual tables with a relational structure.

CUSTOMER_ID	LAST_NAME	FIRST_NAME	CUSTOMER_ORDERS		
75295	Linke	Charles	CUSTOMER_ORDER_ID	ORDER_TIMESTAMP	
			203699	2008-01-16	
			306892	2008-07-21	
			477047	2008-12-09	
103819	Lambert	Larry	CUSTOMER_ORDER_ID	ORDER_TIMESTAMP	
			70675	2008-10-19	
			530223	2008-12-01	
132171	Murphy	Bruce	CUSTOMER_ORDER_ID	ORDER_TIMESTAMP	
			210220	2008-04-21	
			485584	2008-10-14	
			718579	2008-11-23	
			741912	2008-12-24	

FIGURE 3.44

Example of a virtual table according to the extended relational model.

In the *extended relational model*, sometimes referred to as the *non-first normal form model* (NF^2), data is organized in tables that are made up of columns and rows as well. The difference is that in an extended relational model, a cell of a table can hold a simple value, such as a number, string, or date, but it can also hold a table. To illustrate what this might look like, the two relational tables in Figure 3.43 are presented as one table in Figure 3.44. This table contains three rows. The first three columns

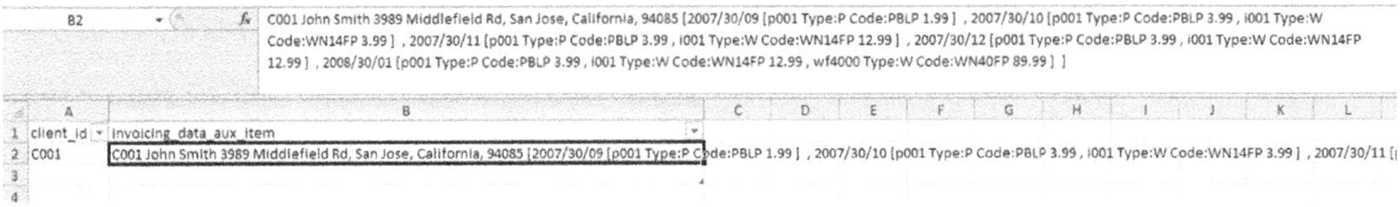

B2	▾	*fx*	C001 John Smith 3989 Middlefield Rd, San Jose, California, 94085 [2007/30/09 [p001 Type:P Code:PBLP 1.99] , 2007/30/10 [p001 Type:P Code:PBLP 3.99 , i001 Type:W Code:WN14FP 3.99] , 2007/30/11 [p001 Type:P Code:PBLP 3.99 , i001 Type:W Code:WN14FP 12.99] , 2007/30/12 [p001 Type:P Code:PBLP 3.99 , i001 Type:W Code:WN14FP 12.99] , 2008/30/01 [p001 Type:P Code:PBLP 3.99 , i001 Type:W Code:WN14FP 12.99 , wf4000 Type:W Code:WN40FP 89.99]]

	A	B	C	D	E	F	G	H	I	J	K	L
1	client_id	invoicing_data_aux_item										
2	C001	C001 John Smith 3989 Middlefield Rd, San Jose, California, 94085 [2007/30/09 [p001 Type:P Code:PBLP 1.99] , 2007/30/10 [p001 Type:P Code:PBLP 3.99 , i001 Type:W Code:WN14FP 3.99] , 2007/30/11 [										
3												
4												

FIGURE 3.45

A value with an embedded table presented in Excel as a complex value.

hold one value for each row, and the fourth column is special. Each row contains a "small" table in this column. Each of these embedded tables represents all the orders of that particular customer. So orders 203699, 306892, and 477047 are all orders of customer Charles Linke.

In a way, tables in the extended relational model organize data in a hierarchical structure. In this example, the customer orders fall hierarchically under customers. The cells of the embedded tables can also hold embedded tables.

When embedded tables are used, the data consumers accessing them should know how to handle these values. Most Java and C# applications won't have any trouble with them, but many reporting tools don't support them. If such a tool does retrieve a value that consists of an embedded table, the data virtualization server presents the whole embedded table as one long string where all the individual values are separated by brackets and colons. It will let the tool decide how to process that value. As an example, Figure 3.45 shows what such a value can look like when retrieved using Excel. For those tools that don't support embedded tables, data virtualization servers offer features to flatten the data and make that data look like ordinary tables.

The third internal data model is the *object model*. In an object model data is organized as objects that are linked together in a network. Figure 3.46 shows what such an object model can look like conceptually. This diagram shows how customer Charles Linke with his orders is presented. The same data is used as in Figure 3.43. Like the extended relational model, the object model has the ability to model hierarchical structures and repeating groups more natively than the relational model.

The extended relational model and the object model offer some advantages over the relational model. Imagine that a data store is a web service that returns an XML document with a hierarchical data structure, and imagine also that a data consumer needs to access the data in XML as well. If the data virtualization server uses a relational model internally, the incoming XML structure has to be flattened first, and when the data is sent to the data consumer, the flattened data has to be transformed to a hierarchical structure. This means that two data model transformations have to be executed. When an extended relational model or an object model is used, no or limited data model transformations are necessary.

To minimize data model transformations, when source tables have a hierarchical structure, it's recommended to first define a virtual table on top of the source table that keeps the hierarchical structure intact by using a virtual table with embedded tables (virtual table V_1 in Figure 3.47). Then, on top of V_1 another virtual table V_2 is defined with a slightly different structure, but that still includes the hierarchical structure. This can be useful for those data consumers that prefer to see the data in a hierarchical structure. For them no real data model transformation takes place. And for those data consumers that prefer to work with relational data, a nested virtual table V_3 is defined in which the data is flattened. So only for them are data model transformations executed.

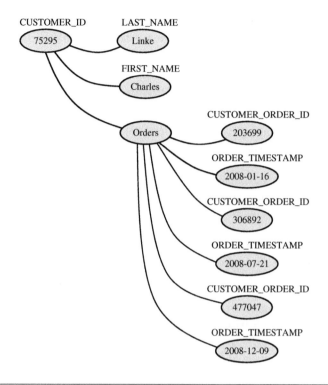

FIGURE 3.46

An object model showing one customer with his orders.

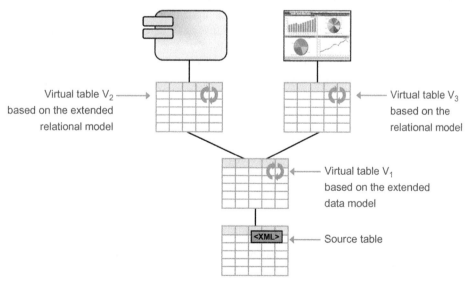

FIGURE 3.47

Two nested virtual tables are defined, one showing the data with its hierarchical structure and the other showing the data in a flat relational form.

Note: Although nonrelational models are being supported, we keep using the term *virtual table* in this book. In addition, in most examples the virtual tables are based on the relational model.

3.11 Updatable Virtual Tables and Transaction Management

The previous sections emphasized querying virtual tables. Evidently, there are data consumers that want to change the data by doing updates, inserts, and deletes. The question that arises is, are virtual tables *updatable*? Can we do updates, inserts, and deletes on the contents of the virtual tables? The answer to this question is not a simple yes or no; it depends. We describe some of the factors determining whether a virtual table is updatable.

The first factor is whether the contents of the source table to which the virtual table points *can* be changed. There can be technical reasons why the data in the data store cannot be changed. For example, if the source table is an MDX cube, some of the MDX products don't allow changes. The only way to insert new data in those cubes is by reloading all the data again—in other words, by doing a total refresh. Another example of a nonupdatable source table is if the data is coming from external HTML webpages. Those are by definition nonupdatable.

The second factor is whether the contents of the source table *may* be changed. Has the data virtualization server been given the proper rights to change the data? Maybe the data virtualization server is allowed to query the data in a particular SQL database, but not to make changes. Additionally, maybe the user who initiates the change doesn't have the proper privileges on the data source.

The third factor is the relationship between the rows in the virtual table and the real records in the source table. To put it differently, if the update, insert, or delete of a row in a virtual table can be translated to an update, insert, or delete of one record in a source table, then changes are almost certainly possible. For example, each row in the V_CUSTOMER virtual table in Example 3.1 points to one row in the source table CUSTOMER. Therefore, an update of the column TITLE or a delete of an entire row in the virtual table can be translated to an update or delete of a record in the source table and is therefore possible.

But if no one-to-one correspondence exists between the virtual rows and the real records, the virtual table is most likely nonupdatable. For example, a virtual table whose contents is the result of a join of two or more source tables is nonupdatable. Therefore, the virtual table defined in Example 3.3 is nonupdatable. The virtual table in Example 3.4, in which data is aggregated, is nonupdatable as well, because each row in the virtual table is fabricated with data from multiple rows from the source tables. By the way, theoretically, this one-to-one correspondence between virtual rows and real records is not required, but this is how it has been implemented in most current data virtualization servers.

Note: In a way, the whole concept of the updatability of virtual tables is very similar to the notion of *updatable views* in SQL databases. Throughout the years, this topic has been extensively researched and discussed in the database field. See [40] for a detailed description of the updatability of views.

Data virtualization servers support *transaction management*. Like in a database server, a transaction in a data virtualization environment can consist of many changes. If a data store supports transaction management, all the changes made are considered to form an *atomic transaction*, which means that all the changes are seen as one *logical unit of work*. They are all committed, or all of them are rolled back, but never are just some of the changes processed; it's all or nothing.

Being able to do a commit or a rollback works well if the data store is, for example, an SQL database server, because all these products support robust transaction management mechanisms. Unfortunately, this is not true for all types of data stores. For example, if a data consumer changes the data of a virtual table defined on a web service, it can be that the web service itself commits the changes. In other words, when the web service is ready, the change is already made permanent and can't be undone anymore by the data virtualization server. Another example is if the virtual table points to a simple sequential file. Most file systems don't support transaction management. You can't ask a file to undo the changes of the running transaction. This means that each change is by definition an atomic transaction. Technically, it's possible that a data virtualization server implements its own transaction mechanism for a file.

Still, data consumers might want to be able to roll back changes on data stores that don't support a transaction mechanism. In this case, a transaction mechanism called *compensation* is required. Compensation means that the data consumers must be able to activate some logic that undoes the changes of the transaction. This logic is called the *compensating transaction*. So when the original transaction inserts data, the compensating transaction deletes it, and when data is deleted, it's inserted back by the compensating transaction. In most systems this usually means that quite some code has to be written to make this possible.

Some data virtualization servers support *distributed transaction management*. In a *distributed transaction* changes are made to multiple data stores, and all are treated as one atomic transaction. All the changes made to all the data stores should be committed or rolled back, or none of them should; again, it's all or nothing. Restrictions apply depending on the data stores. Distributed transactions are supported by data stores that support the *X/Open XA protocol*. It's through this protocol that data virtualization servers control the committing or rolling back of the changes in the various data stores. Most database servers and application servers support this protocol.

But there are many data stores, such as web services and spreadsheets, that don't support XA. A change of a virtual table whose underlying source table resides in an SQL database plus a change of another virtual table whose contents is coming from a spreadsheet can't be treated as an atomic transaction. The changes can be made, but they will have to be made as separate transactions. It is the responsibility of the data consumer to handle this correctly. There is one exception: If n data stores are changed in a distributed transaction and $n - 1$ of them support XA, then a distributed transaction is possible if all the changes in the various data stores are committed in a particular order.

Note: If you want to refresh your memory on atomic and distributed transactions, see [41] and [42].

Data Virtualization Server: Management and Security

4.1 Introduction

This chapter is also devoted to the workings of a data virtualization server. Chapter 3 deals with the concepts used by the designers and developers to set up virtual tables, mappings, and so on. When an environment is up and running, it has to be managed, and security aspects have to be defined. That's the topic of this chapter. These tasks are normally handled by an administrator. The following topics are addressed in this chapter:

- Impact and lineage analysis
- Synchronization of wrapper tables and source tables
- Security of data
- Monitoring, management, and administration

4.2 Impact and Lineage Analysis

A large business intelligence system may consist of many definitions of source tables, virtual tables, mappings, wrappers, and numerous interrelationships. It's important that data virtualization servers bring clarity to such a lattice of objects and can somehow present all the relationships between those objects in a clear way to help the developers and administrators. Because data virtualization servers store the definitions of all the objects and their relationships in a central dictionary (see Section 1.12), it's relatively easy for them to show all these interrelationships between the objects.

It's especially important that a data virtualization server can show the potential effects that changing one object will have on the other objects so the impact of such a change can be studied. This form of analysis is called *impact analysis*. For example, impact analysis makes visible what the effect is if the structure of a source table changes: which mappings and virtual tables will also have to change accordingly; or, it shows which nested virtual tables have to change when the structure or defintion of a particular virtual tables changes. This form of analysis shows for an object all the dependent objects so that developers can determine how much work is involved in implementing a change. As an example, the tree diagram in Figure 4.1 shows the relationship that the table called CLIENT has with all the other tables. It clearly shows that when the structure or mapping of the virtual table CLIENT changes, the objects PERSONAL_DATA, CLIENT_PACKAGE, and CLIENT_PACKAGE_ROWSE could all be affected.

The opposite of impact analysis is *lineage analysis*. Lineage analysis shows the objects on which a particular object is dependent, such as which objects a virtual table is dependent on. For example,

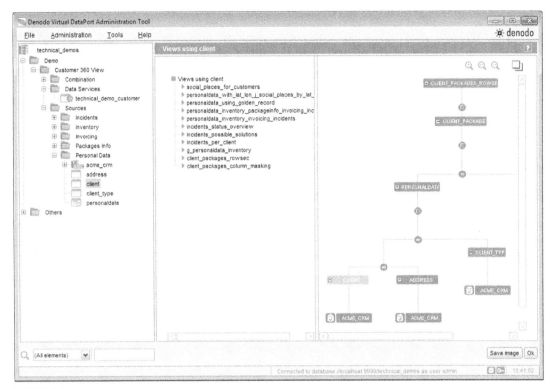

FIGURE 4.1

A tree diagram showing the interdependencies of the table CLIENT.

Reprinted with permission of Denodo Technologies.

Figure 4.2 shows a lineage diagram for the virtual table V_CUSTOMER_PURCHASE. It is clear that virtual table is dependent on the objects V_WCM and V_CUSTOMER_PURCHASES, which is dependent on the objects CUSTOMER_ORDER and CUSTOMER_ORDER_LINE.

Both forms of analysis are important for designers and developers to stay in control of large environments and to be able to determine quickly what the impact of a desired change will be. They increase the transparency of large and complex systems.

4.3 Synchronization of Source Tables, Wrapper Tables, and Virtual Tables

When objects such as source tables, wrapper tables, and virtual tables are interrelated, what happens if the structure of the underlying source table is changed? For example, what does a data virtualization server do when a column is added to a source table, when one is removed, when the data type of a column is changed, or when a column is renamed? The solution is *synchronization*. Some data virtualization servers are able to detect that a source table has changed by periodically comparing the

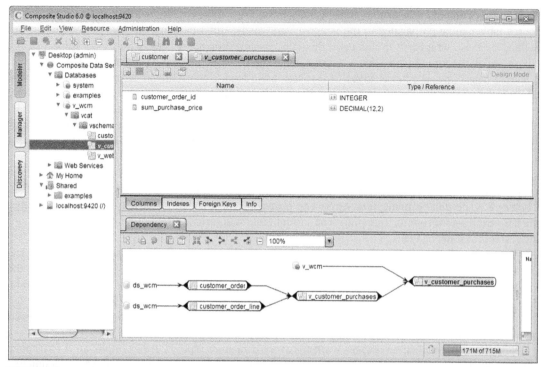

FIGURE 4.2

A lineage diagram showing the interdependencies between objects.

Reprinted with permission of Composite Software.

meta data a wrapper has on a source table with the meta data of the real source table in the underlying data store. They check whether the two are still synchronized.

When a change of a source table has been detected and when a wrapper is bound to that source table, the data virtualization server will ask the administrator what to do. There are three options:

- The dependent wrapper table is removed.
- The dependent wrapper table is invalidated. This means the wrapper is not removed and virtual tables are still bound to it, but it has become inaccessible. Queries on the wrapper are canceled.
- The changes made to the virtual table are automatically *propagated* to the wrapper table. In this case, the data virtualization server determines how the wrapper has to be changed so that it becomes synchronized with the source table again. In most products the change to the wrapper is proposed to an administrator, who decides whether to apply that change.

Example 3.1 shows an example of where propagation can be applied—in this case, where a wrapper called CUSTOMER is defined on the source table CUSTOMER. Imagine the source table is extended with a new column. For a data virtualization server, this change is easy to propagate by extending the wrapper with the new column.

Because wrappers and source tables usually have a one-to-one relationship, most changes on the source table can be propagated to the wrapper very easily. But what happens when virtual tables are defined on these wrappers? In this case, the data virtualization server has to study the impact of the change on all the virtual tables that are directly and indirectly dependent on it. And, as with wrappers, it should determine whether changes of a source table lead to the removal or invalidation of virtual tables or whether the changes can be propagated automatically.

For example, in Example 3.1, when a column is added to the source table, the contents of the virtual table V_CUSTOMER is not affected because no matter what columns are added, it won't influence the mapping of the virtual table. Therefore, the change has no effect on the virtual table and it can be left alone.

Another example of propagation is when the STATUS column is deleted from the DVD_RELEASE source table. (This column is used in the virtual table defined in Example 8.7 in Chapter 8.) The data virtualization server can propagate this change to the virtual table by deleting the case expression from the mapping. The virtual table will have a different content, but the remaining result is still unchanged.

A data virtualization server is not always able to automatically propagate changes to virtual tables. If, for example, the column ORDER_TIMESTAMP is removed from the DVD_RELEASE table, the virtual table defined in Example 3.4 can't be synchronized. The problem is that in this virtual table, data is aggregated on the ORDER_TIMESTAMP column. A data virtualization server will define the virtual table as invalidated. What the designer must do is pick another column to group the data on (if possible) or remove the virtual table.

Note that synchronization doesn't work for every data store type. If, for example, an HTML page changes, it's hard to detect that change. The same applies to some web services and XML documents. Currently, this mechanism works best for SQL database servers.

4.4 Security of Data: Authentication and Authorization

Security in any form is of crucial importance, and this is especially true when it relates to data. It's of utmost importance that the data accessible through a data virtualization server is protected against any form of deliberate or unaccidental unauthorized use. Therefore, data virtualization servers offer a rich set of features to protect the data in the data stores, including authentication, authorization, and encryption. The first two are described in this section.

With respect to *authentication*, users who access a data virtualization server have to present credentials (such as their user ID and password) to identify themselves. In other words, the data virtualization server checks whether the user is really who he says he is. In this case, the data virtualization server is doing the authentication checking. Some data virtualization servers can be configured in such a way that an external system is used for authentication. A data virtualization server will store data on users and passwords in its own dictionary. Some allow this to be stored outside the data virtualization server—for example, in LDAP directories.

It's not likely that every user should have access to all the data. *Authorization* deals with defining who is allowed to do what with which data elements. Some types of data stores, such as database servers, support authorization themselves. For these data stores, data virtualization servers support *passthrough authorization*. All the queries received by the data virtualization server are passed on

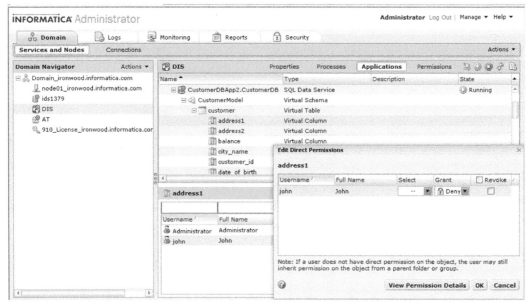

FIGURE 4.3

Assigning privileges to users.

Reprinted with permission of Informatica Corporation.

to the data stores, and it's their responsibility to check whether the data consumer has the right privileges to access the data. In this case, the data virtualization server delegates the responsibility of authorization of the data to the data stores.

All data virtualization servers support authorization as well. Authorization rules can be defined to control which user is allowed to access which data elements. Access privileges for virtual tables can be assigned to users. This is somewhat similar to assigning privileges to users with the GRANT statement in SQL (see [15]). The types of privileges that are normally supported by data virtualization servers are read, write, execute, select, update, insert, and grant. An example of assigning a privilege is shown in Figure 4.3, where privileges are assigned on the column ADDRESS1 of the virtual table CUSTOMER to user John.

Users can be introduced and defined within a data virtualization server, and they can be grouped in domains, roles, and user groups. Unfortunately, in most products, groups can't be nested.

Privileges can be granted on the table level, the column level, the row level, and the individual value level. *Table-level* and *column-level privileges* are supported by all data virtualization servers. If a user receives a table-level privilege, he can see or access all the data in that table. When the user only receives the privilege on a set of columns, some columns will stay hidden.

In some situations, authorization rules have to be defined on a more granular level—namely, on individual rows. Imagine that two users may query the same virtual table, but they are not allowed to see the same set of rows. For example, a manager may be allowed to see the data of all the customers, whereas an account manager may only see the customers for whom he is responsible.

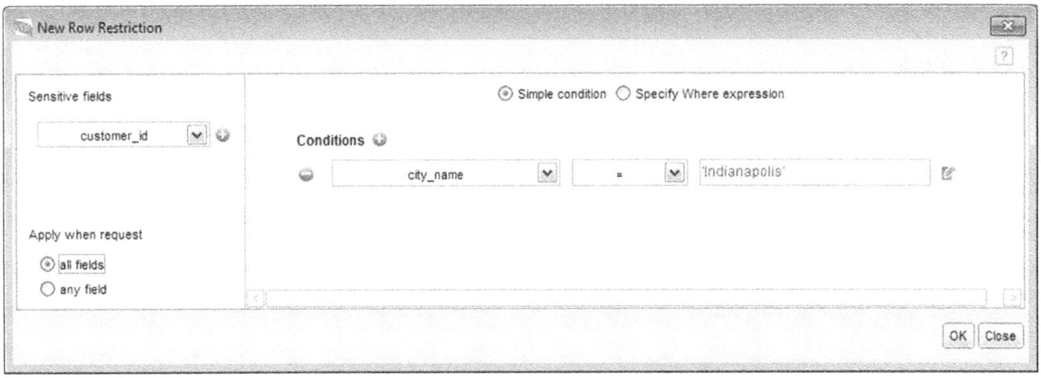

FIGURE 4.4

Assigning row-level privileges to users.

Reprinted with permission of Denodo Technologies.

One way to solve this problem is by defining two separate virtual tables on the same data, one that contains all the customers and one that contains only those customers for which the account managers are responsible. A preferred solution is when only one virtual table is developed and that so-called *row-level privileges* are defined. In this case, if two users retrieve data from the same virtual table, they see different sets of rows. In Figure 4.4, such a row-level rule is defined assigning a user the privilege to only see those customers based in Indianapolis. If necessary, for each user a different rule can be defined.

The most granular form of a privilege is a *value-level privilege*. This allows for defining privileges on individual values in a row. The effect is that some users will have access to particular rows, but they won't see some of the values in those rows, or they will only see a part of the values. This is not the same as column-level privileges, which relate to the values of all the rows in a column. A value-level privilege relates to the values of columns of rows that they do have access to. For example, a value-level privilege can define that a user is allowed to see the annual salaries of all the employees except salaries higher than $100,000. So when these users query the virtual table, they see all the employees in the results of their queries, but the high salary values are masked. Another classic example is when some users may only see the last four digits of all the credit card numbers. Defining value-level privileges is sometimes referred to as *masking*.

When the data store that is accessed supports no security mechanism, the data virtualization server is the only layer of software delivering security. But some types of data stores, such as most database servers, have their own data security mechanisms. In that case, the question is how do the two security mechanisms work together? When the data virtualization server logs on to the database server to access data, what does it use—the user's ID and password or some general user ID that the data virtualization server always uses when accessing the data store? In the former situation, the user needs to have received all the right privileges for all his queries and changes. In the latter, the data virtualization server needs sufficient privileges for all queries and updates executed by all the users.

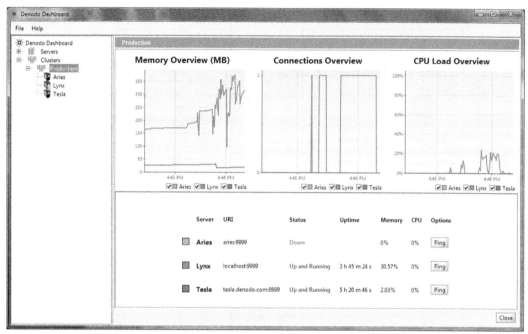

FIGURE 4.5

The monitor of a data virtualization server showing the progress of various servers.

Reprinted with permission of Denodo Technologies.

4.5 Monitoring, Management, and Administration

As indicated in Section 1.12, a data virtualization server consists of two modules: the design and the runtime module. This section focuses on the latter. This runtime module of a data virtualization server has to be monitored and managed in the same way as a database server, an application server, or a network. The reason is very simple: many data consumers rely on the data virtualization server for their data needs. Therefore, it's important that someone or some department within the organization is reponsible for the server. We call this simply the *administrator*. This administrator is responsible for the scalability, availability, and performance of the data virtualization server, and that the data managed, that is accessible via the data virtualization server, is protected against incorrect and unauthorized usage.

If an administrator is responsible for managing a data virtualization server, he needs information on what's happening. In other words, if a data virtualization server would be a black box and would show nothing about the internal processing of all of the requests, it would be hard to manage. Therefore, it's important that a data virtualization server can show how it's performing so the administrator can monitor its state and usage. It should present data on, for example, the number of queries being executed, the performance of the queries, the availability of the data virtualization server, the usage of caches, the speed with which caches are refreshed, and so on. As an example, Figure 4.5 shows the monitor of a data virtualization server. This screenshot shows an overview of memory usage, connections, and the CPU load of three clusters. It also shows that the one called Aries is down.

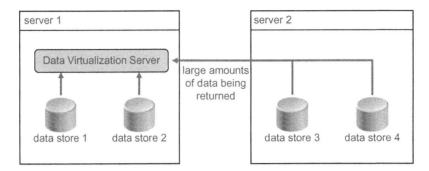

FIGURE 4.6

Accessing remote data stores can lead to quite some network traffic when large results are returned over the network.

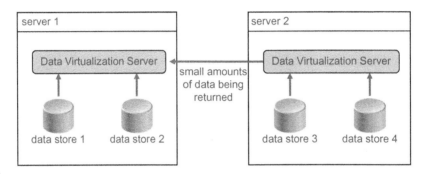

FIGURE 4.7

Installing a data virtualization server on each server where a data store resides can lead to returning small results over the network.

These monitors give administrators a wealth of information on what's happening. They can show information on the usage of caches, the speed of underlying data sources, the progress of individual queries, the efficiency of queries, and so on.

An administrator is responsible for determining how the data virtualization server is installed. Is it installed as one server on one machine, or is it installed as many servers on many machines? Will the data virtualization server be replicated or not? These are just two of the many issues the administrator has to deal with.

The simplest architecture is the one where a data virtualization server is installed on one machine. This server will handle all the access to all the data stores. From a management perspective, this is easy, because there is only one server to manage. However, one server can cause issues when some of the data stores reside on remote servers. This can possibly lead to quite some network traffic in order to retrieve the data from those remote data stores to the data virtualization server, as shown in Figure 4.6. In addition, if only one server has been installed, the entire workload has to be processed by that one server. This can have a negative impact on scalability and performance.

Alternatively, the administrator can decide to install a second data virtualization server on the same server as the remote data stores (Figure 4.7). The advantage of this is that the second server can

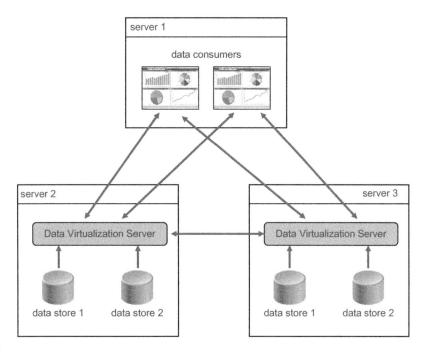

FIGURE 4.8

A replicated data virtualization server architecture.

do most of the transformations and can filter before sending the data to the first server. This might minimize the amount of data sent over the network and therefore might improve performance. By the way, the second server acts as a data store to the first one.

In Figure 4.7 the servers operate independently of one another. They share no specifications, and, as indicated, they see one another as data stores. Some data virtualization servers allow replication of data virtualization servers (Figure 4.8). In this case, the data virtualization server is installed on multiple servers, so technically multiple servers are running, but logically they act as one. In this architecture, the dictionary containing all the mappings, wrappers, virtual tables, and so on is also replicated. New specifications entered in one dictionary are replicated to the other.

The primary advantage of this architecture is increased availability. If one of the servers crashes, the queries of the data consumers are redirected to the other server. A second advantage is that the workload can be distributed. Too many heavy queries being executed concurrently can jam a data virtualization server, which leads to overall bad query performance. An architecture consisting of multiple servers allows for distribution of the workload.

Another aspect administrators are responsible for is the level of performance offered by a data virtualization server. Currently, most data virtualization servers don't offer many parameters that can be set to influence query performance.

One of the other issues for which an administrator is reponsible is *usage limitations*—in other words, limitations set to restrict how many resources are used and how long the processing of a query may take. These limitations can be user dependent. An unacceptable situation would be if a data consumer fires off a query that takes two hours to complete and, while processing, slows down all the queries from the other data consumers. When production systems are accessed, a badly written query can even slow down the overall processing of that system.

Therefore, it must be possible to specify usage limitations. These limitations are preferably specified for data consumers and data stores. For example, a particular data consumer might only run queries that take no more than five seconds to execute, queries may not involve full scans of particular tables, or the queries on a particular data store might not extract more than ten rows per query.

Setting those limitations is relatively easy, and so is enforcing them, but how can the data virtualization server first determine the number of rows returned or the amount of cpu seconds required? The best way to predict this is if the data virtualization server keeps track of statistics on usage, such as the average and maximum performance of each executed query. So a data virtualization server should constantly gather statistical data on usage. The more statistics available, the better the prediction can be.

Data Virtualization Server: Caching of Virtual Tables

5.1 Introduction

Regardless of how efficient a data virtualization server is, it's an extra layer of software that sits between the data consumers and the data stores. It consumes cpu cycles and therefore increases the response time of queries executed by the data consumers. However, for most queries, the added amount of processing time is minimal. The overall performance of a query is determined by the amount of time consumed by the data virtualization server plus the time used by the underlying data store(s), of which the former will only consume a small fraction and the latter most of the processing time. Still, it's important that a data virtualization server optimizes and improves the performance of queries as much as possible.

A data virtualization server can deploy several techniques to improve the performance of queries. These techniques can be classified in two groups: caching and query optimization. This is the third chapter that discusses data virtualization servers and covers caching; Chapter 6 deals with optimization of queries.

5.2 The Cache of a Virtual Table

Most data virtualization servers offer an extensive and flexible *caching* mechanism. Caching means that the contents of a virtual table is retrieved from the underlying source tables by running the mapping and storing the contents on disk or in memory. From then on, when the virtual table is queried, the stored contents is accessed, not the underlying source tables or virtual tables. In addition, transformations are no longer required because the data (the virtual contents) is available in the cache. The side effect of caching is that when querying the virtual table, the data returned may no longer be 100 percent up to date.

Caching is one of the most important instruments a data virtualization server offers to improve query performance, availability, and concurrency, and to minimize interference on source systems. A cached virtual table is sometimes referred to as a *materialized virtual table*.

For every virtual table a cache can be defined that involves nothing more than switching it on. Technically it means that the mappings and queries that make up the definition of the virtual table are executed and that the final result is stored instead of passed on to a data consumer. The next time this virtual table is queried, the data is retrieved from the cache (Figure 5.1).

If virtual tables are nested, caches can be defined on each level. For example, in Figure 5.2, two levels of virtual tables are defined where caches are defined for virtual tables V_1 and V_2. The effect is

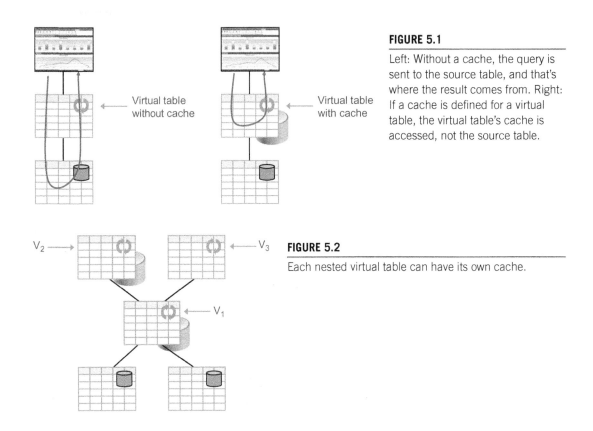

FIGURE 5.1

Left: Without a cache, the query is sent to the source table, and that's where the result comes from. Right: If a cache is defined for a virtual table, the virtual table's cache is accessed, not the source table.

FIGURE 5.2

Each nested virtual table can have its own cache.

that if V_2 and V_3 are queried, the result from the query on V_2 comes from its own cache, and the result from the query on V_3 comes from V_1's cache. Defining a cache for a virtual table and indicating when it should be refreshed are simple tasks in most products; Figure 5.3 shows an example.

5.3 **When to Use Caching**

There can be various reasons for defining a cache:

- *Query performance:* The source system on which the virtual table is defined can be too slow for the performance requirements of the data consumers accessing a virtual table. The reason can be manyfold. It can be that the source is a website from which data has to be extracted by scraping HTML pages, which can be time-consuming. It can also be that the underlying system is just slow by itself. Or the amount of data being accessed is so enormous that every query is slow. In most of these cases, the problem is not so much that the data virtualization server is not fast enough but that the underlying data store is. A cache can help speed up queries on such virtual tables.

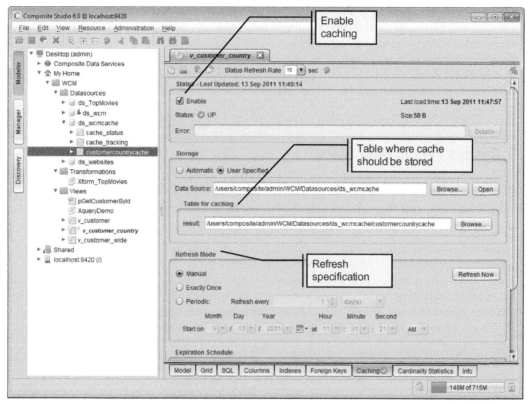

FIGURE 5.3

Defining a cache for a virtual table called v_customer_country.

Reprinted with permission of Composite Software.

- *Load optimization:* A cache can be useful to minimize the load on the underlying system. It can be that a virtual table is defined on source tables in an old system that already has issues with its performance. Additional queries might be too much for this system. By defining a cache, fewer queries are executed on the old system.
- *Consistent reporting:* A cache is also useful if a user wants to see the same report results when running a report several times for a specific period of time (day, week, or month). This is typically true for users of reports because it can be quite confusing when the same report returns different results every time it's run. In this case, a cache might be necessary if the contents of the underlying database is constantly being updated.
- *Source availability:* If the underlying source system is not always available, a periodically refreshed cache might enable a 24×7 operation. For example, the underlying system might be an old production system that starts at 6 a.m. and is shut down at 8 p.m., while the virtual table defined on it offers 24×7 availability. A cache can be the solution. It can also be that the virtual table accesses an external website to extract data. The availability of that website can't be guaranteed. Therefore, a cache can guarantee the right level of availability.

- *Complex transformations:* The transformations that have to be applied to the data might be so complex that executing them on demand might take too long. Storing the transformed result in a cache and reusing the result several times can be more efficient.
- *Security:* Security rules might not allow particular users to query the detailed data in a source system. But they are allowed to query aggregated data. By creating a cache for a virtual table that holds the aggregated data, users won't be able to see the detailed data.

5.4 Caches versus Data Marts

In a way, caches can be compared to the tables in data marts and PDSs. Usually, data marts are developed for most of the same reasons for which caches are used: improved query performance, load optimization, consistent reporting, and so on. Still, there are differences:

- Data marts have to be managed by the developers, whereas caches are managed by the data virtualization server itself. If many caches are created in a database, however, eventually some administrators will have to do some administration work.
- If the need for a cache no longer exists, removal of the cache has no impact on the data consumers accessing the virtual table. Whether or not a cache exists is entirely transparent to them. This is different with data marts. Dropping a few tables in a data mart is definitely not transparent to the data consumers. Dropping them might involve some major redesign and development of the reports.
- Migrating caches to another data store is also transparent to the data consumers. The reason for migration might be that the new data store uses storage technology that improves query performance. Again, migration is transparent for the data consumers, which is not the case with data marts. But there can be other reasons to switch, such as lower license costs of a database server, more security features, and more query capabilities.

To summarize, data marts are a very physical and visible alternative, while caches are more transparent to the data consumers. The latter offers more flexibility.

5.5 Where Is the Cache Kept?

As indicated, depending on the product in use, caches can be stored on disk or in memory. The administrator responsible for the data virtualization environment determines which form is right for which virtual table. If a switch to another storage form is implemented, the data consumers don't notice that. For them the virtual table is still the same virtual table.

If cache data of a virtual table is kept in memory, access is very fast because when the is queried, no read statements to disk are required. Even the process of building up a cache is fast because no write statements to disk are required. A disadvantage might be that the cache is removed the moment the machine on which it resides is stopped. Another disadvantage is that memory is a limited resource and is not cheap. So if the virtual contents of a virtual table is considerable in size, memory might not be the right option. In the future, this might change if the price of solid-state disk technology keeps decreasing.

When cached data is stored on disk, it can be stored in files or in tables inside a database. If files are used, the data virtualization server uses a proprietary format structure that is optimized for fast query processing. Those files are managed by the data virtualization server itself. If the data is stored in a database, it means that the cached data is stored in a dedicated table. Such a table is created by the data virtualization server. The data virtualization server also creates some indexes on that table to be able to optimize certain queries.

Both alternatives have their advantages and disadvantages. The first advantage of using files is that retrieving cached data from files is normally very fast, especially if large subsets of all the records have to be retrieved. The second one is that no database server needs to be installed and managed. In other words, it's a relatively simple solution. Using files is recommended when the amount of cached data is not too large and when the queries on the cache primarily need large amounts of the data. If the cached data is stored in a file, the data virtualization server has to do all the query processing because the only thing the file can do is return all the rows. So the more groupings and complex calculations the query contains, the more processing the data virtualization server has to do. In this case, it might be better to move the cache to a table.

An advantage of storing a cache in a database table is that indexes can be defined on it to speed up particular queries that require a small subset of rows or that contain group-by operations. The second advantage is that queries on the cache can be sent in their entirety to the database server; in other words, the data virtualization server doesn't have to do anything, or hardly anything. A third advantage is that if the amount of data in a cache is large, it's recommended to use tables because they can be indexed. The fourth advantage is that the database administrators can exploit all the storage parameters of the table that holds the cache. This will make it possible to tune the table to improve performance. For example, in Oracle the right value for the freespace parameter can be set to minimize the amount of disk space a cache occupies, or in DB2 the table can be moved to a faster volume to improve I/O speed.

Some database servers, such as IBM's solidDB and Oracle's TimesTen, are *in-memory database servers*. They have been designed and optimized to do most of their database processing in memory. By using these database servers, processing of the caches is memory-oriented as well, speeding up cache access.

A disadvantage of using a database server for holding a cache is that it requires a database server to be installed and managed. A second disdavantage is that when an existing database is used, querying the cache might have a negative impact on the performance of queries on the other tables in that same database.

5.6 **Refreshing Caches**

The longer a cache exists, the bigger the chance that its contents may no longer be in line with the orginal source data. Especially in cases where the source data is a production database that is continuously updated, the cache contents may become obsolete quite quickly. Therefore, caches have to be refreshed to update their contents to bring it in line with the original data.

Data virtualization servers offer different types of triggers to refresh a cache:

- *Construction refresh:* Construction refresh implies that the contents of a cache is determined only once: when it's constructed. After this, the cache is not refreshed anymore. Developing and refreshing a cache only once can be useful for prototyping work.

- *Manual refresh:* Manually refreshing means that an administrator can initiate the refresh of the contents of the virtual table whenever necessary. He should consider what the impact on the data sources is when the refresh starts.
- *Scheduled refresh:* With scheduled refresh, a *refresh rate* is specified which indicates when and how often the contents of the virtual tables should be refreshed automatically. Examples of refresh rates are every 2 hours, every 10 minutes, or every Sunday at 2 p.m. Scheduled refreshing is somewhat comparable to scheduled transformation supported by ETL and ELT tools.
- *Query-driven refresh:* With query-driven refresh, an *expiration date/time* is defined for the contents of a cache. This expiration date/time indicates how old the data in the cache is allowed to be when it's queried. If a query accesses the cache and that cache contains data that is older than the allowed expiration time, the cache is refreshed right before the query is executed. The advantage of this style over scheduled refresh is that the latter can be refreshing a cache while no data consumer accessed it since the previous refresh. The disadvantage of query-driven refresh is that the refresh itself adds to the query performance as perceived by the data consumer. Note that performance degradation only applies to the first query accessing the cache after the expiration date/time.
- *Event-driven refresh:* With event-driven refresh, any event that the data virtualization server can recognize as an event can trigger a cache refresh. Examples of events can be a particular message sent over an ESB, a file being placed in a particular directory, new data being loaded in a table, a transaction committed in a log file, new data coming in from a replication server, and so on. When the event occurs, the cache refresh is started.

It's the administrator's responsibility to determine the correct refresh mechanism for each cache.

5.7 Full Refreshing, Incremental Refreshing, and Live Refreshing

But how does refreshing take place? What happens behind the scenes? The three forms of refreshing are full refreshing, incremental refreshing, and live refreshing. With *full refreshing* the contents of the cache is deleted completely, the query of the cache is executed again, and the new result is stored as the new cache. This is a full replacement of the old contents by the new.

This style of refreshing might look inefficient, but numerous situations exist where this is the preferred approach. If between refresh periods a large percentage of the source data has changed, it's probably efficient to just replace the entire contents. If the amount of data is minimal, a full refresh might also be the preferred approach. Another reason can be that the source system doesn't allow other forms of refreshing, leaving this to be the only alternative.

Incremental refreshing means that during the refresh only the new data is added and the deleted data is removed (incremental refreshing is sometimes referred to as *delta refreshing*). For example, only the customer records added since the last refresh are copied to the cache, and if customers have been deleted, they are removed. This approach makes more sense when only a small percentage of the source data has changed and it's more practical when the amount of source data is high. For example, it would not make sense to do a full refresh of a virtual table with 100 million rows if only a few rows have been added since the last refresh.

Implementing an incremental refresh is more complex than a full refresh because the data virtualization server has to know or determine which data has been inserted, updated, or deleted. Maybe the source system itself keeps track of which records have been changed, possibly by adding timestamps to the records. Those timestamps might indicate when records have been inserted, updated, or deleted. The only thing the data virtualization server has to do is to extract those records with a timestamp later than the previous refresh and apply the same changes to the cache. Another approach for an incremental refresh is that the source data is compared to the contents of the cache. When differences are found, the cache has to be updated accordingly. Note that incremental refresh is not possible on every source system.

Live refreshing means that the moment the source data is changed, inserted, or deleted, that fact is passed on to the caching mechanism. Immediately, the cache is updated (it's sometimes referred to as *trickle feeding* or *instant refreshing*). Note that the update of the cache is not part of the transaction on the source system. The additional copy is done after the actual update has been committed. It probably means that the cache is a few microseconds behind. Technically, this is quite complex; it's as if a replication mechanism (see Section 2.7.3) is used to copy data from the source straight into the cash. Live refreshing might be needed if the users of the cache need to see data that is close to up to date, but they are not allowed to access the source data themselves—for example, for concurrency or availability reasons.

Live refreshing only works if the sources of a virtual table are technically able to keep track of what has changed and to push those changes to the data virtualization server. So, for example, if the source is a spreadsheet or a sequential file, no technology exists that can automatically identify changes made to the data.

5.8 Online Refreshing and Offline Refreshing

With full refreshing a whole table is refreshed. This refreshing process involves three tasks. The first task is that the query making up the mapping of the virtual table is executed to determine new data. The second task involves removing from the current cache the data that has become obsolete. And the third task is inserting the new data into the cache.

Most data virtualization servers support two forms of refreshing: offline refreshing and online refreshing. With *offline refreshing*, a virtual table is made offline for a certain amount of time and can't be accessed by data consumers for the duration of the refresh. This is bad for availability. If refreshing always takes place when there are no live data consumers, this is not an issue. But if that's not the case, the data virtualization server has to come up with a solution.

One way of doing an offline refresh is by first creating the new contents separately. And only when the new contents is created and stored somewhere is the old contents of the virtual table replaced by the new contents. When this switch takes place, for a few microseconds the virtual table can't be accessed.

Some data virtualization servers support *online refreshing*. When online refreshing is used, new data is fed into the virtual table, and concurrently, queries can be executed on the virtual table. There are different ways for a data virtualization server to implement this feature.

A characteristic of online refreshing is that users experience different results. When they run the same query for the second time, the second execution of the query might return a different result if, in between the two executions, an online refresh has taken place. This aspect should be considered when determing whether to use offline or online refreshing.

5.9 Cache Replication

In most cases, for each virtual table only one copy of the cache is set up and managed. For the data virtualization server there might be reasons for creating multiple copies of the same cache. This is called *cache replication*. Note that although there are multiple copies of the cache, logically there is only one virtual table. It's the responsibility of the data virtualization server to keep the caches in sync.

There are different reasons for keeping multiple copies of a cache:

- Cache replication can be useful if the number of queries on the virtual table and/or the number of users accessing the virtual table is high. Maybe the query workload on the database server that stores the cache is getting query performance problems. In that case it might be useful to distribute the query workload over multiple caches stored in different places.
- It could also be that users of a virtual table are geographically dispersed. This can lead to a situation that some users experience network delay. This problem can be solved by placing copies of the cache physically closer to the users.
- By creating multiple copies, the availability of a virtual table can also be raised. If only one cache is created and that cache is stored in a database, the virtual table is not available when that database server is down. Having two or more caches stored in different databases raises the availability level because if one is down, the other might still be available.

Of course, having cache replication increases the time it takes to refresh it. Updating two copies takes more time than updating one cache, regardless of the refresh approach taken.

Data Virtualization Server: Query Optimization Techniques

6.1 Introduction

This is the last of four chapters that discuss the internals of data virtualization servers. Chapter 5 describes caching as a technique to improve the performance of queries. This chapter is devoted to the second technique called *query optimization*. This is the process of determining the best *processing strategy* for a query. Various techniques can be deployed by data virtualization servers for optimizing the queries entered by data consumers.

When working with languages such as SQL, MDX, XSLT, and XQuery, developers only have to specify *what* data they want. They don't have to indicate *how* data should be retrieved from the data stores. That's why they are sometimes called *declarative languages*. For example, with the next SQL query, we're searching for the customers based in Tulsa:

```
SELECT    *
FROM      CUSTOMER
WHERE     CITY_NAME = 'Tulsa'
```

Nowhere in this statement does it say where the table CUSTOMER is stored and whether rows should be retrieved by using an index or not. In a declarative language only the *what* is specified and not the *how*. It's the responsibility of the database server to find the most optimal way of accessing the data; this is called the processing strategy. The module responsible for this task is called the *optimizer*. The better an optimizer is in determining processing strategies, the better the performance of queries will be.

The preceding applies to database servers, but it applies to data virtualization servers as well. Most data consumers in a business intelligence system access a data virtualization server using a declarative language such as SQL. As indicated, such an SQL statement only contains specifications related to the data needed. Therefore, each data virtualization server supports an optimizer as well.

To determine the best processing strategy, every optimizer has to consider the expected amount of I/O and processing seconds. The optimizer of a data virtualization server also has to consider several other aspects that are making it more complex. The first complicating aspect is that the requested data might be stored in multiple data stores and that data from those data stores has to be integrated. Second, those data stores might be using different languages and APIs than the language in which the query is specified, thus (a part of) the incoming query might have to be translated into another query language—for example, SQL has to be translated into XQuery. A third aspect deals with the optimization of the amount of data transmission between the data stores and a data virtualization server.

An optimizer of a database server doesn't have to deal with these three aspects, but the optimizer of a data virtualization does.

This chapter describes how optimizers of data virtualization servers work and explains some of the supported query optimization techniques. It starts with explaining the role of an optimizer, which is followed by factors affecting the query performance. Next, a list of key optimization techniques are explained, including the following:

- Query substitution
- SQL pushdown
- Parallel processing
- Distributed joins
- Ship joins
- SQL override

Most database servers support SQL as the language for database access, and some support XQuery, MDX, or some other language. Because SQL is by far the most popular one, we focus on optimization of that language, but most of what's discussed applies to these other languages as well.

Note: The names assigned in this book to these optimization techniques might differ from those used in particular data virtualization products.

6.2 A Refresher Course on Query Optimization

For those who are not familiar with how optimizers work or for those who haven't studied this topic for some time, we'll begin with an explanation of the workings of a database server's optimizer. We will use a few simple examples to illustrate the internal workings. If you're already familiar with optimizers, you can skip this section.

As indicated, every SQL database server tries to come up with the most efficient way of processing an SQL statement. This analysis is performed by a module within the database server called the *optimizer*. The analysis of statements is referred to as *query optimization*. The optimizer determines a number of alternative *processing strategies* for each statement. Next, it estimates which processing strategy is likely to be the most efficient based on factors such as the expected processing time and the expected amount of data to be accessed. These factors are dependent on how the data is stored, the number of rows in the tables, the distribution of values in columns, the presence of indexes, and so on. Eventually, the database server executes the most efficient processing strategy. We illustrate this optimization process with Example 6.1.

EXAMPLE 6.1

Get all the information on customer 45.

```
SELECT   *
FROM     CUSTOMER
WHERE    CUSTOMER_ID = 45
```

The processing strategy for a query can be represented using a pseudo-programming language. Here is a potential strategy for the previous query:

```
RESULT := [];
FOR EACH C IN CUSTOMER DO
   IF C.CUSTOMER_ID = 45 THEN
       RESULT :+ C;
ENDFOR;
```

Explanation

The variable RESULT represents a set in which rows of data can be temporarily stored. C represents a row from a set—in this case, a customer row. The symbol [] represents the empty set. A row is added to a set with the operator :+.

With this processing strategy, all the rows from the CUSTOMER table are retrieved—in other words, the whole table is scanned. If an index on the column CUSTOMER_ID is available, a more efficient processing strategy would be one where only rows related to customer 45 are fetched. This optimized strategy can be presented as follows:

```
RESULT := [];
FOR EACH C IN CUSTOMER WHERE CUSTOMER_ID = 45 DO
   RESULT :+ C;
ENDFOR;
```

The job of the optimizer is to predict the processing times for both processing strategies. The second one might be the fastest because only the relevant rows are retrieved from disk, while with the first strategy, all the rows are accessed. The second strategy works much more selectively. Although the index has to be accessed first before the rows can be accessed. If CUSTOMER is a relatively small table, it's better to go for the first strategy. If it's a large table, the second one might be faster.

EXAMPLE 6.2

Get the customer number and city of each customer whose ID is less than 10 and who is based in Tulsa. Order the result by customer ID.

```
SELECT   CUSTOMER_ID, CITY_NAME
FROM     CUSTOMER
WHERE    CUSTOMER_ID < 10
AND      CITY_NAME = 'Tulsa'
ORDER BY CUSTOMER_ID
```

A possible strategy is one that is, like the previous example, based on a scan of the entire table:

```
RESULT := [];
FOR EACH C IN CUSTOMER DO
   IF (C.CUSTOMER_ID < 10)
   AND (C.CITY_NAME = 'Tulsa') THEN
     RESULT :+ C;
ENDFOR;
```

If an index is available on the column CUSTOMER_ID, its use might be beneficial:

```
RESULT := [];
FOR EACH C IN CUSTOMER WHERE CUSTOMER_ID < 10 DO
   IF C.CITY_NAME = 'Tulsa' THEN
      RESULT :+ C;
ENDFOR;
```

If a second index exists on the CITY_NAME column, it might be more efficient to first find those customers based in Tulsa:

```
RESULT := [];
FOR EACH C IN CUSTOMER WHERE CITY_NAME = 'Tulsa' DO
   IF C.CUSTOMER_ID < 10 THEN
      RESULT :+ C;
ENDFOR;
```

The optimizer has to determine which one of the last two is the most efficient one. The decisive question to answer is, how many rows is the optimizer likely to find when first all the customers with IDs less than 10 are selected or when all the customers based in Tulsa are selected? This depends on the number of different values and the distribution of the values in those two columns.

The more complex a query is, the more complex the processing strategies will be, and the more difficult it will be for the optimizer to find the most efficient strategy.

EXAMPLE 6.3

Get the ID and last name of each customer based in the same city as customer 45.

```
SELECT   CUSTOMER_ID, LAST_NAME
FROM     CUSTOMER
WHERE    CITY_NAME =
         (SELECT   CITY_NAME
          FROM     CUSTOMER
          WHERE    CUSTOMER_ID = 45)
```

The first strategy:

```
RESULT := [];
FOR EACH C IN CUSTOMER DO
   FOUND := FALSE;
   FOR EACH C45 IN CUSTOMER DO
      IF (C45.CITY_NAME = C.CITY_NAME)
      AND (C45.CUSTOMER_ID = 45) THEN
         FOUND := TRUE;
   ENDFOR;
   IF FOUND = TRUE THEN
      RESULT :+ C;
ENDFOR;
```

An alternative strategy:

```
RESULT := [];
FIND C45 IN CUSTOMER WHERE CUSTOMER_ID = 45;
FOR EACH C IN CUSTOMER WHERE C.CITY_NAME = C45.CITY_NAME DO
   RESULT :+ C;
ENDFOR;
```

Processing a query can be seen as a process consisting of six stages (Figure 6.1). In Stage 1, the query is sent to the database server. In Stage 2, the optimizer of the database server tries to determine the best processing strategy. In Stage 3, the processing strategy is executed by a module of the database server called the *storage engine*. In this stage, commands are sent to retrieve data from disk. The way in which data is retrieved is described in the processing strategy. In Stage 4, the database server receives data from disk. The received data might be too much for the result, so it might still be necessary for the database server to do some extra processing to get the right result. For example, in the first processing strategy of the query in Example 6.1, all the customers are retrieved from disk. In other words, in Stage 4 all the customer data is sent back to the database server, and from that set, customer 45 has to be selected. In addition, extra calculations and transformations might be necessary. If the final result is determined, it's transmitted back to the data consumer in Stage 6.

Each of these stages of the process costs processing time. The time it takes to process a query is equal to the sum of the processing times of these six stages. Usually, Stages 4 and 5 take up most of the time. Therefore, it's important in this whole six-stage process that those two are optimized.

Note: If you want to read more about optimization of queries, see [43] and [44].

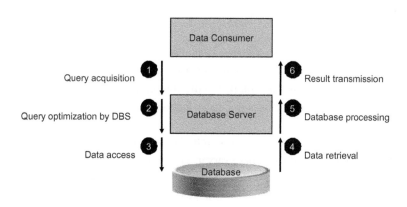

FIGURE 6.1

The six stages making up the processing of a query.

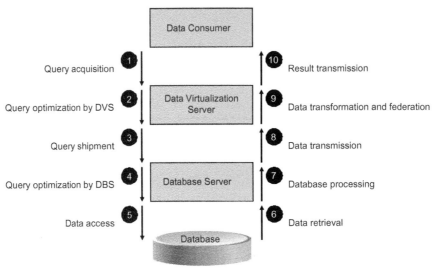

FIGURE 6.2

The ten stages making up the processing of a data virtualization server query.

6.3 **The Ten Stages of Query Processing by a Data Virtualization Server**

If query processing by a database server can be seen as six stages, then query processing by a data virtualization server can be decomposed into ten stages (Figure 6.2). The first five stages deal with getting the data consumers' query to the database. The next five stages are concerned with retrieving data from disk, transforming it into a result, and sending the result back to the data consumer.

What each stage does:

Stage 1: The query is sent from the data consumer to the data virtualization server.

Stage 2: For each virtual table, the optimizer of the data virtualization server determines in which data store it's stored. For each data store, a query is generated. This is an optimization process. (More on this later in this chapter.)

Stage 3: The generated queries are shipped to the correct data stores.

Stage 4: The database server receives the query and optimizes it. The result is a processing strategy.

Stage 5: Low-level access commands are sent to the storage units to retrieve the needed data.

Stage 6: Data is returned to the database server. The unit of I/O is normally pages or blocks of data.

Stage 7: The database server transforms the pages of data into rows of a table, those rows that are requested by the data virtualization server.

Stage 8: The rows are sent back to the data virtualization server.

Stage 9:   The data virtualization server processes the received data. This could mean that rows from different data stores are combined and data is transformed to the right table structure.

Stage 10:   The final result consisting of a set of rows is sent back to the data consumer.

The performance of a query is equal to the sum of the performances of all those ten stages. Stages 1 to 5 don't consume that much processing time. Thus, it doesn't really make sense to optimize them. For example, how much time will it take to send a query from the data virtualization server to the database server, and if it takes too much time, can we optimize it?

Although Stage 2 is not going to cost much processing time, it has an enormous impact on the overall performance of the queries. The data virtualization server has to come up with an efficient strategy for accessing the data stores. One of the most important factors here is to minimize the amount of data sent back from the data stores to the data virtualization server. This is in fact Stage 8. The less data returned, the better the performance. More on this stage in the coming sections.

Stages 4, 5, and 6 are very closely related. Stage 4 is the optimization of the queries by the database server, which is described in Section 6.2. Stage 5 is executed by the storage engine of the database server. The storage engine sends low-level commands to the storage devices to retrieve data. The storage engine retrieves data according to the selected processing strategy.

As with the optimization by the data virtualization server, the optimization of the query by a database server itself (Stage 4) won't cost that much time, but the strategy determined by this optimizer will affect the performance of the query significantly. An important aspect here is to minimize the amount of data retrieved from disk and sent to the database server; this is Stage 6. The processing strategy determined by the optimizer of the database server determines the amount of data transferred from the disks to the database server—in other words, it determines the amount of I/O. For a large part, the amount of I/O determines the overall performance of a query. A data virtualization server has limited influence on this factor, except it should try to send queries that are easy to optimize by the database server.

Stage 7 might be a time-consuming stage. It all depends on how much data is retrieved from disk and how much processing is still required. Maybe all the rows of a table have been accessed, but only a few rows should be returned to the data virtualization server. Maybe in this stage, rows still have to be sorted on a column, or complex calculations are needed.

How much time Stage 8 takes is fully dependent on how much data are transmitted back to the data virtualization server. The more data, the longer it takes. Therefore it's important that the database server tries to return the minimal set of data.

The processing time of Stage 9 primarily depends on how much work the data virtualization server still has to do after receiving the data from the database server. Maybe the only thing the data virtualization server has to do is pass on the result to the data consumer. In this case, Stage 9 barely costs any processing time. However, if, for example, the data has to be merged with data coming from other data sources or has to be grouped, filtered, transformed, and sorted before it can be passed back, then Stage 9 will consume a considerable amount of processing time. So the big question here is, how much work have the underlying database servers already done? The more they have done, the less the data virtualization server has to do.

Finally, in Stage 10 the final result of the original query has to be transmitted back to the data consumer. The performance of this stage depends on what the data consumer requests. If it asks for one row, this stage barely consumes any processing time, but if millions of rows are transmitted, then this stage does require considerable processing time.

6.4 The Intelligence Level of the Data Stores

The optimizer of a database server primarily looks at the usage of I/O and CPU resources when it determines the best processing strategy, but it must consider the following factors as well:

- The "intelligence" level of the data stores
- The amount of data transmitted from the data stores to the data virtualization server
- The processing speed of the data stores

If a data store is a database server, a data virtualization server will let the database server do as much of the work as possible. If, on the other hand, the data store is a spreadsheet or an XML document, the data virtualization server has to do everything itself. For example, if we are looking for all the customers from a particular country and that data is stored in a spreadsheet, the only thing the data virtualization server can do is retrieve all the customers and do the selection (only customers from that country) itself. If the same data is stored in a database server, the data virtualization server can ask the database server for only those customers from that country. The data virtualization server would receive only the relevant rows, which means it can pass the result straight back to the data consumer. A nonintelligent data store, such as a file or web service, can't process any query. The only thing the data virtualization server can ask is "Get all the data." The effect is that it will do most of the processing. So it's important that the optimizer of the data virtualization server knows how "intelligent" a data store is.

Transmitting data from a data store to a data virtualization server takes time. So minimizing the amount of data transmitted is a key aspect in coming up with the best processing strategy. Therefore, one of the goals of an optimizer is to *push down* as much of the processing as possible. This means that the data virtualization server will try to let the database server do as much of all the processing as possible—in other words, the data virtualization server is pushing down work to the database server.

Imagine that a query entered by a data consumer joins two tables stored in the same database. The data virtualization server can come up with a processing strategy in which data from the first table is retrieved first, then all the rows from the second table are obtained, and finally the join of those two tables is performed by the data virtualization server itself. This strategy does lead to the correct result, but it also involves the transmission of a large amount of data from the database server to the data virtualization server. A more efficient strategy would be to let the database server do the join and let it send back the result of the join to the data virtualization server. This technique of push down is discussed more in Section 6.6.

The processing speed of the data store can also affect a processing strategy. Imagine that a data store is capable of grouping a set of rows, but it takes a long time. In that case, it might be better to retrieve all the rows and let the data virtualization server do the grouping itself. Although this might lead to more data transmitted, overall it might improve the query performance. Or what if a data virtualization server is capable of joining two tables faster than the underlying data store?

So besides factors such as required I/O and CPU, a data virtualization server has other factors to consider when optimizing a query. The next section presents various techniques optimizers of data virtualization servers use to develop the perfect processing strategy, taking into account all the crucial factors.

6.5 Optimization through Query Substitution

The first query optimization technique described is called *query substitution*, which involves how queries on nested virtual tables are executed. What is *not* going to happen when a query on a nested

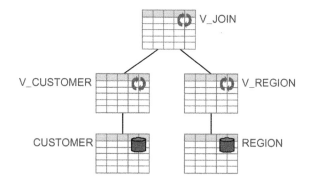

FIGURE 6.3

Queries that make up the mappings of the virtual tables are not executed one by one.

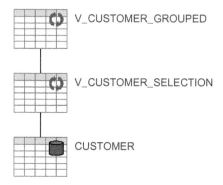

FIGURE 6.4

Two virtual tables defined on the CUSTOMER table.

virtual table is executed, is that query after query are executed sequentially. Let's illustrate this with an example. Imagine that a query is executed on virtual table V_JOIN which is defined on virtual tables V_CUSTOMER and V_REGION. Virtual tables V_CUSTOMER and V_REGION are defined respectively on source tables CUSTOMER and REGION (Figure 6.3). What a data virtualization server won't do is first execute V_CUSTOMER's query on CUSTOMER, then execute V_REGION's query on REGION, then combine and join those results, then execute the query of V_JOIN on that intermediate result, and finally execute the query of the data consumer on that last result. Although this approach does return the correct result, it is very inefficient and will be too slow.

What the data virtualization server does in stead is combine the queries into one query that is passed to the database server for execution. So in our example, the queries making up the mappings of the virtual tables V_CUSTOMER, V_REGION, and V_JOIN, plus the query entered by the data consumer, are combined into one query that leads to a join of the tables CUSTOMER and REGION. The database server will process the join and not the data virtualization server. This combining of queries is called *query substitution*.

Let's illustrate query substitution with a simple example, one that doesn't involve a join (Figure 6.4).

EXAMPLE 6.4

Get all the rows from the V_CUSTOMER_GROUP virtual table where the region ID is between 1 and 20.

```
SELECT   *
FROM     V_CUSTOMER_GROUPED
WHERE    REGION_ID BETWEEN 1 AND 20
```

The virtual table V_CUSTOMER_GROUPED is defined as follows:

```
DEFINE   V_CUSTOMER_GROUPED AS
SELECT   REGION_ID, COUNT(*)
FROM     V_CUSTOMER_SELECTION
GROUP BY REGION_ID
```

And V_CUSTOMER_SELECTION looks like this:

```
DEFINE   V_CUSTOMER_SELECTION AS
SELECT   CUSTOMER_ID, LAST_NAME, FIRST_NAME, REGION_ID
FROM     CUSTOMER
WHERE    CUSTOMER_ID < 1000
```

The query created through query substitution and sent to the database server where source table CUSTOMER resides looks like this:

```
SELECT   REGION_ID, COUNT(*)
FROM     CUSTOMER
WHERE    CUSTOMER_ID < 1000
AND      REGION_ID BETWEEN 1 AND 20
GROUP BY REGION_ID
```

Other queries can be generated that will return the same result:

```
SELECT   *
FROM     (SELECT   REGION_ID, COUNT(*)
          FROM     (SELECT   CUSTOMER_ID, LAST_NAME, FIRST_NAME, REGION_ID
                    FROM     CUSTOMER
                    WHERE    CUSTOMER_ID < 1000) AS TEMP1
          GROUP BY REGION_ID) AS TEMP2
WHERE    REGION_ID BETWEEN 1 AND 20
```

So in the FROM clause of the first query, the call to the virtual table V_CUSTOMER_GROUPED is substituted by its query (its mapping). In short, all the layered queries are coalesced into one single comprehensive query and optimized accordingly. This definitely minimizes the amount of data transmitted between the database server and the data virtualization server. Query substitution is done in

Stage 2. Note that data virtualization servers that do not use SQL as their language use the same optimization techniques. They just do one step first: generate their language to SQL before query substitution takes place.

6.6 **Optimization through Pushdown**

Another technique for optimization is called *pushdown* (also called *query delegation*). As indicated, the goal of a data virtualization server's optimizer is to minimize the amount of data it receives from the source data stores. It tries to push down as much processing to the underlying database servers as possible. This means that selections (i.e., get only the customers from Phoenix), projections (i.e., get only the names and addresses of the customers), and group-by operations are pushed down. A data virtualization server will let the database server process as much of these operations as possible.

EXAMPLE 6.5

Get the customer ID and a concatenation of the first and last name for each customer with an ID less than or equal to 1000 and with a region ID between 10 and 20.

```
SELECT    CUSTOMER_ID, CONCAT(FIRST_NAME, LAST_NAME)
FROM      CUSTOMER
WHERE     CUSTOMER_ID <= 1000
AND       REGION_ID BETWEEN 10 AND 20
```

Imagine that the data virtualization server knows that the data store containing the CUSTOMER table doesn't support the CONCAT function. What it will do is push down the following query:

```
SELECT    CUSTOMER_ID, FIRST_NAME, LAST_NAME
FROM      CUSTOMER
WHERE     CUSTOMER_ID <= 1000
AND       REGION_ID BETWEEN 10 AND 20
```

Almost the entire query is pushed down to the database server. The only remaining task the data virtualization server has to do when the result comes back is to concatenate the values of the columns FIRST_NAME and LAST_NAME. In other words, it has pushed down as much of the processing to the database server as possible, leaving little work for itself to do.

Let's continue with the more complex example in Example 6.6.

EXAMPLE 6.6

Imagine that three source tables are joined. The first two, CUSTOMER_ORDER_LINE and CUSTOMER_ORDER, are stored in one data store, and the third, CUSTOMER, is stored in another one.

```
SELECT   COL.CUSTOMER_ORDER_LINE_ID, CO.CUSTOMER_ORDER_ID, C.REGION_ID
FROM     CUSTOMER_ORDER_LINE AS COL, CUSTOMER_ORDER AS CO, CUSTOMER AS C
WHERE    COL.CUSTOMER_ORDER_ID = CO.CUSTOMER_ORDER_ID
AND      CO.CUSTOMER_ID = C.CUSTOMER_ID
AND      CO.PROMOTION_ID > 10
AND      CO.CUSTOMER_ID < 1000
AND      C.REGION_ID BETWEEN 10 AND 20
```

When pushdown is used, the following query might be sent to the first data store:

```
SELECT   COL.CUSTOMER_ORDER_LINE_ID, CO.CUSTOMER_ORDER_ID, CO.CUSTOMER_ID
FROM     CUSTOMER_ORDER_LINE AS COL, CUSTOMER_ORDER AS CO
WHERE    COL.CUSTOMER_ORDER_ID = CO.CUSTOMER_ORDER_ID
AND      CO.PROMOTION_ID > 10
AND      CO.CUSTOMER_ID < 1000
```

And the next one to the second data store:

```
SELECT   CUSTOMER_ID, REGION_ID
FROM     CUSTOMER
WHERE    CUSTOMER_ID < 1000
AND      REGION_ID BETWEEN 10 AND 20
```

With the first query, the join of CUSTOMER_ORDER_LINE with CUSTOMER_ORDER is pushed down, and with the second one, only relevant rows and columns of the CUSTOMER table are retrieved.

What's special about this second pushed-down query is that the condition CUSTOMER_ID < 1000 has been added. This condition is not explicitly specified in the original query, but it can be derived from the two conditions CO.CUSTOMER_ID = C.CUSTOMER_ID and CO.CUSTOMER_ID < 1000. Adding derived conditions is sometimes called *constraint propagation*.

The data virtualization server tries to add as many conditions to the pushed-down queries as possible to minimize the amount of work it has to do later on (in Stage 9) and to minimize the amount of data that has to be transmitted back to it.

What the data virtualization server still has to do itself is join the results of the two queries, using the following query:

```
SELECT   RESULT1.C1, RESULT1.C1, RESULT2.C4
FROM     RESULT1, RESULT2
WHERE    RESULT1.C1 = RESULT2.C3
```

Evidently, this pushing down of queries is not possible for every data store. Some database servers support a very simple SQL dialect. For example, HiveQL, Apache Hadoop's SQL dialect, is quite limited. Everything that can't be pushed down has to be executed by the data virtualization server. And if the data store is a sequential file, an XML document, or a SOAP-based web service, no optimization can be executed by the data store. In this case, the data virtualization server has to do all the work instead. It will retrieve all the data (unless a cache exists, because then the data is retrieved from that cache).

To summarize, pushing down as much of the query processing to the data stores as possible decreases the processing times of Stages 8 and 9.

6.7 **Optimization through Query Expansion (Query Injection)**

Joining two tables stored in two different data stores requires a smart and efficient processing strategy. An example of an inefficient strategy would be to retrieve all the data from both data stores and to let the data virtualization server do the join. It's inefficient because it involves a considerable amount of data transmission. Techniques exist to process such distributed joins more efficiently. One such technique is called *query expansion* or *query injection*, shown in Example 6.7.

EXAMPLE 6.7

Imagine that the two tables CUSTOMER and WEBSITE are stored in different data stores and are joined with the following query:

```
SELECT   C.CUSTOMER_ID, C.LAST_NAME
FROM     CUSTOMER AS C, REGION AS R
WHERE    C.REGION_ID = R.REGION_ID
AND      R.COUNTRY_ID = 3
```

CUSTOMER is a relatively large table with respect to the number of rows, and REGION is a small one. What a data virtualization server can do is come up with a processing strategy where first all the relevant rows of REGION are retrieved with the following query:

```
SELECT   REGION_ID
FROM     REGION
WHERE    COUNTRY_ID = 3
```

This result consists of 13 rows. The orginal query can then be changed and expanded as follows:

```
SELECT   CUSTOMER_ID, LAST_NAME
FROM     CUSTOMER
WHERE    REGION_ID IN (1,2,3,4,5,6,7,8,9,10,11,12,13)
```

Next, this query is sent to the other database server. The effect of this expansion is that not all the rows of the large CUSTOMER table have to be returned for the join, but only those that have a match in the REGION table. Of course, the entire table REGION is still accessed, but that's a small table, so the amount of data transmission is minimal.

A slightly different optimization technique is one where several queries are generated. In fact, one query is generated for each value returned from the small table. All these queries are then sent in parallel to the other database server. These queries might look like this:

```
SELECT    CUSTOMER_ID, LAST_NAME
FROM      CUSTOMER
WHERE     REGION_ID = 1

SELECT    CUSTOMER_ID, LAST_NAME
FROM      CUSTOMER
WHERE     REGION_ID = 2

And so on
```

Query expansion is a technique executed in Stage 2, and its goal is to minimize the amount of processing to be done in Stage 9.

6.8 Optimization through Ship Joins

Optimization using query expansion is a powerful technique to minimize data transmission when one of the joined tables is relatively small. If two tables stored in different data stores are joined and both are large, a technique called *ship join* can be used. When a ship join is selected, data from one table is transmitted (shipped) to the other data store. Next, this data store is asked by the data virtualization server to join the two tables, and the joined result is then sent back to the data virtualization server. This is shown in Example 6.8.

EXAMPLE 6.8

Imagine that the two tables CUSTOMER_ORDER and CUSTOMER_ORDER_LINE are stored respectively in the data stores DATABASE1 and DATABASE2. These two tables are joined with the following query:

```
SELECT    CO.CUSTOMER_ORDER_ID, COUNT(*)
FROM      CUSTOMER_ORDER AS CO, CUSTOMER_ORDER_LINE AS COL
WHERE     CO.CUSTOMER_ORDER_ID = COL.CUSTOMER_ORDER_ID
GROUP BY  CO.CUSTOMER_ORDER_ID
```

Using the ship join technique, the processing strategy for this query would look somewhat like this:

```
CREATE TEMPORARY TABLE TEMP_CUSTOMER_ORDER IN DATABASE2

INSERT    INTO TEMP_CUSTOMER_ORDER
SELECT    CUSTOMER_ORDER_ID
FROM      DATABASE1.CUSTOMER_ORDER

SELECT    CO.CUSTOMER_ORDER_ID, COUNT(*)
FROM      TEMP_CUSTOMER_ORDER AS TEMP, CUSTOMER_ORDER AS CO
WHERE     TEMP.CUSTOMER_ORDER_ID = CO.CUSTOMER_ORDER_ID
GROUP BY CO.CUSTOMER_ORDER_ID

DROP TEMPORARY TABLE TEMP_CUSTOMER_ORDER IN DATABASE2
```

First, a temporary table is created in CUSTOMER_ORDER_LINE's database DATABASE1. Next, the INSERT statement is executed, which copies data from the CUSTOMER_ORDER table to the temporary table TEMP_CUSTOMER_ORDER. Then, TEMP_CUSTOMER_ORDER and CUSTOMER_ORDER_LINE are joined. The result of that join is sent to the data virtualization server, and finally, the temporary table is dropped. So the ship join technique requires that the data virtualization server and the data stores work closely together. Most of the processing is done in Stage 2.

The question of whether the ship join is an efficient processing strategy determines how long it takes to retrieve CUSTOMER_ORDER from DATABASE2, plus how long it takes to insert that result in the temporary table TEMP_CUSTOMER_ORDER. This has to be compared to how long it would take to transmit both tables from their respective data stores to the data virtualization server and let the latter run the join itself. The optimizer needs a lot of information to make the right decision.

6.9 Optimization through Sort-Merge Joins

If a data virtualization server has to process a join itself, it needs to find a way to optimize its internal join processing. Most of them use a technique called *sort-merge join*. With sort-merge, both tables are retrieved. The queries sent to the data stores are expanded with an ORDER BY clause on the join columns. The effect is that the data stores perform the sorts and the data virtualization server only has to execute the merge. Let's explain this with Example 6.9.

EXAMPLE 6.9

Get the order line ID, the rental price, the customer order ID, and the order timestamp for each customer order line with a purchase price of less than 10.

```
SELECT    COL.CUSTOMER_ORDER_LINE_ID, COL.RENTAL_PRICE,
          CO.CUSTOMER_ORDER_ID, CO.ORDER_TIMESTAMP
FROM      CUSTOMER_ORDER_LINE AS COL INNER JOIN CUSTOMER_ORDER AS CO
          ON COL.CUSTOMER_ORDER_ID = CO.CUSTOMER_ORDER_ID
WHERE     COL.PURCHASE_PRICE < 10
```

The following statement is sent to the first data store:

```
SELECT   CUSTOMER_ORDER_LINE_ID, CUSTOMER_ORDER_ID, RENTAL_PRICE
FROM     CUSTOMER_ORDER_LINE
WHERE    PURCHASE_PRICE < 10
ORDER BY CUSTOMER_ORDER_ID
```

And a comparable statement is sent to the other:

```
SELECT   CUSTOMER_ORDER_ID, ORDER_TIMESTAMP
FROM     CUSTOMER_ORDER
ORDER BY CUSTOMER_ORDER_ID
```

Explanation
Note that both queries have been extended with an ORDER BY clause in which the result is sorted on the same column CUSTOMER_ORDER_ID. Merging the two results now is straightforward for a data virtualization server. The advantage of this approach is that the two data stores can retrieve and sort the data in parallel in the sort-step and that the merge-step should not take that much processing time. Still, a large amount of data is transmitted.

6.10 Optimization by Caching

For the optimizer of a data virtualization server, the existence of a cache (see Chapter 5) has a direct impact on which processing strategy it will select. For example, if a data consumer is looking for all the customers from a particular region, and if a cache for the CUSTOMER table exists, the data virtualization server creates a processing strategy in which that cache is accessed.

In principle, if a cache can be used, it will be used. It can become somewhat more complex if some of the tables being accessed are cached and some aren't. For example, when the tables CUSTOMER, REGION, and WEBSITE are joined and a cached virtual table is available on the join result of CUSTOMER and REGION, the data virtualization server performs a join of WEBSITE with the data in the cache. If that cache is small, the data virtualization server might use the ship join technique to join them.

But what can we do when, in the same situation, a query only accesses the REGION table? Imagine also that there is no cache defined for this source table, but a cache on the join of CUSTOMER and REGION exists. The optimizer must decide to access the small table REGION or to access the cached version. However, that cached version is the result of a join with CUSTOMER, which probably makes it a big cache. So what is faster—accessing a small source table or a large cached table? The optimizer uses preprogrammed rules to make the right decision.

6.11 Optimization and Statistical Data

For most of the decisions the optimizer of a data virtualization server must make, it requires quantitative data on the tables, such as the number of rows in a table (cardinality), the number of different values in each column, the number of nulls in each column, the average width of the rows, and whether columns have been indexed. In addition, it requires information on the speed of data transmission and the intelligence level of the data stores. This type of data is called *statistical data*.

It's important that statistical data on data stores collected by a data virtualization server is as accurate as possible. The more accurate the statistical data is the more likely that the optimizer does come up with the best processing strategy. So periodically, a data virtualization server accesses data stores to check whether the statistical data it holds is still in sync with the data in the data stores.

It's relatively easy for a data virtualization server to collect statistical data on a data store when it's an SQL database server. Some data stores, however, can't offer this type of data. For example, XML documents and SOAP services can't answer questions concerning the number of rows they contain. In that case, some data virtualization servers allow statistical data to be entered manually.

By entering statistical data manually, developers can influence the optimization process. For example, imagine that an optimizer decides to use the ship join technique for a particular join because it assesses that both tables are large. If a developer knows that it's better to use the query expansion technique, he can set the cardinality of one of the two tables to an artificially low number just to force the data virtualization server to go for query expansion. Care should be taken with this technique of improving query performance, however, because it requires in-depth knowledge of the internal workings of a data virtualization server's optimizer.

6.12 **Optimization through Hints**

If developers feel that a data virtualization server's optimizer isn't coming up with the best possible processing strategy, some of these products allow them to specify *hints* in these mappings. Hints are specifications included in a mapping that indicate what the best processing strategy is. Although the term doesn't suggest this, with hints, the optimizer is forced to use a specific strategy. A hint can be a specification that indicates which index to use when the rows of a source table are accessed, one that indicates to which data store a table should be shipped to execute a ship join, or one that indicates not to use the ship join but to use the query expansion technique.

Figure 6.5 shows a part of the processing strategy of a complex query. In this query, multiple tables are being joined. The middle of the diagram shows how the join type for a particular join can be selected by a developer. In this example, the developer can select between five different join types. When the hint has been selected, the query optimizer uses this join type even if it thinks another join type is better.

6.13 **Optimization through SQL Override**

In principle, a data virtualization server generates standard SQL: an SQL dialect supported by many SQL database servers. However, several SQL database servers have extended their SQL implementations with proprietary features, such as special functions and SQL constructs, to improve the query performance. Unfortunately, in most cases those proprietary extensions are not generated by a data

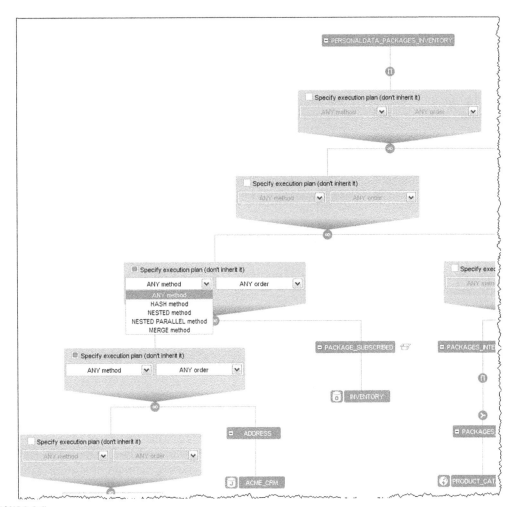

FIGURE 6.5

Developers can enter hints in mappings to indicate how a query should be processed.

Reprinted with permission of Denodo Technologies.

virtualization server. If developers know they can improve query performance by replacing the generated SQL statement by custom code, they can do so by using *SQL override*. With this feature, developers instruct a data virtualization server not to use the generated SQL but the custom SQL code. The effect is that the generated code is replaced by the custom code, which is then passed straight on to the underlying database server without any modifications. Some products call this feature *SQL passthrough*.

The big advantage of SQL override is that the full power of the SQL dialect of a particular data store can be exploited. A disadvantage is that the code can't be ported to another data store. So it becomes the responsibility of the developers to know which SQL dialect is supported by which data store. If they make mistakes, the SQL statement can't be processed. With SQL override, the concept of encapsulation is lost. Therefore, when SQL override is used, it's recommended to isolate the custom code as much as possible. For most data virtualization servers, when SQL override is used, the query can't be a join of tables from different data stores.

6.14 **Explaining the Processing Strategy**

The previous sections cover the various query optimization techniques. This final section describes how data virtualization servers are capable of showing how a query is executed. In other words, they can explain what the processing strategy of the query is. This allows developers to evaluate the effectiveness of query optimization. In most products this is called the *Explain feature*. Figure 6.6 shows the result of invoking this feature to get an understanding of how a query is processed. The boxes represent all the individual steps to be taken.

The details of how queries are expanded and broken into smaller queries and how they are shipped to different data stores, and so on, can help a developer understand why the performance is the way it is. For example, if the performance of a query is poor when the developer expected it to be fast, the explain feature can indicate what's wrong.

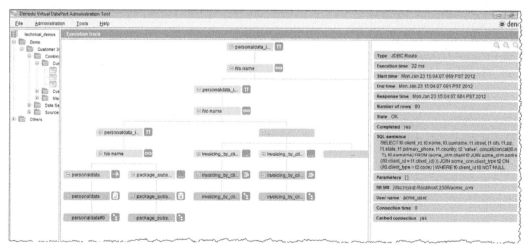

FIGURE 6.6

An example of a query processing strategy.

Reprinted with permission of Denodo Technologies.

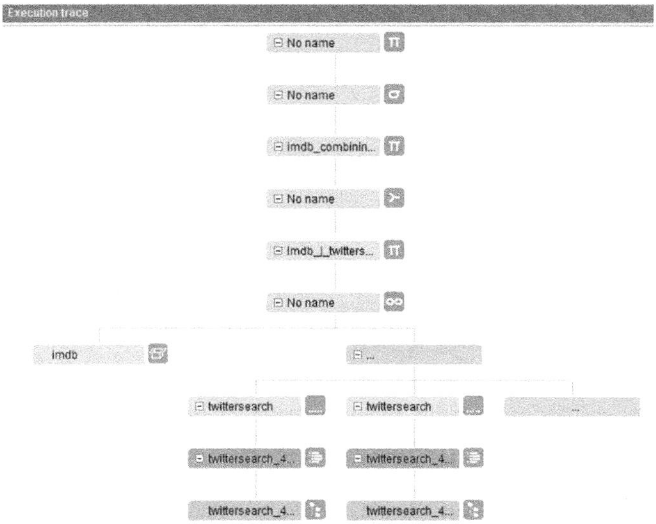

FIGURE 6.7

The processing strategy of a join of an unstructured data source with a semistructured data source.

Reprinted with permission of Denodo Technologies.

If developers can come up with a better processing strategy themselves, some data virtualization servers allow developers to change the order in which particular operations are executed. This is like manual query optimization. In this case, the result of Explain is not merely a diagram for viewing but a representation of the real strategy.

Figure 6.7 shows the processing strategy of the join of the IMDB website and Twitter (see Section 3.5 in Chapter 3). It shows that for each movie it finds on the website, it tries to find all the relevant tweets. This diagram shows that access to Twitter is parallelized.

Deploying Data Virtualization in Business Intelligence Systems

7.1 Introduction

Chapters 1, 3, 4, 5, and 6 explain what data virtualization is, how data virtualization servers work internally, and which techniques they support to improve performance. Chapter 2 gives an overview of business intelligence and data warehousing. In this chapter we're bringing the topics together. We'll examine how a data virtualization server can be used in a business intelligence system. The advantages and disadvantages of data virtualization are described. In addition, the following questions are answered: Why does deploying data virtualization in a business intelligence system make the latter more agile? What are the different application areas of data virtualization?

7.2 A Business Intelligence System Based on Data Virtualization

Deploying data virtualization in a business intelligence system means that data consumers are accessing the data stores, such as the central data warehouse, data marts, and personal data stores, via a data virtualization server (Figure 7.1). The data virtualization server hides for the data consumers from which data stores the data is retrieved from.

Figure 7.1 might give the impression that when a data virtualization server is deployed, all the data stores normally found in business intelligence systems will still be there. This doesn't have to be the case; on the contrary, the intention is to remove some of those data stores so a simpler architecture evolves. Figure 7.1 only illustrates that all those data stores can be accessed, but it's neither a requirement nor a goal. For example, if all the data in a personal data store is also stored in a data mart or data warehouse, it can be removed. Only the mappings of the virtual tables that are pointing to the personal data store have to be redirected to source tables in the other data store. The same might apply for a report retrieving data from a data mart. If all the data accessed is also available in a data warehouse, the data mart might not be needed anymore. And if data stores are removed, the storage structure of the business intelligence system becomes simpler and thus more flexible.

Introducing a data virtualization server has impact on various aspects of a business intelligence system. First, the developers of the reports won't know which data store is accessed. They only see this one large database in which all the data is integrated. They develop their reports on top of the virtual tables, but they won't have to know what the mappings look like and where and how data is stored.

Second, when a data virtualization server is deployed, specifications related to the data that would normally end up in the reports now end up in the definitions and mappings of virtual tables and are

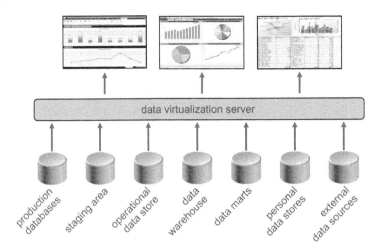

FIGURE 7.1

Data virtualization and a business intelligence system.

managed by that data virtualization server. As indicated in Section 3.7, in which the concept of shared meta data specifications is introduced, by letting these specifications be managed by a data virtualization server, all reporting tools (even if they are from different vendors) accessing the data via a data virtualization server use them. So all reports share the same set of specifications.

Third, in a classic business intelligence system, a lot of transformation and integration logic has to be developed to get the data in a form suitable for the reporting tools. Normally, most of that logic ends up in ETL scripts. When a data virtualization server is used, that logic is implemented in the mappings. Nevertheless, ETL will not disappear completely. For example, data still has to be copied from the production databases to the staging area periodically, and possibly from there to the data warehouse as well.

Something that won't change is what the users see and experience. In this new architecture, users don't see that data access is suddenly handled by a data virtualization server. They see their familiar reports and they don't see whether the accessed data store is a data mart loaded with data using ETL scripts or whether it's data accessed through a data virtualization server. Do realize that it's not important for users to know from which data store data is retrieved. As long as the data is the right data, has the right quality level, and is returned with an acceptable performance or, in other words, as long as the data meets all their requirements, they are satisfied.

7.3 Advantages of Deploying Data Virtualization

Why should organizations adopt data virtualization in their business intelligence systems? This section lists the advantages of deploying this technology in a business intelligence system. The advantages are grouped in three categories: advantages resulting from decoupling, from shared meta data specifications, and from working with on-demand transformations.

Most reporting and analytical tools require *meta data specifications* to be entered before reports can be developed. Some of those specifications are *descriptive*, and others are *transformative*. Examples of descriptive specifications are definitions of concepts—for example, a customer is someone who has bought at least one product, and the northern region doesn't include Washington State. Alternative names for tables, columns, and definitions of relationships between tables are also examples of descriptive specifications. Examples of transformative specifications are "how country codes should be replaced by country names" and "how a set of tables should be transformed to one wide dimensional table." In a data virtualization server, those specifications are centrally managed and can be shared. The advantages resulting from shared meta data specifications are as follows:

Increased speed of report development: Because most specifications already exist within the data virtualization server and can be reused, it takes less time to develop a new report. In other words, the time-to-market for new reports is significantly shortened. Development can focus primarily on the use of the specifications and on creating user interfaces that fit the needs of the users perfectly. The effect is that new user requirements and demands can be implemented faster.

Easier maintenance of meta data specifications: Unfortunately, with most reporting and analytical tools, descriptive and transformative specifications can't be shared. So if two users use different reporting tools, the specifications have to be replicated. The advantage of using a data virtualization server is that most of those specifications can be defined once within the mappings of the virtual tables and can be used by all the tools. Therefore, maintaining existing and adding new meta data specifications is easier.

Consistent reporting: If a data virtualization server is used, all reporting and analytical tools can use the same specifications to create results. The advantage is that those results will be consistent even if the tools are from different vendors. So even if some users use SAP/Business Objects and others use SpagoBI, they see the same data. This improves the perceived quality of and trust in a business intelligence system.

As indicated, with a data virtualization server, the data consumers are *decoupled* from the data stores. This means that they don't know which data stores are being accessed: a data warehouse, a data mart, or an operational data store. Neither do they know which data store technologies are being accessed: an Oracle or IBM database or maybe Microsoft Analysis Service. The advantages resulting from decoupling are as follows:

Cost reduction due to simplification: If a data virtualization server is installed in an existing business intelligence system—for example, one based on the CIF (corporate information factory) architecture—the architecture can be simplified considerably. Many physical data marts and personal data stores can probably be removed because all of their data is available in the data warehouse as well. When those data stores are removed, existing reports have to be redirected to another data store, which is easy to do with a data virtualization server. The advantage of this simplification of the architecture is cost reduction: fewer database server licenses, fewer ETL scripts to develop and manage, and fewer database management and optimization activities to perform.

Increased flexibility of the business intelligence system: When data stores are removed, the overall system consists of less code, fewer specifications, fewer servers to manage, and so on, and thus a simpler system. A simpler system is easier to change. This seriously increases flexibility. When new data stores have to be added or when data structures change, those changes are easier to implement.

Easier data store migration: A data virtualization server offers data store independency. Reports accessing a particular data store can easily be migrated to another. The reports' queries can be redirected through the data virtualization server to that other data store. For example, if a report is currently accessing a data mart, migrating it to the data warehouse doesn't require any changes in the report definition. So on the data storage level, data virtualization makes a business intelligence system more agile.

Seamless adoption of new technology: Recently, powerful new analytical database servers and storage technology have been introduced. As indicated, because a data virtualization server separates data consumers from data stores, replacing an existing data store technology with a new one is relatively easy and has no impact on the reports, except for a better performance. For example, if the need exists to migrate from an SQL database to MDX-base technology, or if a classic SQL database server has to be replaced by a fast analytical database server, these changes can be implemented without having any impact on the reports. In short, if a data virtualization server is in place, migration to another data store technology is relatively easy. The data virtualization server hides all the specifics of a particular database technology. Numerous reasons can exist why an organization wants to migrate. For example, they may want to switch to database technology that offers faster query performance or data storage is outsourced and needs to be accessed differently.

Data model-driven development: Adopting data virtualization has an impact on data modeling. In fact, data modeling becomes the driving force behind development. More on this in Chapter 11.

Transparent archiving of data: Eventually, data warehouses might become so massive that "older" data has to be archived. Normally, this involves taking data from the original data store and moving it to another. But even if the data is old, it doesn't always mean users don't want to access it anymore. If the data is archived, those reports that still want to work with that data has to be rewritten to access the data store that contains the archived data. If a data virtualization server is in place, it can hide whether the data is archived and where and how it's archived. If users are still interested in all the data, a data virtualization server can combine the nonarchived data with the archived data store. Depending on the implementation, the effect might be that the performance is somewhat slower, but the good thing is that reports don't have to be changed. Again, the data virtualization server transparently hides the fact that some data has been archived. Changing archiving solutions can also be hidden from the data consumers.

As indicated in Chapter 1, in a data virtualization server, data is transformed and integrated when the data is being accessed: on-demand transformation. The advantages resulting from on-demand transformations are as follows:

Access to operational data: Some data consumers need access to live data; they want to see what's happening in the business processes, and they don't want delays. For operational management in particular, being able to see live data can be of significant value. Normally, before data in production databases can be used for reporting, it has to be transformed. The transformations can be done by using ETL or by a data virtualization server. When an ETL tool is used, the result of the transformation is stored, which means the reports won't be accessing live data. A data virtualization server offers on-demand transformation. When the report asks for the data, the production data is retrieved and transformed live. To summarize, because a data virtualization server supports on-demand transformations, developing reports that present operational data becomes a possibility. Note that when operational systems are being accessed, care must be taken to avoid interference.

Mixing operational and historical data: If a data virtualization server is allowed to access production databases and to access data warehouses, operational data from the former can be joined with historical data coming from the latter. This allows for comparing the current with the historical situation. For example, how do the current sales figures relate to those of the previous weeks?

7.4 **Disadvantages of Deploying Data Virtualization**

Every technology has advantages and disadvantages, and it's no different with data virtualization. The following are the disadvantages of deploying data virtualization in a business intelligence system:

Extra layer of software: A data virtualization server is an extra layer of software located between the data consumers and the data stores and consumes cpu seconds. Parsing the incoming queries, executing on-demand transformations, and processing results all cost time, but whether they have a negative impact on performance depends on several factors. First of all, if a nonintelligent data store is accessed, such as a sequential file or a web service, a data virtualization server has to do little work. However, if a data virtualization server isn't being used and the reporting tool accesses the data store directly, the reporting tool itself has to do all the processing. Most likely, both execute that same logic in the same time. If, on the other hand, an intelligent data store is accessed and if a large part of a query can be pushed down to the data store, it's predominantly that data store that determines what the performance is. In this case, most of the processing time is spent by the data store on retrieving data from the disks. To summarize, in most cases a data virtualization server just adds a minimal amount of time to the total processing time.

Repeated processing of transformations: An ETL tool transforms data and stores the result in a data store. This transformed result can be reused many times. With on-demand transformations, results are not reused repeatedly. Every time a virtual table is accessed, the transformations in the mappings are executed. In other words, the transformations are executed repeatedly. Note that by defining a cache, the number of times a transformation is executed is minimized.

Proprietary development language: Because no international standard exists for data virtualization servers, every tool uses a proprietary language for specifying the mappings and wrappers. Therefore, switching from one data virtualization server to another is not simple. It involves a lot of development, which is clearly a disadvantage. Note that the same disadvantage applies for most types of products used in business intelligence systems, including reporting tools, statistical tools, ETL and ELT tools, and replication tools. All of them use proprietary languages as well. In general, the use of proprietary languages in business intelligence systems is high.

Management of data virtualization servers: Like database servers and application servers, data virtualization servers have to be managed technically as well; they have to be installed, tuned, and managed. Someone or some department has to be responsible for such a product. The performance, availability, and scalability have to be monitored; security rules have to be managed; and so on. Management of a data virtualization server costs time.

Limited experience: At the time of writing, experience with data virtualization servers is still limited. The expectation is that this will change quickly now that organizations have discovered the value of data virtualization and have started to adopt it.

7.5 **Strategies for Adopting Data Virtualization**

This section describes a number of strategies for adopting data virtualization in a business intelligence system. The first strategy can be used if an existing business intelligence system has to be extended with data virtualization, and the others apply when a new business intelligence system is developed.

Whatever strategy is selected, it has to address the following key questions:

- Where and how is data transformed?
- Where and how is data cleansed?
- Where and how is data from different sources (production systems) integrated?
- How do we offer the data consumers the right table structures?
- How is historical data handled, and how are different versions of the same data implemented?
- Does the solution have the right load performance and query performance?

Note: The three strategies described are just examples. All three have been successfully used in real-life projects, but other strategies can be applied as well. It's also possible to mix the strategies described in this chapter. When a strategy is selected, be sure that the preceding questions are covered.

7.5.1 Strategy 1: Introducing Data Virtualization in an Existing Business Intelligence System

Many organizations have a business intelligence system already in use: data stores have been designed, ETL scripts have been developed, and reports are up and running. In such a situation, does adopting data virtualization require a revolution? Does it mean that large portions of the architecture have to be thrown away and redesigned? The answer to both questions is no. Data virtualization can be introduced step by step with little to no disturbance for the existing data consumers. It's more evolution than revolution. This section describes how data virtualization can be adopted in such a situation.

Step 1: A data virtualization server is installed, source tables are imported, and wrappers and virtual tables are defined for each of the relevant source tables in all the data stores of the business intelligence system (Figure 7.2). Reports are not changed in this step and are still accessing the data stores directly. Most of the virtual tables developed in this step have a one-to-one correspondence with the source tables. So no mappings with complex transformations are developed.

Step 2: One by one, the data consumers are redirected to access their data stores via the data virtualization server (Figure 7.3). The effect is that they still access the same source tables in the same data stores and their queries stay unchanged. The difference is that the queries are now processed via the data virtualization server. To make this possible, in Step 1 virtual tables are created that have the same structure and virtual contents as the source tables they originally accessed.

Step 3: For some data consumers, the mappings of the virtual tables they're accessing are changed in this step (Figure 7.4). For example, a virtual table that accesses some source tables in a data mart can now be redirected to access the data warehouse holding the same data but organized in a different set of tables. This change is transparent to the data consumers.

The tables in the orginal data stores are probably filled with data using ETL scripts. These scripts contain the transformation logic used to transform the data from the source tables to the original tables. This logic is used in the mappings of the new virtual tables. All this logic has to be translated to guarantee that the new virtual tables have the same structure and the same virtual contents as the original tables.

Step 4: This step focuses on simplifying the architecture by removing duplicate data from the data stores (Figure 7.5).

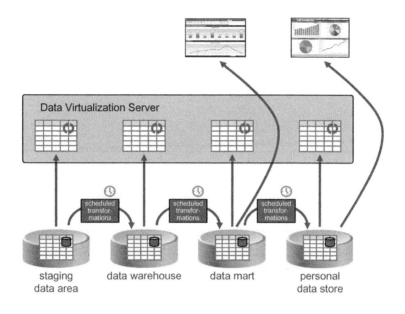

FIGURE 7.2

Step 1: The data virtualization server is installed and the source tables are imported.

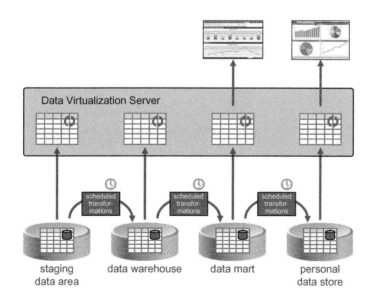

FIGURE 7.3

Step 2: The data consumers are redirected to access virtual tables.

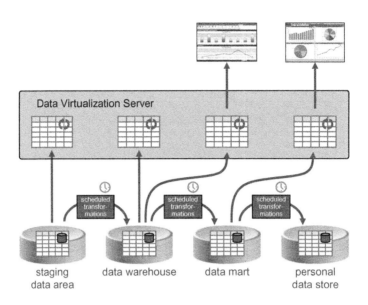

FIGURE 7.4

Step 3: The virtual tables are changed to access other source tables.

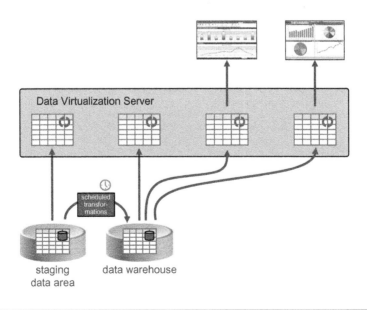

FIGURE 7.5

Step 4: Duplicate data is removed.

When source tables are no longer being accessed because the queries have been redirected to other tables (in other data stores), they've become superfluous and can be removed. In addition, the ETL scripts loading these source tables can also be removed. If sufficient source tables have been removed, then eventually whole data stores, such as personal data stores and data marts, can be removed as well.

It could also be that some source tables contain derived data. For example, the customer table might hold the total number of rented movies in the last year for each customer, or the customer order table might contain a value that shows the sum of its rental price. This type of derived data is usually added to improve query performance and might have been added to tables in the data warehouse, data marts, or personal data stores. In this step, derived data is removed. The logic used to calculate the derived data is moved to the mappings of the virtual tables that used to access that derived data.

Up to this step, nothing in the existing reports is changed. The reports still show the same data and present the same results as before data virtualization was introduced. Nevertheless, maybe the performance of the reports has changed; it might be somewhat slower or faster depending on the database and hardware technology used.

Step 5: This step is like a cleanup step (Figure 7.6). Because the structures of the virtual tables created in Step 1 are identical to the structures of the original source tables, those structures might not be perfect. It can be beneficial to normalize a structure of a virtual table somewhat or to design it in such a way that it is according to design standards. Virtual tables with comparable structures and contents might be "merged." If virtual tables are changed, the report definitions must be changed accordingly.

Step 6: Due to the approach taken, many virtual tables are linked to source tables straight on. For development, maintenance, and consistency reasons, it's recommended that you identify common

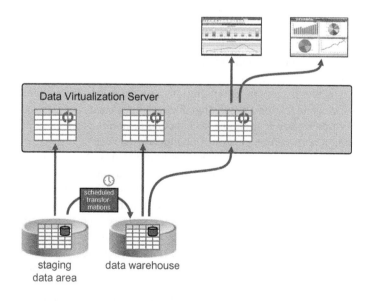

FIGURE 7.6

Step 5: Identify and merge comparable virtual tables.

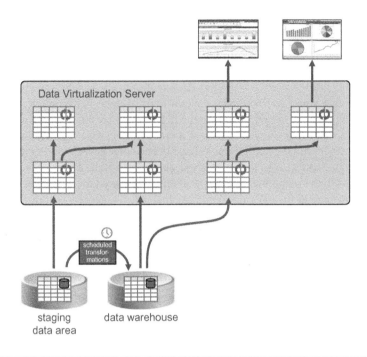

FIGURE 7.7

Step 6: Identify common virtual tables and nest virtual tables.

specifications and implement them as shared specifications in new virtual tables (Figure 7.7). The existing virtual tables then become nested virtual tables.

Step 7: Enable caching for those virtual tables for which query performance is unacceptable. The benefit of this strategy is that it's a seamless migration; in other words, it's an evolution and not a revolution. Existing data consumers don't notice that changes have been made on the data store level. In addition, when data virtualization is used, the architecture is significantly more agile. So new reports and changes to existing reports can be implemented much faster.

With respect to the key questions listed at the beginning of this chapter, the following statements can be made: Most of the data transformation, cleansing, and integration in this strategy are performed by the ETL scripts already in use. If ETL scripts for loading duplicate tables or data stores have been removed, and if those scripts contained logic for transformation, cleansing, and integration, comparable logic has been implemented in the mappings of the virtual tables. Historical data is still handled the same way as in the original architecture. Because there will be less loading going on, load performance won't be an issue if it wasn't an issue before. Query performance, however, can be a big challenge. Therefore, it might be necessary in Step 7 to introduce caches to get the required performance.

This strategy can be applied as described: step by step. But a more iterative approach can be applied as well. For each report or set of reports, the seven steps can be executed.

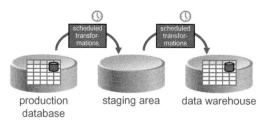

production
database   staging area   data warehouse

FIGURE 7.8

Step 1: Develop the staging area and the data
warehouse and use scheduled transformation to load
them.

7.5.2 Strategy 2: Developing a New Business Intelligence System with Data Virtualization

When an organization wants to develop a new business intelligence system that exploits data virtualization, a different set of steps is recommended.

Step 1: Start by developing a system consisting of a minimal set of data stores, preferably only a data staging area and a data warehouse (Figure 7.8). Use ETL, ELT, or replication for loading the data staging area and the data warehouse.

Two important decisions have to be made when designing this part of the system: First, how much data cleansing should be done? Second, how much data integration should take place? With respect to the first decision, implement most of the cleansing operations in the two loading steps. Each cleansing operation not implemented in these steps leads to implementing them in the mappings of the virtual tables.

The rule here is that the more data cleansing is handled *upstream*, the better it is. With upstream we mean as close to the source as possible. Cleansing data *downstream* (closer to the reports) is more complex and can be quite cpu intensive. In an ideal world, data cleansing is fully handled by the production systems themselves. These systems should be developed in such a way that it becomes close to impossible for users to enter incorrect data. And if incorrect data is entered, somehow the production environment should resolve that issue before the data is copied to the staging area. To summarize, data stored in the data warehouse is cleansed, transformed, and normalized.

With respect to the design of tables in the data warehouse, try to normalize them as much as possible, with each fact stored only once. If the structures of the tables in the production systems are not really normalized, it's recommended to let the ETL scripts transform the data into a more relational structure. For example, if a table in a production database contains a repeating group, such as all the telephone numbers of an employee, a separate table should be created in the data warehouse for these telephone numbers. In this example, the effect is that data from that employee table in the production databases is copied to two tables in the data warehouse.

The tables in the data warehouse should have a structure that can hold multiple versions of the same object. For example, the customer table should be able to hold the current address of a customer, as well as all of its previous addresses. In other words, the tables should be able to store historical data, and the ETL scripts should know how to load new data and make existing data historical data. Different design solutions exist to handle this correctly and efficiently.

Step 2: Install a data virtualization server and import from the data warehouse and the production databases all the source tables that may be needed for the first set of reports that have to be developed (Figure 7.9).

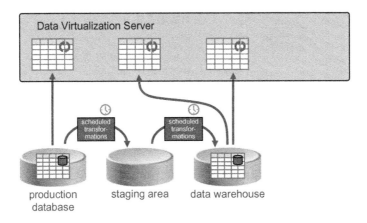

FIGURE 7.9

Step 2: Define the first layer of virtual tables responsible for cleansing and transforming the data.

Make sure that the contents of these virtual tables is *filtered*. Filtered in this context means that the data in the virtual tables conforms to particular rules. The developers implement these filtering rules in the mappings of the virtual tables. For example, known incorrect values are replaced by correct ones, and incorrect values that can't be replaced by correct ones are flagged as incorrect or those rows are filtered out and don't show up in contents of the virtual table. (Section 8.2 describes filtering and flagging in detail.) An example of an incorrect value is one that falls outside acceptable boundaries, such as 1899 being the birth year of an employee.

To develop the right filters, it might be necessary to create special tables that help with transforming incorrect to correct values. These tables have to be stored as source tables in the data warehouse itself and are not loaded with data from the production environment. These correct codes are entered and updated separately and are managed by the data virtualization server.

There are two reasons for verifying data and for including filters. The first reason is to increase the quality level of the data used by all the data consumers. Implementing these filters within the mappings of the first layer of virtual tables means that all the data consumers see the cleansed and verified data, regardless of whether they're accessing the lowest level of virtual tables or some top levels (defined in the next steps). The second reason is to improve the consistency of reporting across all reporting tools and all users. The structures of these virtual tables should be comparable to those of the underlying source tables. They should have a one-to-one correspondence with the source tables.

Eventually, the structures of tables in the data warehouse will change. Hopefully, this first layer of virtual tables hides these changes. Of course, this only applies when existing structures are changed and when existing columns are removed. When new columns or tables are added, and if that data is needed by the reports, the virtual tables have to be changed in order to show the new data.

So to summarize, the first layer of virtual tables is responsible for improving the quality level of the data, improving the consistency of reporting, and hiding possible changes to the tables in the production systems.

Step 3: Create a second layer with virtual tables where each table represents some business object or a property of some business object (Figure 7.10). Examples of business objects are customers,

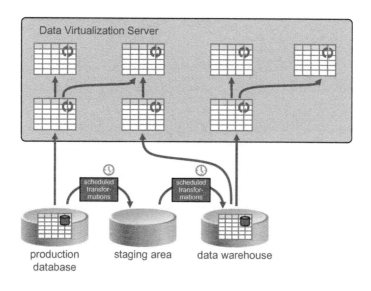

FIGURE 7.10

Step 3: Define virtual tables that represent business objects.

products, and invoices. This can mean that data from multiple virtual tables is joined into one larger virtual table. For example, when customer data is spread out over multiple production databases, it's integrated here to form one virtual table showing all the customers with all their data.

It might be necessary to integrate data from multiple data warehouse tables to create one integrated view. For example, one set of customers is stored in one production system and another set in another system. Both source tables exist in the data warehouse, and for both, a virtual table is defined, but on this second level of virtual tables, there is only one. A mapping combines those tables. In other words, this layer of nested virtual tables is responsible for integrating data and for presenting that data in a more business object-oriented style. This layer of virtual tables represents an enterprise view. It contains the data in a neutral or canonical way. Because of this, it's sometimes referred to as a *canonical model*.

If business objects are subsets of other business objects, this step can lead to multiple levels of nested virtual tables. For example, on a virtual table called V_CUSTOMER (holding all the customers), a nested one called V_GOOD_CUSTOMER might be defined that holds only those customers who adhere to a particular requirement. The set of rows of V_GOOD_CUSTOMER table forms a subset of those of V_CUSTOMER. To be able to develop nested virtual tables, the definitions of the business objects should be clear to all parties involved.

Step 4: Develop a third layer of virtual tables that are structurally aimed at the needs of a specific data consumer or a group of data consumers (Figure 7.11). For example, it might be that one tool can only access data if the tables form a star schema. Another wants to work with business objects that are derived from business objects on the second level. A data consumer may not work with all the customers in the virtual tables but only with the ones from a specific region. Or another data consumer doesn't want to see historical customer data, only current data which means that historical data has to be filtered out.

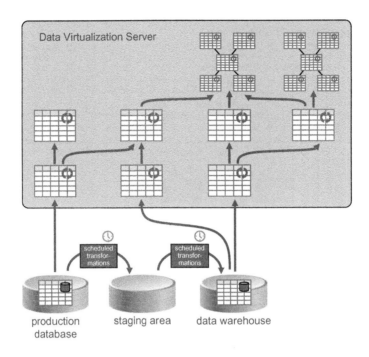

FIGURE 7.11

Step 4: Define virtual tables that fit the needs of the data consumers.

The virtual tables in this layer can be regarded as forming a *virtual data mart*. In a *physical data mart*, the structures of the tables are also aimed at the use of the data. For these virtual tables making up virtual data marts, the same applies. More on virtual data marts in Section 7.6.2.

To summarize, developers are completely free in designing a structure that fits the needs of the user. This virtual solution is easy to change, and if the right design techniques are applied, many mapping specifications can be reused. Compared to physical data marts, virtual data marts form an extremely flexible solution and are cost-effective.

Step 5: Develop the reports on the top layer of virtual tables (Figure 7.12). In some cases, when reports are developed, changes have to be applied to the top layer of virtual tables due to new insights.

Step 6: It might be necessary to enable caching for particular virtual tables (Figure 7.13). There might be different reasons for doing this, such as poor query performance, too much interference on the production systems, and data consumers that want to see consistent data content for a particular duration. See also Section 5.3 for a more detailed description of reasons for enabling caching. If caching doesn't solve the problems, create physical data marts and use ETL scripts to load them.

The diagrams in Figures 7.12 and 7.13 might give the impression that only the top-level virtual tables are accessible for the data consumers, but that's not the intention of these diagrams. If reports require detailed data in a form that closely resembles that of the original data, they can be given access to the lowest level of virtual tables.

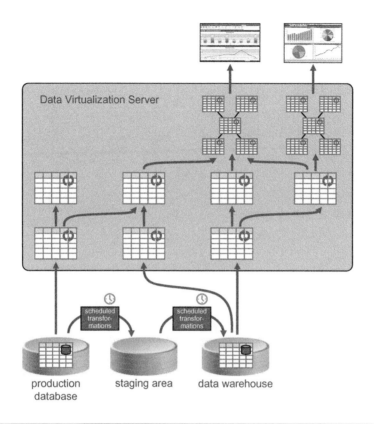

FIGURE 7.12

Step 5: Develop the reports and modify the virtual tables when needed.

7.5.3 **Strategy 3: Developing a New Business Intelligence System Combining Source and Transformed Data**

A disadvantage of the second strategy is that no virtual table can give data consumers access to the original data as it has been entered and stored in the production databases. The reason is that the data has been transformed and cleansed. If some data consumers need to see the original data (including all the incorrect values), a different strategy has to be applied. We describe this third strategy by explaining the differences with the previous strategy.

Notice that the need to access operational data doesn't imply a need to access the production database. Maybe business users want to see what an invoice looked like two years ago in its untransformed and uncleansed form.

Step 1: Start with an architecture consisting of a minimal set of data stores, preferably a data staging area and a data warehouse only (see Figure 7.8). Use ETL, ELT, or replication for loading the staging area.

Initially, the data coming from the production systems is not cleansed or transformed. The tables in the data warehouse are designed in such a way that the original operational data is stored and can

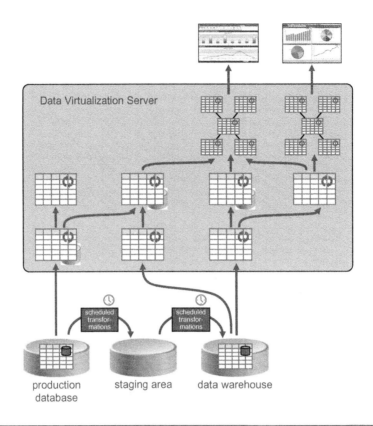

FIGURE 7.13

Step 6: If needed, enable caching.

be retrieved. To make this possible, the structures of the tables in the data warehouse will resemble those of the production systems. If possible, normalize these tables as much as possible.

Use an ELT approach for loading the data warehouse. Unchanged data is first loaded into the data warehouse. This can be seen as the first version of the data. It represents the data as it is (or was) stored in the production systems. Next, the data is cleansed and transformed. The changed data is regarded as a new version of the data. So the data warehouse contains the first untransformed and transformed version of the data. Transformed and cleansed data always forms a next version. This makes it possible to support data consumers who need to work with cleansed and transformed data, and also to support data consumers who need to see the original data the way it was entered in the production system. Section 8.10 shows what these tables could look like.

Step 2: Install a data virtualization server and import all the source tables of the data warehouse and the production databases that are needed for the first set of reports that have to be developed (see Figure 7.9).

Step 3: Define virtual tables and filter the contents (in the same way as with the second strategy). It might be necessary to develop two sets of virtual tables: one that presents only the original data and one that contains the transformed and cleansed data.

Steps 4–6: These steps can be executed in a similar way as with the previous strategy.

7.6 **Application Areas of Data Virtualization**

This section describes a wide range of application areas where data virtualization can be applied in business intelligence systems. Some of these application areas can be implemented in a business intelligence system with a more classic architecture as well, but in most cases they will be (much) more difficult and more time-consuming to implement. Chapter 9 covers application areas of data virtualization that don't deal with business intelligence but that relate to service-oriented architectures.

7.6.1 **Unified Data Access**

The primary application area of data virtualization is to supply data consumers with the right data, at the right time, and in the right form. This data is retrieved from various data stores, including data warehouses, data marts, operational data stores, and external data sources (see Figure 7.1). This application area can be summarized with the term *unified data access*. Data consumers accessing the data via a data virtualization server see one logical data store in which all the data coming from multiple data stores is unified. The data virtualization server is responsible for integrating and transforming the data. Unified data access is the most common application area of data virtualization in business intelligence systems.

7.6.2 **Virtual Data Mart**

In most business intelligence systems, if data marts exist, they usually handle the majority of all the reporting and analytics. In general, the reasons for developing a data mart are as follows:

- The most dominant reason for organizations to develop data marts is query performance. Without data marts, all the queries have to be executed on a data warehouse or some other central data store. This query workload might be too heavy for the database technology in use, leading to long waiting times for the users. By implementing data marts, most of the queries are offloaded from the central data warehouse to these data marts, and by distributing the query workload over multiple data marts, the performance of queries improves.
- Certain reporting or analytical tools require accessed data to be organized in a particular way. For example, a tool might need data to be organized in tables according to a star schema. If the tables in the data warehouse are normalized, that tool won't be able to access the data. In this case, a data mart is used to present the same data in the right structure. In such a system, ETL scripts are used to transform the normalized data to a star schema arrangement.
- If users are geographically dispersed, accessing a central data store might lead to considerable network delay when the query results are returned, making the reports slow. In this situation, it's better to move data physically closer to where the users are located, taking network traffic out of the equation.

These are all excellent reasons for creating a data mart, but there are also disadvantages—namely, they have to be designed, developed, and managed. All these activities cost time and money.

With a data virtualization server, the existence of a data mart can be simulated. Such a data mart is called a *virtual data mart* (Figure 7.14). In a data virtualization server, virtual tables can be developed with the same structure as those developed for a physical data mart. However, with a data virtualization server, the data is not physically stored. When the virtual data mart tables are accessed, data is copied from, for example, a central data warehouse through on-demand transformation to the data consumers. Instead of actually creating a data store for a physical data mart and writing ETL scripts

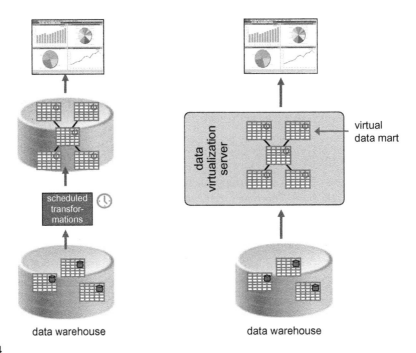

FIGURE 7.14

Virtual data marts (right) as an alternative to physical data marts (left).

for periodically refreshing the data mart, virtual table structures and mappings are defined in the data virtualization server.

The principal advantages of virtual data marts over physical data marts are development speed, agility, and lower costs.

Development speed: Table 7.1 lists most of the activities for setting up a physical data mart versus a virtual one. It clearly shows that setting up a physical data mart requires much more work. Some activities have to be done, regardless of whether a physical or virtual data mart is developed, such as designing the required data structures and defining the needed transformations. But for a physical data mart environment, that's not where it stops. Database servers have to be installed and tuned, data must be refreshed periodically, and so on. More activities mean more development time.

Agility: Changing a virtual table in a virtual data mart involves altering a mapping and nothing more. Making a comparable change in a physical data mart might lead to changing the data structures, redefining ETL scripts, unloading and reloading data, possibly changing the existing indexes structures, and retuning and reoptimizing the database. In other words, it involves more work, which reduces agility. Virtual data marts, on the other hand, involve less work, and less means more agile.

Lower costs: Developing and changing physical data marts is more expensive than developing and changing virtual data marts. The main reason is, again, there's less work.

A potential advantage of a physical data mart is that its performance can be better than that of a virtual alternative. However, the performance of a virtual data mart can be improved by enabling caching (see Chapter 5). In this case, a comparable performance can be obtained. Note that in all the strategies explained in Section 7.5, it's recommended to create virtual data marts.

Table 7.1 Activities Required to Set Up Physical and Virtual Data Marts

Activities for Setting Up a Physical Data Mart	Activities for Setting Up a Virtual Data Mart
Define data structures (probably with a star schema)	Design data structures
Define ETL logic to copy data from data warehouse to data mart	Define mappings
Prepare a server	—
Install a database server	—
Create a database	—
Implement the tables	Define virtual tables
Physical database design, tuning, and optimization	Enable caching (if needed)
Load the tables periodically	—
Tune and optimize the database regularly	—
Make a DBA responsible	—

7.6.3 **Virtual Data Warehouse—Based on Data Marts**

Imagine that a business intelligence system of an organization consists of data marts only and doesn't include a central data warehouse. Suppose that this organization wants to develop reports for which data from multiple data marts has to be integrated. In that case, a data virtualization server can be useful to develop a *virtual data warehouse*.

A virtual data warehouse can combine data stored in multiple physical data marts. It can do that the moment a report asks for the data: on-demand data integration. Note that it is required that the accessed data marts support conformed dimension tables (see Section 2.6.3). This means they must have columns on which tables can be joined (possibly after transformations). For example, if one data mart contains sales data and the other weather-related data and a need exists to join these two based on a common dimension called region, it's necessary that both support a dimension table using the same codes to identify regions. Only if data marts contain such conformed dimensions is a join possible and can a virtual data warehouse be developed (Figure 7.15).

Another approach would be to periodically copy data from the data marts to an extra data store. This data store would be accessed by the reports that need the integrated view. The advantage of using a data virtualization server is that the existing architecture doesn't have to be changed, nor do extra data stores have to be developed and managed.

7.6.4 **Virtual Data Warehouse—Based on Production Databases**

Another way of developing a virtual data warehouse is by defining a data virtualization server on top of all the production databases (Figure 7.16). Technically this is feasible—but under two conditions. First of all, the production databases should contain all the data needed by the users of the reporting environment; this includes historical data. Second, the queries executed on the production databases should not cause too much performance and concurrency problems for the production applications.

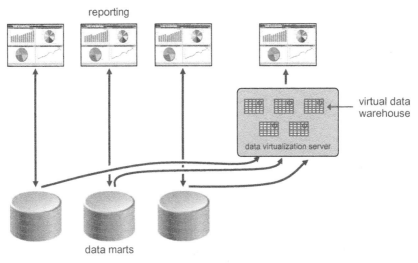

FIGURE 7.15

A virtual data warehouse can be derived by integrating multiple data marts.

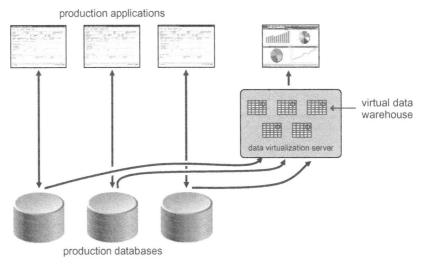

FIGURE 7.16

A virtual data warehouse can be derived by integrating multiple production databases.

Developing a virtual data warehouse on production databases requires a thorough study of its feasibility. Such a study should involve an analysis of the reasons described in Section 2.5.1 for why (physical) data warehouses are developed in the first place.

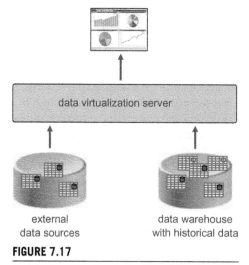

FIGURE 7.17

Developing an extended data warehouse by using a data virtualization server for combining external data sources and the data warehouse.

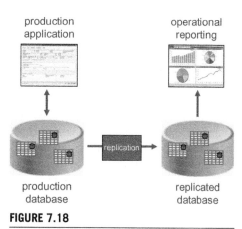

FIGURE 7.18

Operational reporting using replication.

7.6.5 **Extended Data Warehouse**

For reports that have to extend data from the data warehouse with data from other data sources, such as production databases, external sources, and local files, a data virtualization server can offer an integrated view of all those data stores—hence the name *extended data warehouse* (Figure 7.17). This way there is no need to copy the data from those other data stores to the data warehouse.

The ability to create wrappers on non-SQL data sources, such as web services, XML documents, and Java components, makes it relatively easy to offer access to those external data sources. The reports will be able to access them in the same way they access virtual tables holding internal data.

How easy it is to join columns from virtual tables defined on external sources with columns from virtual tables in the data warehouse depends a large part on whether sources use key values that are consistent with the ones used in the data warehouse.

7.6.6 **Operational Reporting and Analytics**

Users who need reports based on operational data need access to operational data, meaning they probably need access to the production databases, because those data stores contain the most up-to-date state of the data.

Roughly three approaches exist to implement *operational reporting* and *analytics*. The first approach is the most straightforward: let the reports access the production databases directly. With the second approach, data is copied from the production databases to other data stores using replication (see Section 1.11). These replicated data stores are accessed by the reports (Figure 7.18). With this approach, data is copied one-to-one. The result is that the structure and the contents of the tables in the replicated data store is identical to those of the original production database; the replicated data is not transformed.

Although both approaches sound feasible, they lead to the following complexities:

- The table structures in a production database may not be suitable for reporting. They might have been designed to support production applications, but not operational reports. These structures can lead to complex reporting code.
- The tables in a production database might contain data that needs to be corrected or recoded. Usually, this is handled by ETL scripts. With operational reporting, the reporting tools have to handle this; they become responsible for on-demand cleansing and on-demand transformations. Most reporting tools have not been designed to handle such tasks. If they are, all that code is replicated across multiple reports accessing the same operational data.
- If data from multiple production systems has to be integrated for a report, it's the reporting tool itself that has to include all the integration logic. Again, most reporting tools are not properly equipped for this. If they are, all that integration logic is replicated across multiple reports accessing the same operational data.
- Queries on production databases can cause performance problems, especially if they are complex, statistical queries. The query might cause so much I/O that operational users trying to insert or update data will have to wait. Note that this problem applies to the first approach only, but not to the second, because here the queries are run on the replicated data store.
- Reporting on production databases can also cause concurrency issues. Running a report might lead to locking of data, resulting in operational users waiting for data to become available. On the other hand, updates by the operational users might lead to queries that have to wait before they can be executed. Note that this problem applies to the first approach only, but not to the second, because the replicated data store is accessed.

In fact, the preceding list is also a short summary of the reasons why data is normally copied to a data warehouse before it is used by the reporting tools. All the issues that we normally deal with during the copying process now must be handled by the reporting tool. Most of them do not support sufficient functionality to deal with these issues easily and elegantly. For some, it is impossible.

The third approach for implementing operational reporting is by deploying data virtualization. A data virtualization server offers the reports direct access to the production databases (Figure 7.19). It is responsible for handling the complexities listed above. In fact, these products have been designed to handle such complexities. By defining the right virtual tables and mappings, they can present a more suitable data structure, transform incorrect data, integrate data from different production databases, and optimize access in such a way that the problems of performance and concurrency are minimized or are resolved completely. An additional benefit of using data virtualization is that all the specifications entered in the data virtualization server are shared by all the tools that need access to the operational data; the specifications are being reused.

The queries of a data virtualization server can have a negative impact on the ongoing operational work. These same queries can also lead to concurrency problems. Caching may not be the solution here, because if the reports really need to access the most up-to-date state of the data, they have to be executed on the production databases. In this case, an approach where data virtualization and replication are used is preferred (Figure 7.20).

7.6.7 Operational Data Warehouse

The reports described in the previous section only needed access to operational data. When the need exists to combine operational data with historical data, the reporting tools need access to production

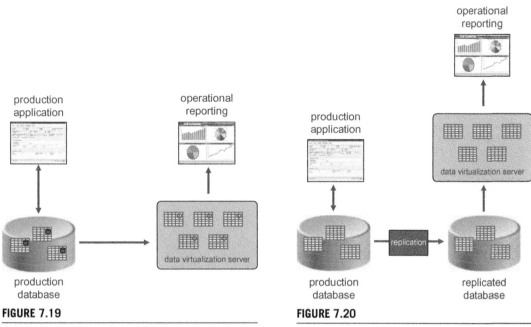

FIGURE 7.19

Operational reporting using data virtualization.

FIGURE 7.20

Operational reporting using data virtualization and replication.

databases and a data warehouse. Most tools are technically able to access multiple data stores, so most of them are able to access the production databases and the data warehouse. However, the tools will have to deal with all the issues described in the previous section, plus they have to know how to integrate the data coming from those two different data stores.

A more effective approach is to deploy data virtualization and let a data virtualization server combine the actual data from production databases with the historical data available in the data warehouse (Figure 7.21). This simulates what some call an *operational data warehouse* and others call an *online* or a *near-online data warehouse*.

When a data virtualization server is used for this application area, it has to solve a number of issues. First of all, to be able to join data in the data warehouse with data from production systems, they must have consistent key values on which the join can be executed. This requires that the keys from the production systems are copied to the data warehouse environment. Second, if data in the data warehouse has been cleansed, whereas the data in the production system has not, inconsistenties can occur. Third, accessing a production system can lead to the same performance and concurrency problems described in the previous section.

7.6.8 **Virtual Corporate Data Warehouse**

In some large organizations, several business intelligence systems are created independently of one another, each with its own central data warehouse and its own operational data store and data marts. Possible reasons why multiple systems exist are a merger of two organizations that already had

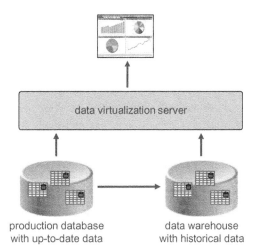

FIGURE 7.21

An operational data warehouse is simulated by letting a data virtualization server join data from a production database and a data warehouse.

business intelligence systems in use and each unit of an organization in a different country decided to develop its own system.

In these situations, eventually the need arises to compare or combine data from all those environments. For example, production numbers of different countries have to be compared, or sales numbers of all organizations have to be summarized. A solution is the *virtual corporate data warehouse*.

When a report needs to access data stored in all these central data warehouses, a data virtualization server is the most practical solution. The solution is very similar to the virtual data warehouse solution on data marts. However, instead of combining data from multiple data marts to form one virtual data warehouse, data from multiple data warehouses (and/or data marts) is combined to form one virtual corporate data warehouse.

7.6.9 Self-Service Reporting and Analytics

As described in Section 2.9.3, self-service reporting and analytics have become popular. Users want to develop their own reports and do their own analytics. They don't want to wait for the IT department to set up an environment on which they can build the reports.

In the ultimate form of self-service, users are given access to any data store. They can determine which tables in which data stores they want to access. The risk of this approach is whether the users are manipulating the data correctly. Are they combining tables on the right columns? Do they know how history has been implemented in particular tables? Do they understand the values used in some columns? Do they know that some columns still have incorrect codes, and do they know how to transform them?

A data virtualization server allows an IT department to meet the users halfway. Virtual tables can be defined. Transformation, integration, and cleansing rules can be implemented in mappings. By predefining the right virtual tables, users are given access to a consistent set of tables. If they need more tables, or if table structures have to be changed, access can be given quickly and in a controlled way. In other words, with a data virtualization server, virtual tables can be set up and adjusted rapidly because they are virtual and not physical concepts. The ability of the IT department to react quickly fits perfectly with the nature of self-service business intelligence.

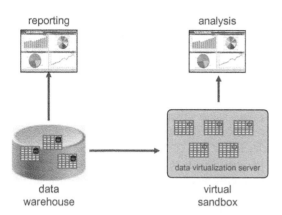

reporting   analysis

data
warehouse

data virtualization server

virtual
sandbox

FIGURE 7.22

A virtual sandbox using data virtualization.

In a nutshell, by deploying data virtualization, users can still have their flexible self-service environment, while still giving the IT department control over data access without losing agility. Data virtualization can turn self-service reporting into *managed self-service reporting*.

7.6.10 Virtual Sandbox

The term *sandbox* (besides being a box full of sand for kids to play in) refers in the world of business intelligence to a stand-alone and somewhat isolated environment set up for analysts and data scientists to study data and find answers to unclear or poorly defined questions. In such a sandbox, any form of analysis or reporting can be executed without disturbing other users. The analysts can change table structures if they think that's useful, they can run queries that can take hours of processing, and so on. It's a playground. It's not uncommon to throw the sandbox away when the analysts have their results.

Currently, in most organizations, when a sandbox is needed, a physical environment is set up, consisting of a server, a database server, a data store, and analysis software. The data store is loaded with all the data the analysts think they need. Setting up such a *physical sandbox* costs time and money. In addition, if more data is needed than initially planned for, special ETL scripts are developed to extract and load that new data.

With a data virtualization server, a *virtual sandbox* can be set up in a fraction of the time (Figure 7.22). This solution demands less work in advance and a smaller investment than when an actual physical sandbox is created. In addition, if more data is needed, only extra virtual tables have to be defined. To summarize, a virtual sandbox is more agile than a physical sandbox, which fits the temporary nature of a sandbox better.

7.6.11 Prototyping

Developing a new business intelligence system or extending it with new functionality can be quite time-consuming. Existing data stores have to be studied, table structures have to be designed, the required transformation and integration operations have to be determined, ETL scripts have to be designed and implemented, and so on.

All these activities have to be completed before any result can be shown to a user for verification. Then, if the user discovers that data has been transformed or handled incorrectly, or if the wrong definition of a business object has been implemented, many changes have to be applied. In fact, a considerable amount of time gets lost just from going back and forth between development and talking to users.

Valuable time can be saved when a *prototype* is developed first, but one that doesn't use ETL scripts or any extra data stores. A prototype can more easily be developed using data virtualization. Virtual tables and mappings can be defined quickly, and the result can be shown to the users right away. If something is not to their liking, the mappings and table structures can be changed quickly, maybe even on the spot. Very swiftly, such a prototype gives a clear insight into the problems that exist with regard to transformations, integration, and cleansing.

Later on, the final version can be developed by using the insights that have been gained by developing the prototype. This can even mean that a business intelligence system with a more classic architecture is developed consisting of a physical data warehouse and physical data marts. In this case, data virtualization has been used as a prototyping instrument that offers a more dynamic environment in which user changes can be implemented easily.

7.6.12 Analyzing Semistructured and Unstructured Data

Sections 3.8.6 and 3.8.7 show how virtual tables can be defined on semistructured and unstructured data sources, respectively. When those tables exist, their contents can be analyzed. Some data virtualization servers support advanced functions for analyzing text, such as sentiment analysis, language detection, and keyword lookup. By using this technology and defining virtual tables that present this data, business users can analyze all the nonstructured data using their favorite reporting and analytical tools. The example shown in Section 3.8.7, in which data from the Twitter and the IMDB websites are combined, is a clear example of integrating two nonstructured data sources and querying the result using a standard reporting tool. When the virtual tables are defined, users can even integrate structured data from the data warehouse with nonstructured data.

An alternative solution to using data virtualization is one where all the data needed for reporting is extracted from the data sources and stored in a separate data store. The disadvantage of this solution is that the data store has to be designed and managed, and its content has to be refreshed periodically. With the solution based on data virtualization, there is no need to create a separate data store. It may be necessary to create a cache, but if that's the case, it's managed by the data virtualization server that also takes care of the refreshing.

A solution based entirely on data virtualization is not always possible. As with production databases that don't keep track of historical data (see Section 7.6.4), something similar might apply to some external, nonstructured data sources. Although it's not the case that data is updated in these sources, it can get old and be deleted or become inaccessible. Let's illustrate this with an example based on Twitter. Imagine a report should show the total number of positive tweets in which an organization's name appears per month for the last four years. This form of trend analysis is only possible if the source (Twitter in this example) keeps tracks of all the tweets ever published and if they allow access to that full history. However, maybe only tweets of the last few months can be retrieved and not the older ones. In this case, it's necessary to copy the required tweets periodically to a local data store and analyze that data store. In this example, ETL can be used to extract all the relevant tweets and load those tweets in the data store, and a data virtualization server is used to analyze the data and turn it into a structure that can be analyzed by various reporting tools (Figure 7.23). When the source with nonstructured data is internal, no data is thrown away, and all the data remains accessible; then such a solution as the one described for Twitter is probably not required.

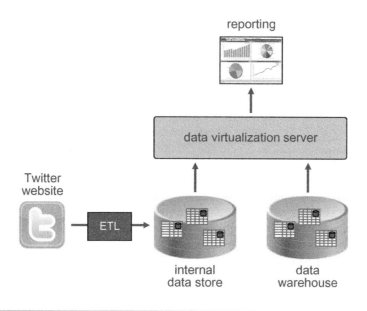

FIGURE 7.23

Using ETL and data virtualization together to extract structure from nonstructured data sources.

Note, however, that the coding of values, the semantical meaning of the data, and the correctness of the unstructured data in the external sources might not be consistent with the internal data or might not have the form or level of detail the report needs. Because these external data sources fall outside the responsibility of the business intelligence department, care should therefore be taken when using this data.

7.6.13 Disposable Reports

More and more often, business intelligence departments are confronted by users who need to run a new report that will only run once or twice. In most cases these reports have to be developed urgently as well. We call these reports *disposable reports*.

Given the urgency, there is no time to design a complete physical environment consisting of a data mart, ETL scripts, and so on. Plus, even if the time for all that work would be available, it would make it too expensive.

More fitting is to use data virtualization. Here, a few virtual tables can be developed quickly and easily to support the report. After the report has been developed and executed, the virtual tables can be removed. This requires a minimal investment, especially compared to a more physical solution.

Performance problems are not an issue here. Even if executing this report takes many hours, it wouldn't make sense to optimize it afterward because the report won't be executed again. Optimizing and tuning of queries only make sense for queries that are executed repeatedly.

7.6.14 Extending Business Intelligence Systems with External Users

More and more organizations offer *external users* access to the data available in the business intelligence system. For example, suppliers are allowed to check stock levels of their products in retail stores (reporting). In addition, they want to see what the sales pattern is for their products to predict how much of their products should be shipped (analytics). Another example is where independent insurance agents want to see the state and full details of insurance policies they sold to their customers. For this they might need access to the data managed by the insurance companies. The third example deals with an airline where customers want to see how many frequent flyer mile points they have collected on which flights so far, and they want to see a prediction based on their current travel characteristics on when they will reach platinum status.

As these examples show, the queries from external users can range from relatively simple ones to some that can be categorized as complex analytical queries. All these queries need access to the data stored in internal data stores, such as production systems, data warehouses, and data marts. However, we can't give external users access to the data stores in the same way we do it for internal users. There are various reasons, and we will look at three of them.

First, external users are not allowed to see all the data; they must be restricted to seeing only their own data and nothing else. They can definitely not see the data related to other users, so it's important that they are all compartmentalized with respect to the subset of the data they can access. Assigning the right privileges to external users is even more important than when assigning them to internal users. Data access should be restricted to only those rows and values they are really allowed to see. Row-level and value-level privileges are a requirement here.

Second, external users might be using a wide variety of technical interfaces and languages to query the data. For example, one is using a reporting tool that uses SOAP messages, another is using a Java-based analytical tool that prefers JSON, and a third has a tool that sends SQL statements through an ODBC interface. Many technical interfaces should be supported.

Third, the query workload generated by external users can be enormous and highly unpredictable. Especially in cases where there are many external users, keeping the performance stable and acceptable is a challenge. In the case of the airline, there might possibly be thousands of customers. Together they can create a massive query workload, possibly causing interference, scalability, and concurrency problems.

By letting all external users access data via a data virtualization server, these three issues can be managed (Figure 7.24). Data virtualization servers support the privileges needed for external users. To each external user or group of users, different authorization rules can be assigned that specifically indicate who is allowed to see which rows and which values. With respect to the second issue, as explained in Chapter 1, the key characteristics of data virtualization are encapsulation and abstraction. Using these characteristics, the right API and language (encapsulation) can be offered to external users, and the right data at the right level of aggregation can be presented to them (abstraction). For each virtual table defined for external users, multiple technical interfaces can be published. Note that a virtual table with its mapping and column structure is only defined once. And the third issue can be managed by defining caches and refresh rates that support a large workload.

To summarize, the authorization and other security features, the ability to define multiple technical interfaces for one and the same virtual table, and the caching features make data virtualization the right technology for extending business intelligence systems with external users.

7.7 Myths on Data Virtualization

In some articles, books, and blogs, statements on data virtualization can be found that are partly or not at all correct. Because some of them are repeated by others, they become like myths. This chapter ends with a list of some of these myths and explanations for why they do or do not make sense.

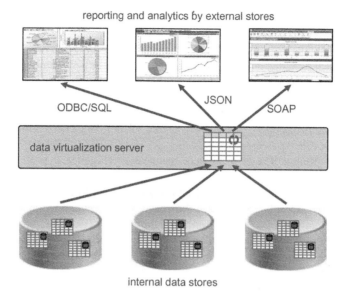

reporting and analytics by external stores

JSON

ODBC/SQL

SOAP

data virtualization server

internal data stores

FIGURE 7.24

Extending a business intelligence system by allowing external users to access data using data virtualization.

Myth 1: Data virtualization servers slow down queries.

A data virtualization server is an extra layer of software that does consume processing time. So in a way, it does make queries perform slower. However, as indicated in this book, every data virtualization server supports features to make the processing of queries and the transmission of data as efficient as possible, and they all support caching to improve query performance. In addition, usually the amount of processing time a data virtualization server consumes is marginal compared to the processing performed by a database server. Especially if a large amount of data has to be retrieved, the amount of processing time consumed by the data virtualization server is relatively minimal.

Myth 2: When data virtualization is deployed in a business intelligence system, no data warehouse is needed.

Usually, when data is updated in production systems, old data is overwritten by new data, and when a record is deleted, it's really removed from the database. For many reports, access to historical data is crucial. So when historical data is deleted from the production databases, a separate data store is needed to store it somewhere. Depending on the architecture of a business intelligence system, there has to be at least one data store for storing the historical data. This can be a data warehouse or a set of data marts. So data virtualization doesn't imply that a data warehouse is not necessary, because a data warehouse might be needed as a storage point for historical data to develop the reports that need to analyze historical data. In other words, it's not the intention of deploying data virtualization to get rid of data warehouses but rather to design the simplest architecture possible to increase the flexibility level.

Myth 3: When data virtualization is deployed in a business intelligence system, no data marts are needed.

This myth is very much like the previous one. If a business intelligence system doesn't consist of a data warehouse and if all the data marts are removed, then where is all the historical data stored?

It's the same with the previous myth: one or more data stores are required to store the data that is not stored by the production databases but are needed for reporting.

Myth 4: The goal of data virtualization is to create a virtual data warehouse.

If all the data needed by data consumers is available in data marts (assuming these data marts support conformed dimension tables), it should be possible to simulate a data warehouse by developing virtual tables on all the data marts. However, this is not the goal of data virtualization. If organizations want to build it like this, then technically that can be done. For conceptual and practical reasons it's recommended to do it the other way around: create virtual data marts on top of a physical data warehouse.

Myth 5: If data virtualization is used in a business intelligence system, ETL is not needed anymore.

This is almost certainly not true. ETL (or ELT) is probably still necessary to copy data from one data store to another. For example, it might still be desired to periodically copy data from the production databases to the data staging area or from the data staging area to the data warehouse. ETL is probably a much better alternative for this than data virtualization. In this respect, data virtualization and ETL are more complementary. In some situations, ETL is the preferred choice, and in others, it is data virtualization.

Myth 6: Data virtualization is a synonym for data federation.

This myth is understandable because various vendors of data virtualization products used to call their products data federation products. But because new features have been added, they changed the name of the product category. (See Section 1.5.3 for a description of both concepts.) In summary, data federation is an aspect of data virtualization. In other words, data virtualization involves much more than data federation.

Myth 7: Data virtualization works for small environments only. Occasionally, this myth is extended with the statement: for larger environments, ETL is and always will be required.

Compared to database servers and application servers, most data virtualization products are relatively young, although some products have been available for at least ten years. New products normally need a few years to scale. This is probably still true for most data virtualization products. Nevertheless, various organizations have created business intelligence systems with data virtualization at the heart, and these systems are supporting massive amounts of data, large numbers of users, and complex distributed queries. In other words, data virtualization products scale today and are also suitable for large environments.

Myth 8: Due to the concept of on-demand transformations, data virtualization can only support limited data cleansing features.

Section 8.2 describes guidelines on how incorrect data can be handled by data virtualization servers. Some of them support the same set of features for data cleansing as ETL products do; so this myth is not correct. The question is, however, do we want to let a data virtualization server be responsible for data cleansing? As recommended in Section 7.5.2, regardless of how data virtualization is deployed in business intelligence systems, it's best to handle data cleansing as much as possible upstream. In other words, it should be handled by the production systems or as close to them as possible. Let a data virtualization server be responsible for transforming values from different systems (from different owners) so that they can be integrated, because cleansed data is easier to integrate than incorrect data.

Design Guidelines for Data Virtualization

8.1 Introduction

This chapter describes a number of guidelines for designing a business intelligence system based on data virtualization. These design guidelines are based on experiences from real-life projects in which data virtualization was deployed. They address the following questions:

- Where and how should incorrect data be handled?
- How many levels of virtual tables should be defined?
- At which level should data from multiple systems be integrated?
- Should virtual tables be normalized?
- How can access to production systems be made more efficient?
- How is the archiving of data designed?

Note: Because this book doesn't focus on one particular data virtualization product, this chapter restricts itself to the more general design issues that apply to most products. Because all products are different in what they can do and how their internal architecture works, for each product extra design guidelines apply. For those, we recommend consulting the vendor's manuals and documentation.

8.2 Incorrect Data and Data Quality

The data stored in production systems is not always correct. Names are spelled incorrectly, numeric values are outside realistic boundaries, values in two fields have accidentally been switched, stored values don't represent reality, and particular values or rows are completely missing. If no actions are taken, this incorrect data is copied to the data warehouse and is presented by the data virtualization server to the data consumers. The consequence is that incorrect data is used for decision making. The quality of business decisions is for a large part dependent on the quality of the data. Therefore, data quality is an important consideration when designing business intelligence systems.

Many studies have shown that organizations suffer from poor data quality. In 2002, the Data Warehouse Institute estimated that data quality problems cost US businesses $600 billion each year (see [45]). Therefore, whether a business intelligence system is developed with a more classic architecture or by using data virtualization, data quality is a crucial design aspect that should receive considerable attention.

Data virtualization servers offer a number of alternative approaches to handle and clean incorrect data. Before we look at some of them, we examine the different types of incorrect data and then the concept of integrity rule.

8.2.1 Different Forms of Incorrect Data

The following are some types of incorrect data.

Missing data: The first form of incorrect data is absent data. Absent data does not automatically signify a data quality problem. Maybe some values don't exist in reality. For example, if the middle name of a customer is absent, it doesn't automatically imply a data quality issue because this customer might not have a middle name.

But absent data is a problem if it involves mandatory data. For example, in an organization the rule holds that the gender value of employees is mandatory. If, in that situation, the gender value is missing, then a data quality problem does exist. Absent mandatory data is referred to as *missing data*. And missing data is considered a data quality problem. Besides missing values, whole rows can be missing as well. For example, due to technical problems, all the transactions of a specific date have been lost.

Missing data can't always be reconstructed automatically. In most cases missing data can only be reconstructed by going back to the source. This could mean, for example, calling up customers and asking them for their address if that data is missing. It can also mean importing files from external data suppliers to get, for example, the correct telephone number of a particular customer.

In most cases, reconstructing missing data falls outside the scope of a business intelligence system. This should be handled by the owners of the production systems.

Misspelled data: The second form of incorrect data is when values are, somehow, spelled incorrectly. The most common example of misspelled data is inconsistent coding. In this case, values are used that are not in the list of standardized codes or names. For example, the incorrect state code FLA is used to indicate the state of Florida instead of the correct code FL. Or three different codes have been used to indicate that customers are male: M, Male, and Man. This type of incorrect data is called *misspelled data*.

Incorrect spellings of names, such as the names of products, customers, products, and cities, are also classic examples of misspelled data. For example, in a production system the city name Brussels is spelled as Brusels and Brussel, and New York is spelled as NewYork.

Misspelled values might represent the correct value, but it could be the wrong spelling was used. For example, if the code FLA is used to indicate the state of Florida, we know exactly what the value should have been. For some of these misspelled values, such as FLA, it's possible to automatically derive the correct value, but not for every value. In cases where numeric values representing measurements are misspelled, for example, how do we, first of all, determine that the value is misspelled, and next, how do we determine what the value should be?

False data: Imagine that in a database March 15, 1879 is stored as the birth date of theoretical physicist Albert Einstein. This value looks correct. It probably conforms to any integrity rule we specify, it's spelled correctly, and most people who look at this date will assume it's correct. The value, however, is not correct. Einstein's birth date is March 14, 1879. In other words, this value is not according to reality. Data that is not according to reality is called *false data*. Another example of false data is if a database contains Sydney as the capital of Australia. This might look like a correct value, but it isn't. Canberra is the capital of Australia.

The hard part about dealing with false data is how can you detect it? How do you know for sure that a customer's birth date is really the right one? And when it can be detected as false, how is the correct value determined? Sometimes false data can be discovered when values are somehow related to one another. For example, if a customer's first name is given as Sandra, the maiden name has been filled in, and the gender is indicated as male, we know one of those values is incorrect—probably the value for gender. We know that because Sandra is usually a woman's name, and only women have maiden names.

Another way of discovering false data is by defining acceptable boundaries. For example, if the birth year of an employee is 1856, that value is unrealistically low and falls outside acceptable boundaries. Or it is indicated that a receptionist in a hotel worked over 80 hours in a week. Again, this value is probably too high. Still, in most cases it's difficult to use software to detect false data. In this book, the term *incorrect data* is used for all forms of missing, misspelled, and false data that can be detected as such.

8.2.2 Integrity Rules and Incorrect Data

To be able to improve the quality of data, rules have to be specified that relate to the quality of the data. Those rules are called *integrity rules* (sometimes called *integrity constraints*). These are the rules to which data should adhere; they define which values are allowed and which are not. Examples of integrity rules are: an email address should contain a @ symbol; the price of a DVD release should be less than $1,000; each customer order line should always belong to one customer order; and if the country is Canada, the postal code should consist of seven characters, of which the middle one is a blank. Data that doesn't satisfy integrity rules is by definition incorrect.

The first design guideline is to analyze and specify all the integrity rules that apply to the data. Discuss them with the users and test them. Be as comprehensive as possible. The concept of defining too many integrity rules doesn't exist. Define these integrity rules and explain which forms of incorrect data they deal with.

Design Guideline 1: Analyze and specify all the integrity rules that apply to the data processed by the data virtualization server.

Although it's important that integrity rules are being analyzed, they won't solve the entire problem of incorrect data. For example, it's impossible to specify an integrity rule that guarantees that all customer names are spelled correctly, nor is it possible to formulate an integrity rule that detects false data, such as the incorrect birth date of a customer. Also, missing data can't be reconstructed. Nevertheless, the more time spent on analyzing and implementing integrity rules, the better it is for the quality of the data presented to the users.

8.2.3 Filtering, Flagging, and Restoring Incorrect Data

When ETL scripts are used to copy data from production systems to a target data store, such as a data warehouse or data mart, integrity rules can be implemented within those scripts to check the correctness of data. The effect is that the correct data is copied to the target data store and the incorrect data is in a separate data store (the garbage bin). Afterward, this data store should be studied by analysts to determine what to do with the incorrect data. Should more transformation rules be implemented, or should the owner of the data be warned about the incorrectness of the data and asked to correct it? This doesn't work for data virtualization. When on-demand transformation is used, each mapping has only one result, and that result is returned to the data consumer. In other words, there is no "second" data store where the incorrect data can be found after executing the tranformations. Thus, the question is, what should be done with the incorrect data? The following are five ways to handle incorrect data:

1. *Doing nothing:* No logic is added to detect incorrect data, and the data is returned to the data consumers uncorrected. In this case, it's the responsibility of the data consumer to detect incorrect data and to determine what to do with it. From the perspective of the data virtualization server, this is the easiest approach, but from the perspective of the quality of decision making, it probably isn't the best solution.
2. *Filtering rows:* For detecting incorrect data, as much logic as possible is added to the mappings of the virtual tables. Every row that contains one or more incorrect values is removed from the result. Data consumers see only the rows with correct data.
3. *Filtering values:* A slightly different version of filtering is when values are filtered instead of rows. If an incorrect value is detected, the row remains in the result, but the value is removed. The value can be replaced by a null value or by a special code indicating that the original value is incorrect and has been removed.
4. *Flagging:* If incorrect values are detected, in an extra column, codes are inserted indicating that particular values are incorrect. The codes in this extra column are the flags. For example, this column can have the value NAM,CIT indicating that the values in the NAME and CITY columns are incorrect. One can also add a special flag column for each column that can hold incorrect data. It's up to the data consumer to determine what to do with these flags and the data.
5. *Restoring:* All of the preceding approaches do not correct incorrect data. Replacing an incorrect value with a correct one is called restoring.

Design Guideline 2: For every virtual table accessed by data consumers, the preferred approach for handling incorrect data is filtering, flagging, or restoring.

If different data consumers want to handle incorrect data differently, it's best to implement flagging at the lowest layer of virtual tables. The effect is that all the data is still there, and the flags indicate which values are incorrect. A nested virtual table on this virtual table can hide all the flags and present all the data untransformed, a second one can filter out all the rows for which a flag has been raised showing only correct data, and a third one can use restoring to replace the detected incorrect value with the right values.

Regardless of the approach, it's recommended to implement as many integrity rules as possible for those virtual tables that access the source tables. In other words, implement detection of incorrect data on nonnested virtual tables.

Design Guideline 3: Implement as many integrity rules as possible to increase the data quality level of the contents of the virtual tables.

8.2.4 Examples of Filtering Incorrect Data

As indicated in the previous section, two styles of filtering exist: one that filters out rows and one that filters out individual values. Usually, filtering rows is the easiest to implement. Filters are added to the mappings of the virtual tables. These filters are all based on relevant integrity rules.

Note: In this chapter we use SQL again as the language for defining the mappings. All these mappings can also be defined with data virtualization products that support other languages. We use the tables from the sample database described in Section 1.14.

EXAMPLE 8.1

The following integrity rule holds for the CUSTOMER_ORDER table: date values in the ORDER_TIMESTAMP column should all be greater than 31 december 1999. The reason is that the company didn't exist before that date. Define a virtual table that implements this integrity rule as a filter:

```
DEFINE    V_CUSTOMER_ORDER_FILTERED_V1 AS
SELECT    *
FROM      CUSTOMER_ORDER
WHERE     ORDER_TIMESTAMP > DATE('1999-12-19')
```

Explanation

All the rows with a timestamp that is too old are removed from the result. So data consumers retrieving data from this virtual table don't see those rows.

This integrity rule is executed in a straightforward way. If, for example, a data consumer retrieves all the customers from the cities New York and Los Angeles, the query sent to the database server looks like this:

```
SELECT    *
FROM      CUSTOMER_ORDER
WHERE     CITY_NAME IN ('New York', 'Los Angeles')
AND       ORDER_TIMESTAMP > DATE('1999-12-19')
```

The optimization technique called query substitution is used to merge the mapping with the integrity rule with the data consumer's query (see Section 6.5). Adding this condition doesn't have a negative impact on perfomance; in fact, it can even make the query a little faster, because less data is transmitted from the database server to the data virtualization server. Multiple integrity rules can be implemented as filters in the mapping of a virtual table, as is shown in Example 8.2.

EXAMPLE 8.2

The following integrity rules hold for the DVD_RELEASE table: the value X for RATING is incorrect, the column ASPECT should not contain the values LBX and VAR, and STATUS should be equal to one of the values Cancelled, Discontinued, Out, Pending, Postponed, or Recalled. Define a virtual table that implements these three integrity rules as filters:

```
DEFINE    V_DVD_RELEASE_CHECKED_V1 AS
SELECT    *
FROM      DVD_RELEASE
WHERE     RATING <> 'X'
AND       ASPECT NOT IN ('LBX', 'VAR')
AND       STATUS IN ('Cancelled', 'Discontinued', 'Out',
                     'Pending', 'Postponed', 'Recalled')
```

The following table shows some of the rows and columns of the CUSTOMER table that are not part of the contents of the V_DVD_RELEASE_CHECKED_V1 virtual table:

```
DVD_RELEASE_ID  RATING  ASPECT  STATUS
--------------  ------  ------  ------
          2453  X       1.66:1  Discontinued
          2520  X       1.33:1  Out
         16769  NR      VAR     Out
         16770  NR      VAR     Out
        145377  UR      1.33:1  Discontineud
```

Evidently, the filters defined in the previous examples are relatively simple. Filters can be complex. For example, to check an integrity rule, a join with other tables or complex calculations may be necessary. Be careful, since complex filters can slow down query processing. Caching might have to be considered. In any case, a decision should be made concerning what's more important: performance or data quality.

An alternative to filtering of rows is filtering of individual values. This means that all the rows remain in the result, but incorrect values are removed and replaced by special values; see Example 8.3.

EXAMPLE 8.3
Implement the integrity rule specified in Example 8.1 as a filter for values.

```
DEFINE   V_CUSTOMER_ORDER_FILTERED_V2 AS
SELECT   CUSTOMER_ORDER_ID,
         CUSTOMER_ID,
         PROMOTION_ID,
         CUSTOMER_FIRST_NAME,
         CUSTOMER_MIDDLE_INITIAL,
         CUSTOMER_LAST_NAME,
         SHIPPING_CITY_NAME,
         SHIPPING_ADDRESS1,
         SHIPPING_ADDRESS2,
         SHIPPING_POSTAL_CODE,
         CASE
            WHEN ORDER_TIMESTAMP > DATE('1999-12-19') THEN ORDER_TIMESTAMP
            ELSE NULL END AS ORDER_TIMESTAMP_FILTERED,
         STATUS_LOOKUP,
         SHIPPING_REGION_ID
FROM     CUSTOMER_ORDER
```

Explanation
If the value for ORDER_TIMESTAMP is too old, the value is replaced by a null value. Another value can be selected as well. The result of this virtual table contains all the rows of the underlying table.

EXAMPLE 8.4

Implement the three integrity rules specified in Example 8.2 as filters for values.

```
DEFINE     V_DVD_RELEASE_CHECKED_V2 AS
SELECT     DVD_RELEASE_ID,
           TITLE,
           STUDIO,
           RELEASED,
           CASE
              WHEN STATUS IN ('Cancelled', 'Discontinued', 'Out',
                              'Pending', 'Postponed', 'Recalled') THEN STATUS
              ELSE NULL END AS STATUS_FILTERED,
           SOUND,
           VERSIONS,
           PRICE,
           CASE
              WHEN RATING <> 'X' THEN RATING
              ELSE NULL END AS RATING_FILTERED,
           YEAR,
           GENRE,
           CASE
              WHEN ASPECT NOT IN ('LBX', 'VAR') THEN ASPECT
              ELSE NULL END AS ASPECT_FILTERED,
           UPC,
           RELEASE_DATE,
           TIMESTAMP
FROM       DVD_RELEASE
```

This table shows a few rows and columns of the contents of this virtual table:

DVD_RELEASE_ID	STATUS_FILTERED	RATING_FILTERED	ASPECT_FILTERED
2453	Discontinued	?	1.66:1
2520	Out	?	1.33:1
16769	Out	NR	?
16770	Out	NR	?
145377	?	UR	1.33:1

Explanation

Incorrect values in the columns STATUS, RATING, and ASPECT are removed and null values are inserted. In this mapping the column names are extended with the keyword FILTERED.

Design Guideline 4: Use filtering when the data consumers don't want to see and work with incorrect data.

8.2.5 Examples of Flagging Incorrect Data

Flagging of incorrect data in separate columns is very much like filtering of values. In other words, the integrity rules can be implemented in a similar way. In the first example we show how flagging is done by introducing an extra column for each column for which integrity rules apply.

EXAMPLE 8.5

Define a mapping that implements the integrity rule of Example 8.1 but now using flagging.

```
DEFINE   V_CUSTOMER_ORDER_FLAGGED AS
SELECT   CUSTOMER_ORDER_ID,
         CUSTOMER_ID,
         PROMOTION_ID,
         CUSTOMER_FIRST_NAME,
         CUSTOMER_MIDDLE_INITIAL,
         CUSTOMER_LAST_NAME,
         SHIPPING_CITY_NAME,
         SHIPPING_ADDRESS1,
         SHIPPING_ADDRESS2,
         SHIPPING_POSTAL_CODE,
         ORDER_TIMESTAMP,
         CASE
            WHEN ORDER_TIMESTAMP > DATE('1999-12-19') THEN NULL
            ELSE 'Incorrect' END AS ORDER_TIMESTAMP_FLAG,
         STATUS_LOOKUP,
         SHIPPING_REGION_ID
FROM     CUSTOMER_ORDER
```

Explanation

The result of this virtual table includes the column ORDER_TIMESTAMP, which contains untransformed values, and it includes a new column called ORDER_TIMESTAMP_FLAG. The essential difference between filtering of values and flagging is that with the former, the incorrect values are removed, and with flagging, the incorrect values are still visible, but a special value indicates that the value is incorrect. It's up to the consumer of the data to determine what to do with this data.

For each column for which an integrity rule is specified, a separate flag column can be defined. In Example 8.6, we show how flagging for multiple columns can be applied in just one column.

EXAMPLE 8.6

Implement the three integrity rules specified in Example 8.2; use flagging in one extra column.

```
DEFINE    V_DVD_RELEASE_FLAGGED AS
SELECT    DVD_RELEASE_ID,
          TITLE,
          STUDIO,
          RELEASED,
          STATUS,
          SOUND,
          VERSIONS,
          PRICE,
          RATING,
          YEAR,
          GENRE,
          ASPECT,
          UPC,
          RELEASE_DATE,
          TIMESTAMP,
          CASE
             WHEN STATUS IN ('Cancelled', 'Discontinued', 'Out',
                             'Pending', 'Postponed', 'Recalled') THEN ''
             ELSE 'STA,' END ||
          CASE
             WHEN RATING <> 'X' THEN ''
             ELSE 'RAT,' END ||
          CASE
             WHEN ASPECT NOT IN ('LBX', 'VAR') THEN ''
             ELSE 'ASP,' END AS FLAGS
FROM      DVD_RELEASE
```

This table shows a few rows and columns of the contents of this virtual table:

DVD_RELEASE_ID	STATUS	RATING	ASPECT	FLAGS
2453	Discontinued	X	1.66:1	RAT,
2520	Out	X	1.33:1	RAT,
16769	Out	NR	VAR	ASP,
16770	Out	NR	VAR	ASP,
145377	Discontineud	UR	1.33:1	STA,

Explanation

If a row contains an incorrect status, rating, and aspect, the value is set to STA,RAT,ASP, in the FLAGS column.

Design Guideline 5: Use flagging when the data consumers want to see which data values are incorrect.

8.2.6 **Examples of Restoring Misspelled Data**

When filtering or flagging is used, data is not corrected. The incorrect data is removed or it's flagged as being incorrect. Mappings can be used to replace incorrect data by correct data. In fact, these mappings clean the data. This technique can only be used for restoring misspelled data. Example 8.7 shows how restoring of values can be implemented using mappings.

EXAMPLE 8.7

Define a virtual table that implements integrity rules for the columns STATUS, SOUND, RATING, and ASPECT. Restore as many values in those columns as possible.

```
DEFINE  V_DVD_RELEASE_RESTORED AS
SELECT  DVD_RELEASE_ID,
        TITLE,
        STUDIO,
        RELEASED,
        CASE STATUS
           WHEN 'Discontineud' THEN 'Discontinued'
           ELSE STATUS END AS STATUS_EDITED,
        CASE SOUND
           WHEN '4.0 DTS/4.0' THEN '4.0/DTS'
           WHEN '4.0/4.0 DTS' THEN '4.0/DTS'
           WHEN '4.1 DTS/4.1' THEN '4.1/DTS'
           WHEN '4.1/DTS 4.1' THEN '4.1/DTS'
           WHEN 'DTS 5.0'     THEN '5.0/DTS'
           WHEN '5.0/DTS 5.0' THEN '5.0/DTS'
           WHEN '5.1 DTS'     THEN '5.1/DTS'
           WHEN '5.1 HD-DTS'  THEN '5.1 DTS-HD'
           ELSE SOUND END AS SOUND_EDITED,
        VERSIONS,
        PRICE,
        CASE RATING
          WHEN 'PA'   THEN 'PG'
          WHEN 'UN'   THEN 'UR'
          WHEN 'UR/R' THEN 'R/UR'
          ELSE RATING END AS RATING_EDITED,
        YEAR,
        GENRE,
        CASE ASPECT
          WHEN '1.781' THEN '1.78:1'
          ELSE ASPECT END AS ASPECT_EDITED,
        UPC,
        RELEASE_DATE,
        TIMESTAMP
FROM    DVD_RELEASE
```

This table shows a few rows and columns of the contents of this virtual table:

```
DVD_RELEASE_ID  STATUS_EDITED  SOUND_EDITED  RATING_EDITED  ASPECT_EDITED
--------------  -------------  ------------  -------------  -------------
         18739  Out            5.0/DTS       NR             1.85:1
         67143  Out            4.0/DTS       NR             1.78:1
        117175  Recalled       5.1           R/UR           1.78:1
        127720  Out            5.1           R              1.78:1
        144253  Out            2.0           PG             1.33:1
        145377  Discontinued   2.0           UR             1.33:1
```

Explanation

The column STATUS contains one misspelled value Discontineud, which is transformed to Discontinued. For the columns SOUND, ASPECT, and RATING, the same type of transformation is applied.

This solution works well, but its restriction is that new incorrect values entered in the production system are not automatically discovered and added to the mapping. Someone has to keep an eye out for this.

In this example, the solution selected is a mapping that is fully responsible for all the transformations. Another approach is to create a dedicated table that holds all the incorrect values and their correct counterparts. For example, the following SOUND_CODES table with the following contents can be developed:

```
SOUND_MISSPELLED  SOUND_CORRECT
----------------  -------------
4.0 DTS/4.0       4.0/DTS
4.0/4.0 DTS       4.0/DTS
4.1 DTS/4.1       4.1/DTS
4.1/DTS 4.1       4.1/DTS
DTS 5.0           5.0/DTS
5.0/DTS 5.0       5.0/DTS
5.1 DTS           5.1/DTS
5.1 HD-DTS        5.1 DTS-HD
```

Instead of the long CASE expression, the transformation looks like this:

```
IFNULL(SELECT    SOUND_CORRECT AS SOUND_EDITED
       FROM      SOUND_CODES
       WHERE     SOUND_INCORRECT = SOUND), SOUND)
```

Explanation

If the code is misspelled, the expression returns the correct code from the SOUND_CODES table, or it returns the value of the SOUND column itself.

The advantage of the approach with a translation table is that if new misspelled codes are detected, the mapping doesn't have to be changed; only the SOUND_CODES table must be updated. It's an approach that is more maintainable.

In the examples in this section, the number of misspelled values is relatively low. The problem is harder to fix when it concerns names such as those of companies, customers, and cities. Neither solution (case expression or translation table) works in this situation. To determine whether a name has been spelled correctly, more advanced technology, such as fuzzy matching, is needed. Access to data sets with correct data is needed as well. For example, even if the names of a city, street, and state are spelled correctly, the three might still not belong to one another. The only way to detect that the address doesn't exist is when we have access to all the correct addresses.

Most data virtualization servers can access web services. This feature can be used to access data sets and services that help with correcting data. Figure 8.1 shows an example in which incorrect address data is corrected. The incoming address contains spelling errors, and the data virtualization server returns the right data. For example, in row four, the city name San Mateo is changed to Palo Alto, and in row five, San Antonio Rd is changed to San Antonio Ave. These corrections are done by invoking a Google service that checks whether an address is correct and returns the correct values. This service is invoked in the mapping like any other function that the data virtualization server supports. The developer doesn't see that it's an external service.

Design Guideline 6: Use restoring when data consumers are not interested in original data but in data of the highest possible quality.

8.3 Complex and Irregular Data Structures

Tables in production systems might have structures and solutions that are so complex or irregular that they need to be transformed significantly before their data can be accessed by reporting and analytical tools. This section discusses some of the more complex and irregular data structures and explains how to handle or transform them.

8.3.1 Codes without Names

Many production systems contain columns with codes (sometimes quite cryptic), such as product group codes, state codes, and region codes. Maybe some data consumers prefer to use names instead of those codes. If the production systems also contain tables that hold the names for all these codes, replacing the codes by the names is easy; see Example 8.8.

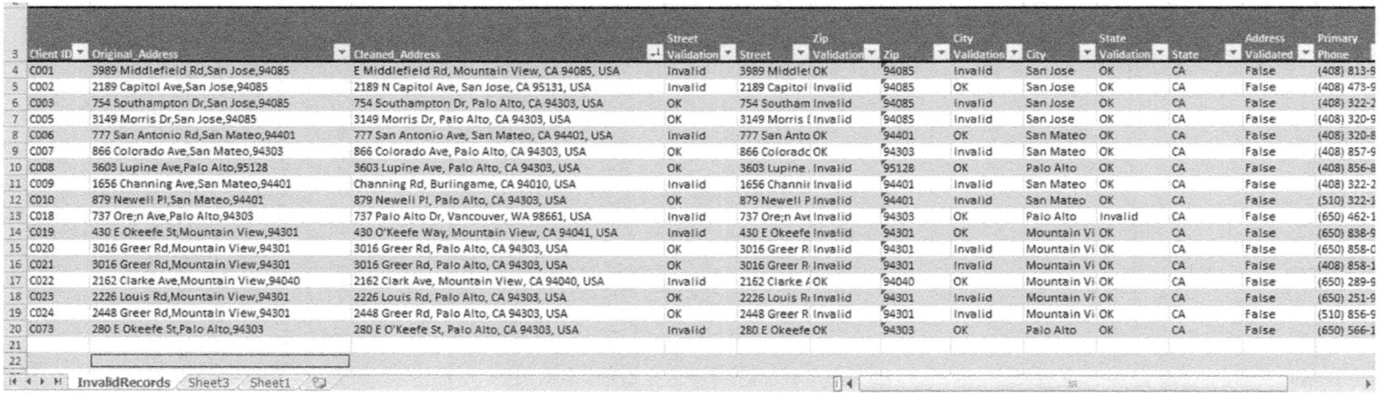

	Client ID	Original Address	Cleaned Address	Street Validation	Street	Zip Validation	Zip	City Validation	City	State Validation	State	Address Validated	Primary Phone
4	C001	3989 Middlefield Rd,San Jose,94085	E Middlefield Rd, Mountain View, CA 94085, USA	Invalid	3989 Middle	OK	94085	Invalid	San Jose	OK	CA	False	(408) 813-9
5	C002	2189 Capitol Ave,San Jose,94085	2189 N Capitol Ave, San Jose, CA 95131, USA	Invalid	2189 Capitol	Invalid	94085	OK	San Jose	OK	CA	False	(408) 473-9
6	C003	754 Southampton Dr,San Jose,94085	754 Southampton Dr, Palo Alto, CA 94303, USA	OK	754 Southam	Invalid	94085	Invalid	San Jose	OK	CA	False	(408) 322-2
7	C005	3149 Morris Dr,San Jose,94085	3149 Morris Dr, San Jose, CA 94085, USA	Invalid	3149 Morris	Invalid	94085	Invalid	San Jose	OK	CA	False	(408) 320-9
8	C006	777 San Antonio Rd,San Mateo,94401	777 San Antonio Rd, San Mateo, CA 94401, USA	Invalid	777 San Anto	OK	94401	OK	San Mateo	OK	CA	False	(408) 320-8
9	C007	866 Colorado Ave,San Mateo,94303	866 Colorado Ave, Palo Alto, CA 94303, USA	OK	866 Colorado	OK	94303	Invalid	San Mateo	OK	CA	False	(408) 857-9
10	C008	3603 Lupine Ave,Palo Alto,95128	3603 Lupine Ave, Palo Alto, CA 94303, USA	OK	3603 Lupine	Invalid	95128	Invalid	Palo Alto	OK	CA	False	(408) 856-8
11	C009	1656 Channing Ave,San Mateo,94401	Channing Rd, Burlingame, CA 94010, USA	Invalid	1656 Channin	Invalid	94401	Invalid	San Mateo	OK	CA	False	(408) 322-2
12	C010	879 Newell Pl,San Mateo,94401	879 Newell Pl, Palo Alto, CA 94303, USA	OK	879 Newell P	Invalid	94401	Invalid	San Mateo	OK	CA	False	(510) 322-1
13	C018	737 Oren Ave,Palo Alto,94303	737 Palo Alto Dr, Vancouver, WA 98661, USA	Invalid	737 Oren Av	Invalid	94303	OK	Palo Alto	Invalid	CA	False	(650) 462-1
14	C019	430 E Okeefe St,Mountain View,94301	430 O'Keefe Way, Mountain View, CA 94041, USA	Invalid	430 E Okeefe	Invalid	94301	OK	Mountain Vi	OK	CA	False	(650) 838-9
15	C020	3016 Greer Rd,Mountain View,94301	3016 Greer Rd, Palo Alto, CA 94303, USA	OK	3016 Greer R	Invalid	94301	Invalid	Mountain Vi	OK	CA	False	(650) 858-0
16	C021	3016 Greer Rd,Mountain View,94301	3016 Greer Rd, Palo Alto, CA 94303, USA	OK	3016 Greer R	Invalid	94301	Invalid	Mountain Vi	OK	CA	False	(408) 858-1
17	C022	2162 Clarke Ave,Mountain View,94040	2162 Clark Ave, Mountain View, CA 94040, USA	Invalid	2162 Clarke	OK	94040	OK	Mountain Vi	OK	CA	False	(650) 289-9
18	C023	2226 Louis Rd,Mountain View,94301	2226 Louis Rd, Palo Alto, CA 94303, USA	OK	2226 Louis R	Invalid	94301	Invalid	Mountain Vi	OK	CA	False	(650) 251-9
19	C024	2448 Greer Rd,Mountain View,94301	2448 Greer Rd, Palo Alto, CA 94303, USA	OK	2448 Greer R	Invalid	94301	Invalid	Mountain Vi	OK	CA	False	(510) 856-9
20	C073	280 E Okeefe St,Palo Alto,94303	280 E O'Keefe St, Palo Alto, CA 94303, USA	Invalid	280 E Okeefe	OK	94303	OK	Palo Alto	OK	CA	False	(650) 566-1

InvalidRecords / Sheet3 / Sheet1

FIGURE 8.1

An example of correcting address data by invoking external services.

Reprinted with permission of Denodo Technologies.

EXAMPLE 8.8

Define a virtual table that replaces in the CUSTOMER table the region ID by the region name and the website ID by the website title.

```
DEFINE     V_CUSTOMER_EXTENDED AS
SELECT     C.CUSTOMER_ID,
           C.FIRST_NAME,
           C.MIDDLE_INITIAL,
           C.LAST_NAME,
           C.DATE_OF_BIRTH,
           C.MAIDEN_NAME_MOTHER,
           C.GENDER_LOOKUP,
           C.CITY_NAME,
           C.ADDRESS1,
           C.ADDRESS2,
           C.POSTAL_CODE,
           C.EMAIL_ADDRESS,
           C.TELEPHONE_NUMBER,
           C.PASSWORD_HASH,
           W.WEBSITE_TITLE,
           C.BALANCE,
           C.DATE_REGISTERED,
           C.DATE_UNREGISTERED,
           C.TIMESTAMP_CHANGED,
           R.REGION_NAME
FROM       CUSTOMER AS C, REGION AS R, WEBSITE AS W
WHERE      C.REGION_ID = R.REGION_ID
AND        C.WEBSITE_ID = W.WEBSITE_ID
```

Explanation

The title of the website and the name of the region are retrieved respectively from the WEBSITE and the REGION table.

Unfortunately, not all production systems contain a special code table. Sometimes the explanation of the codes is coded inside the application and therefore not accessible for a data virtualizaton server. In that case, there are two options. First, the code in the application can be invoked by the data virtualization server and is wrapped. Next a virtual table is defined on top of that wrapper and a cache is defined to speed up queries. Second, a code table is developed within the data virtualization environment. Practically, this means that a separate (small) database has to be set up that contains those code tables. The data virtualization server will be the only user of this database.

8.3.2 Inconsistent Key Values

In some organizations, data on the same business objects are stored in multiple systems. For example, the Sales system contains a customer table and the Finance system has one as well. This doesn't

Customer table in Sales System

ID	Name	Initials	City	State
12345	Young	N	San Francisco	CA
23324	Stills	S	New Orleans	LA
57657	Furay	R	Yellow Springs	OH
65461	Palmer	B	Boston	MA
...	...	...	...	...

Customer table in Finance System

ID	Name	Initials	Email address	Balance
C5729	Young	N	young@xyz.com	100
LA781	Stills	S	stil@stil.org	200
J7301	Furay	R	buf@spring.com	150
K8839	Palmer	B	bass@spring.com	200
...	...	...	...	...

FIGURE 8.2

Two tables with customer data from two different production systems: Sales and Finance.

Customer join table

ID	Sales ID	Finance ID
MD12	12345	C5729
MD13	23324	LA781
MD14	57657	J7301
MD15	65461	K8839
...	...	...

FIGURE 8.3

A join table holding the keys from the two customer tables.

have to be a problem, but it will be when different key values are used in these tables to refer to the same customer; see the two tables in Figure 8.2. For example, in the Sales system, customer Young has 12345 as key value, and in the Finance system, C5729 is used to represent him. A reason for this unwanted situation can be that the company recently acquired another company. Each company had its own customer management system. The two companies share the same customers, but the keys assigned to those customers are different. These are called *inconsistent key values*.

With inconsistent key values, bringing data together from different systems is difficult and sometimes close to impossible. Instead of joining the two tables on keys, we can join them on last name and initials. If we look at the four rows in Figure 8.2, the result is probably correct. But if the customer table holds thousands of customers, this join might return incorrect results because there can be multiple customers with the same last name and initials, or, in the second table, the spelling of some last names is incorrect, leading to incorrect joins.

What is needed is a dedicated table that links the right customer rows from the two tables together; see Figure 8.3. With this table the two other tables can be joined together, and a more complete virtual table can be presented to the data consumers; see the table in Figure 8.4. We call this a *join table*, and its only purpose is to, as the name suggests, join tables. In this join table, an extra key is added as well, but this is not necessary.

This approach works, but it is very labor-intensive. First of all, who manages this join table? Who indicates that particular records refer to the same customer? How is this join table updated when customers are deleted, updated, and inserted in the original customer tables? Procedures are necessary to keep this join table in sync with the original data.

Design Guideline 7: Design a join table to be able to join data from tables using inconsistent key values.

Customer table

ID	Sales ID	Finance ID	Name	Initials	City	State	Email address	Balance
MD12	12345	C5729	Young	N	San Francisco	CA	young@xyz.com	100
MD13	23324	LA781	Stills	S	New Orleans	LA	stil@stil.org	200
MD14	57657	J7301	Furay	R	Yellow Springs	OH	buf@spring.com	150
MD15	65461	K8839	Palmer	B	New York	NY	bass@spring.com	200
...	...	...	...	...	...	...	...	...

FIGURE 8.4

A virtual table can be defined that joins the two customer tables with the join table to show an integrated view of the customers' data.

Note: Chapter 10 discusses master data management. If an organization has implemented master data management, it's recommended to make that function responsible for the join tables.

8.3.3 Repeating Groups

In some older production systems, data might be stored as *repeating groups*, meaning that a set of comparable values is stored "next to each other" instead of "underneath each other." For example, if we store the total sales values for each quarter in one row of a table, those four columns form a repeating group. Figure 8.5 shows a table DS_PIVOT with a repeating group formed by the four columns called data1 up to data4.

Most reporting tools have difficulties in processing repeating groups, so these structures have to be transformed in such a way that data is presented underneath each other in four different rows. This transformation process is sometimes called *pivoting*. Pivoting such a table into a virtual table in which those four values are presented underneath each other, as separate rows, is done differently by the various data virtualization products.

One data virtualization product uses *procedures* for transforming the repeating groups to a more normalized structure. A procedure is a piece of code that returns a set of rows. The code is written in a procedural language that resembles PL/SQL of Oracle and Transact-SQL of Microsoft SQL Server. With this procedure, language wrapper tables can be developed. As an example, Figure 8.6 shows the procedure that pivots the table in Figure 8.5. The code is short and not too complex. This particular procedure returns a table of rows in which each row contains one value. Its content is shown at the bottom right-hand side of Figure 8.5. Procedures can also be used for very complex transformations for which procedural code is the only solution.

Design Guideline 8: Don't copy repeating group structures from the source tables to the virtual tables because they are difficult or impossible to process by most reporting and analytical tools.

8.3.4 Recursive Data Structures

Some tables in production systems contain *recursive data structures*. An example of a recursive data structure is formed when the relationships among customers are stored. Is one the father or the mother of another one, or is one a daughter or a brother? The sample database doesn't contain such

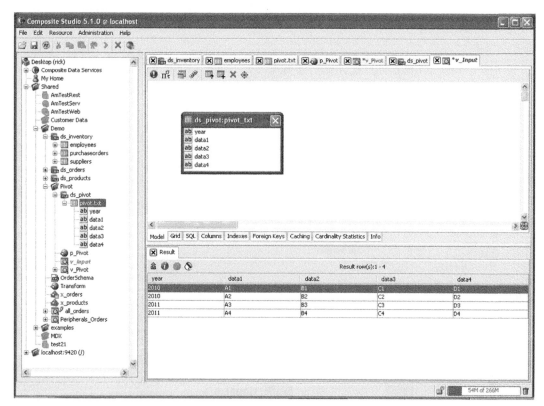

FIGURE 8.5

A table with a repeating group.

Reprinted with permission of Composite Software.

a recursive structure, but there are numerous databases that do. For example, imagine the following PARTS table:

SUPER	SUB	QUANTITY
P1	P2	10
P1	P3	5
P1	P4	10
P2	P5	25
P2	P6	5
P3	P7	10
P6	P8	15
P8	P11	5
P9	P10	2
P10	P11	25

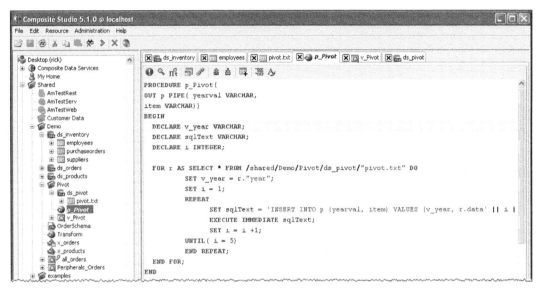

FIGURE 8.6

A procedure that transforms a repeating group into a relational structure.

Reprinted with permission of Composite Software.

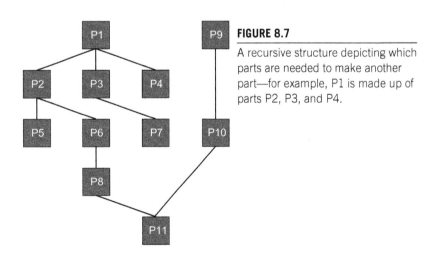

FIGURE 8.7

A recursive structure depicting which parts are needed to make another part—for example, P1 is made up of parts P2, P3, and P4.

This table represents a *bills-of-material* example in which parts consist of smaller parts. Figure 8.7 contains a graphical representation of the parts stored in this table. In this example, P1 consists of parts P2, P3, and P4, and P2 consists of P5 and P6.

Example 8.9 shows a recursive query.

EXAMPLE 8.9

Get all the parts that directly and indirectly make up part P2.

```
WITH      PARENTS (SUPER, SUB) AS
          (SELECT  SUPER, SUB
          FROM  PARTS
          WHERE  SUPER = 'P2'
          UNION ALL
          SELECT  P.SUPER, P.SUB
          FROM  PARTS AS P, PARENTS AS PAR
          WHERE  P.SUPER = PAR.SUB)
SELECT    *
FROM      PARENTS
```

The result is:

```
SUPER  SUB
-----  ---
P2     P5
P2     P6
P6     P8
P8     P11
```

Most data virtualization servers and most reporting and analytical tools don't support recursive queries. The first group isn't able to process recursive queries. If a data consumer sends a recursive query to a data virtualization server, it rejects the query because it doesn't support the SQL dialect that allows for recursive queries. The reporting and analytical tools don't send recursive queries to the data virtualization servers. These tools generate SQL statements but never statements containing a recursion. Still, if the data does have a recursive structure, a solution must be found.

There are roughly two solutions. The first solution is that reporting tools use SQL override (see Section 6.13). In this case, the reporting tool sends a recursive query to the data virtualization. When the data virtualization server receives this query, it passes it straight on to the underlying database server without even reading the query. It doesn't even know it's passing a recursive query from the data consumer to the database server. The database server processes the query, and the reporting tool receives the result. This solution works, but only if the reporting tool in this case is able to generate recursive queries.

The second solution is to define a virtual table (or wrapper table) with a mapping that holds a recursive query that uses SQL override. The contents of that virtual table contains the recursive data but in a nonrecursive and more flattened form. In other words, the recursive query flattens the whole recursive structure. For example, the PARTS table can be flattened as follows:

```
SUPER  SUB  STEPS  LOCATION
-----  ---  -----  --------
P1     P1   0      top
P1     P2   1      top
P1     P3   1      top
P1     P4   1      top
```

(Continued)

```
P1    P5    2    top
P1    P6    2    top
P1    P7    2    top
P1    P8    3    top
P1    P11   4    top
P2    P2    0    middle
P2    P5    1    middle
P2    P6    1    middle
P2    P8    2    middle
P2    P11   3    middle
P3    P3    0    middle
P3    P7    1    middle
P4    P4    0    bottom
P5    P5    0    bottom
P6    P6    0    middle
P6    P8    1    middle
P6    p11   2    middle
P7    P7    0    bottom
P8    P8    0    middle
P8    P11   1    middle
P9    P9    0    top
P9    P10   1    top
P9    p11   2    top
P10   P10   0    middle
P10   P11   1    middle
P11   P11   0    bottom
```

Each row in this table repesents a link between a part and a direct or indirect subpart, or a link between a part and itself.

If the data is accessible in this form, the data consumers can ask recursive questions without having to use recursive queries. For example, the query in Example 8.9 looks like this:

```
SELECT    SELECT  SUPER, SUB
FROM      PARTS_FLATTENED
WHERE     SUPER = 'P2'
AND       SUPER <> SUB
```

The advantage of this second solution over the first is that all reporting and analytical tools can use recursive queries on the recursive data. It's a more generic solution.

Note: Because it's not supported by most data virtualization servers, this solution, in which an SQL feature is hidden within a mapping or wrapper, is used regularly.

The flattened version of the PARTS table can be generated with the following recursive query:

```
WITH      PARENTS (TOP, SUPER, SUB, STEPS) AS
          (SELECT  SUPER, SUPER, SUB, 1
           FROM    PARTS
           UNION ALL
           SELECT  PAR.TOP, P.SUPER, P.SUB, PAR.STEPS+1
           FROM    PARTS AS P, PARENTS AS PAR
           WHERE   P.SUPER = PAR.SUB)
```

(Continued)

```
SELECT     DISTINCT TOP, SUB, STEPS,
           CASE WHEN TOP NOT IN (SELECT SUB FROM PARTS)
             THEN 'top'
             WHEN TOP NOT IN (SELECT SUPER FROM PARTS)
             THEN 'bottom'
             ELSE 'middle' END
FROM       PARENTS
UNION
SELECT     DISTINCT SUPER, SUPER, 0,
           CASE WHEN SUPER NOT IN (SELECT SUB FROM PARTS) THEN 'top'
             WHEN SUPER NOT IN (SELECT SUPER FROM PARTS) THEN 'bottom'
             ELSE 'middle' END
FROM       PARTS
UNION
SELECT     DISTINCT SUB, SUB, 0,
           CASE WHEN SUB NOT IN (SELECT SUPER FROM PARTS) THEN 'bottom'
             WHEN SUb NOT IN (SELECT SUb FROM PARTS) THEN 'top'
             ELSE 'middle' END
FROM       PARTS
ORDER BY 1, 2
```

Evidently, this query can be expanded and adapted based on the needs of the data consumers.

Design Guideline 9: If the reporting and analytical tools don't support recursive queries, a virtual table should be defined that presents the data with a flattened, nonrecursive structure.

8.4 Implementing Transformations in Wrappers or Mappings

Wrappers on SQL database servers are usually straightforward. In principle, in such a wrapper the data passes one-to-one from the relational source table to the relational virtual table. For wrappers on non-SQL data stores, such as XML documents and web services, it might be a different story. Languages such as XPath, XSLT, or XQuery are used to transform the nonrelational structure of the data store. If those languages are indeed used, extra processing can be added to those wrappers. For example, selections can be added to minimize the amount of data returned, projections can be added to minimize the number of columns returned, transformations can be added to change values, and so on.

This allows designers to choose whether particular transformations should be included inside the wrappers or inside the mappings of the virtual tables. This choice can have a serious impact on performance. If the module executing the wrapper executes the transformations faster than the data virtualization server can execute the mapping, then including them in the wrappers can speed up performance. Moving transformations to the wrapper can also minimize data transmission (Stage 8), but this only applies if the wrapper is really executed on the data store side.

Design Guideline 10: Include transformations in wrappers if the module executing them can do this faster than the data virtualization server can.

8.5 Analyzing Incorrect Data

When filtering or flagging is used, incorrect data is removed from the result of a virtual table or is flagged as being incorrect. The effect is that data consumers don't see that incorrect data. It also means that the incorrect data is not shown. Within an organization, there always exists (or should exist) a group of specialists responsible for the quality of data. This group definitely needs access to the incorrect data. If they can see which data values are false, missing, or misspelled, they may want to go back to the owners of the production data and discuss how it should be fixed. Hopefully, the result of such an exercise is that the overall quality of the data improves.

To support these data quality specialists, dedicated virtual tables can be defined that show the incorrect data. These virtual tables show the filtered, flagged, or incorrect data. Using SQL defining this type of virtual table is relatively easy, as Example 8.10 illustrates.

EXAMPLE 8.10
Define a virtual table that shows all the data filtered out in Example 8.2.

```
DEFINE      V_INCORRECT_DVD_RELEASE AS
SELECT      *
FROM        DVD_RELEASE
MINUS
SELECT      *
FROM        VT_DVD_RELEASE
```

Explanation
The result of the first part of the query returns *all* the DVD releases, and the second one all the DVD releases that are correct. If they are subtracted from each other, what remains are the rows that contain incorrect data.

The same approach works for filtering of values and restoring of values. If a table contains filtered values (incorrect values replaced by null values) and the restored values are subtracted from the original table, the result has a set of rows containing incorrect values.

As indicated, doing this in SQL is relatively easy. It might not be that easy using other mapping languages. Still, it's recommended to define these virtual tables next to the ones presenting all the correct data.

Design Guideline 11: For data quality specialists define dedicated virtual tables that make incorrect data visible.

8.6 Different Users and Different Definitions

In the same organization, different user groups might be using different definitions for the same business object (see Chapter 10). For an organization, it's better if everyone uses the same definition. Unfortunately, that's not always the case, and forcing users to use the same definition can be difficult and sometimes even impossible.

The second best approach is to implement both definitions using data virtualization. Implementing them with a data virtualization server is done by defining one virtual table that holds the common specifications of the two (or more) definitions and by defining two nested virtual tables on that first virtual table. These two nested virtual tables hold the specifications that are unique to the two alternative definitions.

For example, department D1 uses the following definition for the concept of a good customer: someone who has been a customer for at least the last five years, who has ordered at least three times per quarter, and who has sent only one complaint in the previous year. Another department D2, on the other hand, utilizes the following definition: someone who has been a customer for at least the last five years and who has ordered at least once per month. Although these two definitions are different, they have two things in common. First, both require that a good customer is someone who has been a customer for at least the last five years, and second, both require that a good customer has ordered at least three times per quarter.

The recommended approach for designing this situation is to include the common specifications in a virtual table that is used by both departments. This virtual table contains the specifications that those two groups share.

Next, for department D1, a nested virtual table is defined on the first virtual table. The mapping of this virtual table contains an extra condition: each customer should have sent only one complaint during the previous year. For D2, a separate nested virtual table is defined on the shared virtual table with the following extra condition: each customer should have ordered at least once every month.

The advantages of this approach are, first of all, that each user group sees the data according to their own definition, and second, it's clear why they might see different results. In other words, user groups use different definitions, but in a controlled manner.

Design Guideline 12: When different definitions are used, include the common specifications of those definitions in a shared virtual table, and place the unique specifications in separate, nested virtual tables.

8.7 **Time Inconsistency of Data**

When data from a production system and a data warehouse is joined by during the mapping of a virtual table, the problem of *time inconsistency* may arise. The best way to explain this type of problem is with an example.

Imagine that the decision has been made *not* to copy all the data from the production system to the data warehouse. Data in the CUSTOMER table is copied to the data warehouse, but not the data in the CUSTOMER_ORDER and CUSTOMER_ORDER_LINE tables (Figure 8.8). Copying the customer data is done once per 24 hours, at midnight. In addition, a virtual table is defined that joins the three tables from the two data stores.

The problem with this design is that when the virtual table is accessed and the query is executed, the result might show a state of the data that has never happened. Imagine as an example a report that is based on the following query: For each region (column REGION_ID in the CUSTOMER table), get the sum of the rental price (column RENTAL_PRICE in the CUSTOMER_ORDER_LINE table). Imagine that the following activities occur on a particular day:

1. From 9:00 a.m. to 12:00 noon, a customer moves to a new home in another region.
2. At 5:00 p.m., when he is done unloading his truck, he rents a video from a store in his new region.

The effect is that when the report is run at the end of that same day, the result is incorrect. The CUSTOMER_ORDER and CUSTOMER_ORDER_LINE tables show the most up-to-date state of the data, including the video rental. However, the CUSTOMER table in the data warehouse hasn't

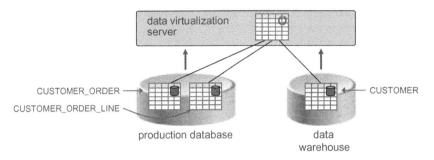

FIGURE 8.8

Some tables are stored in the production database, and one is stored in the data warehouse.

been updated yet. According to the data warehouse, the customer still lives in the former region. So his latest rental is added to his old region when it should have been added to his new region. If the same report is run the next day, this problem will be gone.

The trouble is that the tables being accessed (two in the production system and one in the data warehouse) are temporarily inconsistent, hence the name time inconsistency. Designers have to be aware of this type of problem and have to cater to them. A possible solution would be to access the CUSTOMER table in the production system, too, and not in the data warehouse. Another solution would be to refresh the CUSTOMER table more often.

Design Guideline 13: If the data accessed is distributed over multiple data stores, care should be taken with respect to possible time inconsistencies.

A comparable situation can arise when two virtual tables are joined, but a cache has been defined only for one of them. This can also lead to time inconsistencies if the cache is refreshed with long intervals in between, while the other table holds operational data.

Design Guideline 14: If cached data and noncached data is integrated, care should be taken with respect to possible time inconsistencies.

8.8 Data Stores and Data Transmission

A problem that every business intelligence project has to deal with is query performance. In many studies, users indicate that the performance of their business intelligence system is poor. This is not going to be different if a business intelligence system exploits data virtualization. Therefore, when a business intelligence system is designed, attention has to be paid to performance aspects. Performance problems, however, can be caused by various reasons. For example, the reason can be that too much data is being accessed that, by itself, leads to performance problems, too many concurrent queries can also be an issue as well as the complexity of the queries. In this section we focus on one aspect that definitely influences performance: Where do all the data transformations take place?

The data stored in the production databases has a particular structure and quality level. Whatever architecture is selected, somewhere that data has to be transformed and cleansed by a data virtualization server to a structure suitable for reporting and analytics. Where this is done depends heavily on the points of data storage used in the architecture. Figure 8.9 shows six different solutions. In this diagram the fatness of the arrows indicates where most of the transformation work takes place.

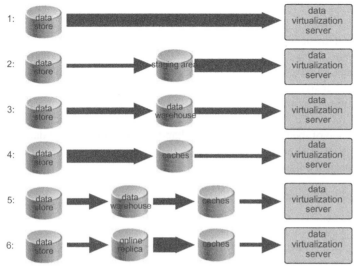

FIGURE 8.9

Where data transformations take place depends on the points of data storage; the fatness of the arrows represents how much data transformation takes place.

For each alternative we describe what the impact is on interference (disturbance of the production workload), concurrency (whether reporting and analytics block the production workload, or vice versa), and performance (the performance of queries from the data consumers).

Solution 1: In this solution, no intermediate data store is introduced, not even a data warehouse. The data virtualization server extracts data directly from the source data stores. The entire business intelligence workload runs directly on the data stores. If this is really possible, if the data stores contain all the necessary data for reporting and analytics, then this is one of the leanest, most agile, and probably cheapest solutions imaginable. However, all the required transformation operations have to be executed live. They have to be executed when the reports are run by the user. This can cause serious performance, concurrency, and contention problems.

Solution 2: With Solution 2, data is first copied to a staging area that is accessed by the data virtualization server. This means that some of the transformations don't have to be processed by the data virtualization server anymore; they are handled by the ETL script copying the data to the staging area. However, in most situations, data is only transformed in a limited way when copied to a staging area, so most of it will still be the responsibility of the data virtualization server. This solution does solve the concurrency and interference problems of Solution 1, because the data virtualization server is not accessing the production databases anymore, but it will only improve performance minimally (compared to Solution 1).

Solution 3: This solution resembles Solution 2, except the staging area is replaced by a data warehouse. The advantage of this approach over Solution 2 is that more transformations are handled before the data is stored in the data warehouse. Thus, the data virtualization server has to perform fewer transformations. Like Solution 2, this improves concurrency and performance and minimizes interference. The only problem might be that the whole query workload has to be handled by the data warehouse.

Solution 4: This solution is like Solution 1, except that caches are defined for the virtual tables accessing the production databases. In this solution, data is transformed when the caches are loaded. The queries in the reports from the data consumers don't have to do that much work anymore. This solution is significantly different from Solution 2, because there, all the transformations are processed when the data is accessed by the reports. This solution does improve the performance, it's good for concurrency, and it minimizes interference. However, the assumption made for Solution 1 applies here as well: the production databases have to contain all the necessary data for reporting and analytics.

Solution 5: This solution is a combination of Solutions 3 and 4. Data is first copied to a data warehouse. In the data virtualization server, virtual tables with caches are defined that access the data warehouse. In this solution some of the transformations are handled when loading the data warehouse and some when loading the cache. It's good for concurrency and performance, and it minimizes interference. The performance improvement over Solution 3 is that the query workload is distributed over multiple caches.

Solution 6: Here, data is first copied to an online replica. This replica can't be called a staging area because it's really just that: a copy. No form of transformation takes place during this copying process. Virtual tables with caches are defined to access the replica. Most of the transformations are handled in this step. The effect is that when the caches are accessed, most of the data already has the structure the data consumers need. Again, the assumption made for Solution 1 applies here as well: the production databases do have to contain all the necessary data for reporting and analytics. This solution is good for performance and concurrency, and it minimizes interference.

Note that these are not all the potential solutions. In fact, it's relatively easy to come up with others. For example, Solution 7 could be based on a source data store, an ODS, a data mart, a personal data store, and a cache. We only described six solutions, but the number of solutions is almost endless. But this discussion should give you an idea of how to evaluate such solutions.

Design Guideline 15: Design an architecture in which interference is low and performance and concurrency are high by selecting the right place to execute all the data transformations.

8.9 Retrieving Data from Production Systems

Some reports need access to operational data, data that is 100 percent up to date. In some environments, the only way to implement this is by accessing the production systems. This can potentially lead to interference, performance, and concurrency problems. Therefore, it's important that care is taken on how those systems are accessed. A design is required that minimizes these problems or completely rules them out.

There are roughly three different styles of how production systems are accessed by data virtualization servers:

- Accessing detailed data on one business object—for example, retrieving all the detailed data making up an invoice or an order.
- Updating, inserting, or deleting detailed data on one business object—for example, the update of an order or the delete of a customer. This style is not common in a business intelligence system, but it is quite common when a data virtualization server is used for developing data services of an SOA (see Chapter 9).
- Querying a set of business objects—for example, retrieving all the customers from a particular region or all the rentals of one customer.

For the first two styles, it's important that the data virtualization server has access to the primary key value of the business object it's trying to retrieve or manipulate. By accessing the data in the production system via the key values, the database server probably accesses the required data via an index. The effect is that the interference is minimal, and performance is as good as the performance of the production systems themselves because the data virtualization server is undoubtedly accessing the production data in the same way the production applications are. But the important aspect here is that the data virtualization server knows what the keys are. If it has to find, for example, a customer in a production system based on that customer's name and/or address, and if no index or other direct access mechanism has been defined on those columns, all of the customer data is scanned. This leads to poor performance, and it interferes with the production systems. To summarize, when accessing production data, the data virtualization server should mimic the style of access used by the production systems themselves.

In summary, when designing the tables in the data warehouse, include the keys of the production systems. In addition, the virtual tables in the data virtualization server should also include these keys. Only then does the data virtualization server have access to the keys used in the production systems and can use those keys to access the operational data with a decent performance and limited or almost no interference.

For the third style of data access, there is a bigger chance of interference. These types of queries return a set of business objects. What has to be avoided is that these queries are executed without any form of direct access, a scan of data should be prohibited. Therefore, it might be necessary for extra indexes to be defined on tables in the production systems purely to support the queries coming from the data virtualization server. If this is impossible, caching is probably required. Note, however, that if a cache is used, the data is no longer 100 percent up to date.

Design Guideline 16: If data consumers need access to the data in the production systems, the data has to be accessed via the keys from those production systems as much as possible.

8.10 Joining Historical and Operational Data

A design issue very much comparable to the one described in the previous section is when a report needs to analyze historical and operational data while the former is stored in a data warehouse and the latter is stored in a production system. To be able to join data from those different systems, access to keys appearing in both systems is a prerequisite. This requires that the keys of the production systems have to be included in the design of the virtual tables.

Let's take the example shown in Figure 8.10 to illustrate the issue. In this example, the CUSTOMER_ORDER table (of which just a few rows and columns are shown) is stored in a production system called Sales, and the CUSTOMER table is stored in the data warehouse. The CUSTOMER table keeps track of history. That's why the columns START_DATE and END_DATE have been added. Rows two and three in this table show two versions of the same customer. The column called CUSTOMER_ID is the new key assigned to customers in the data warehouse environment, whereas SALES_ID contains the ID of the customer as used in the Sales system. The CUSTOMER_ORDER table contains no historical data; it represents the state of customer order data as it currently is. Now imagine that we want to calculate how much has been sold per state. This requires a join of the two tables. If the CUSTOMER table would not contain the customer_id as used

Customer table in Sales System

ID	Name	Initials	City	State
12345	Young	N	San Francisco	CA
23324	Stills	S	New Orleans	LA
57657	Furay	R	Yellow Springs	OH
65461	Palmer	B	Boston	MA
...	...	...	...	...

Customer table in data warehouse

Customer_id	Start_date	End_date	Sales_id	Name	Initials	City	State
1	2001-01-01	?	12345	Young	N	San Francisco	CA
2	2001-11-01	?	23324	Stills	S	New Orleans	LA
3	2004-01-01	2006-04-15	57657	Furay	R	Yellow Springs	OH
3	2006-04-16	?	57657	Furay	R	Palo Alto	CA
4	2005-05-01	?	65461	Palmer	B	New York	NY
...	...	...	...	...	...	...	...

FIGURE 8.10

Keys from the production systems are copied to the data warehouse.

in the Sales system (SALES_ID column), we would have no way to join the two tables. Therefore, it's important that those keys are included.

Design Guideline 17: To be able to integrate operational data with historical data, include the keys from the operational data in the design of the virtual tables.

8.11 Dealing with Organizational Changes

Organizations are dynamic objects. They merge, they acquire others, they break up, and so on. But every time an organization changes, the IT department might face a real challenge. Imagine that the organization BigO buys the organization LittleO. BigO possesses a table containing all its customers. Many reports and applications have been written that access that table. LittleO has a customer table as well. However, its structure is somewhat different. Of course, that table contains comparable data to BigO's customer table but also some unique columns. BigO's IT department has to make a choice: (1) The customer data from LittleO is transformed and copied into BigO's customer table. For the new, unique columns, new columns are added to the BigO's customer table. (2) A virtual table is defined that forms the union of BigO's customer table and LittleO's customer table (Figure 8.11).

A disadvantage of Option 1 is that the applications of LittleO have to be ported as well. They have to be redeveloped so they access BigO's customer table. The question is whether this is technically feasible.

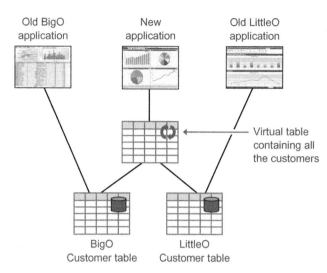

Old BigO
application

New
application

Old LittleO
application

Virtual table
containing all
the customers

BigO
Customer table

LittleO
Customer table

FIGURE 8.11

A virtual table is used to make two different customer tables look like one.

Option 2 has the advantage that BigO's and LittleO's existing applications can continue to run, while those applications that want to process all the customer data can access the data through the virtual table. The advantage of this approach is that the existing systems don't have to be changed to make reporting on all the customers possible. This lowers the threshold to integrate data from new systems. In other words, the business intelligence system doesn't force the production systems to be changed. Virtual tables hide the new tables. The solution allows more source tables to be slid in and out as cartridges. But they stay managable chunks of data. In addition, working with a data virtualization server means that the decision to port LittleO's applications can be postponed. A more gradual migration of LittleO's applications is now possible.

Design Guideline 18: Develop virtual tables in such a way that new tables can easily be attached to existing virtual tables to present a complete view of all the data.

8.12 Archiving Data

Some data warehouses are so immense in size that they become unmanageable, and the performance of queries significantly deteriorates because so much data have to be processed. This asks for *archiving* of a portion of the data. Archiving data in a data warehouse implies that "older" data, sometimes called "cold" data, is removed from the tables and moved to another storage area, one that is cheaper and, therefore, probably slower to access. By removing some data from the original tables, the environment becomes easier to manage, and it improves the performance of queries because there is less data to process.

Imagine that a table with call detail records contains five years of history and consists of millions of records. Most reports probably query the data of the last 12 or 24 months. Occasionally, a few reports query the full five years. In such a situation, it makes sense to move, for example, the two oldest years of data to an archive. However, just taking it out of the database and storing it somewhere on tape is

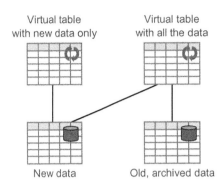

Virtual table with new data only

Virtual table with all the data

New data

Old, archived data

FIGURE 8.12

Archived data is stored in a separate table, but all the data is still accessible for the data consumers as one table.

no option for the reports still occasionally interested in querying that older data. It might mean that for them to be able to access the older data, it might have to be reloaded. This takes too long.

A better solution is to create two tables with identical structures: one containing the new data and the other the old data. Periodically, old data is moved from one to the other. For the reports, two virtual tables are created: one that is a full copy of the table that contains the new data and one that contains the union of the two tables (Figure 8.12).

Spreading data over two source tables has three advantages. First, queries on virtual table 1 aren't slowed down because all the old data has been removed. Second, the table with the old data can be stored on cheaper storage devices but still remains accessible for queries. Third, all of the data is stored only once.

Design Guideline 19: If data is archived, define virtual tables that present the nonarchived data and virtual tables that contain all the data.

Note: Some database servers support features to handle archiving of data. When a table is designed, both hot and cold data in the same table can be placed in different physical areas. This makes archiving fully transparent to all applications and even to a data virtualization server. When a database server supports transparent archiving of data, then this is the preferred approach. Likewise, some storage devices come with multiple storage technologies built in. What we perceive as one big disk can in fact be a combination of very slow disks and SSDs. The storage device itself, depending on particular specifications, determines where the data is stored. These storage systems are normally referred to as *hybrid storage systems*. They also form a perfect solution for archiving. Again, if this type of storage technology is available, then this is the preferred approach over using a solution of separate tables in a data warehouse.

Data Virtualization and Service-Oriented Architecture

9.1 Introduction

Business intelligence is a key application area for data virtualization. The data-oriented nature of data virtualization fits the data-oriented nature of business intelligence very well. But other important application areas do exist for data virtualization. One of them is *service-oriented architecture* (SOA), the topic of this chapter.

In an SOA, applications, services, and databases are being integrated. In that respect, data warehousing and SOA have something in common: both deal with integration. Although the focus in an SOA is on *application integration* and in a business intelligence system on *data integration*, they do have to solve similar problems with respect to transformation, cleansing, and integration of data.

Data virtualization servers can be deployed in an SOA for integrating applications more easily. Using them for developing so-called data and composite services improves development productivity and eases maintenance.

9.2 Service-Oriented Architectures in a Nutshell

Many books and articles have been written on SOA. Instead of trying to repeat all that literature, this section restricts itself to a short summary. For more detailed descriptions of SOA and related topics, see [46] and [47].

Wikipedia (on December 19, 2011) defines SOA as follows:

A service-oriented architecture is a set of principles and methodologies for designing and developing software in the form of interoperable services.

This definition clearly shows that the main building block of an SOA is a *service*. In [48], Boris Lublinsky describes a service as follows:

Each service represents a certain amount of functionality. In the simplest case, a service can be defined as a self-contained, independently developed, deployed, managed, and maintained software implementation supporting specific business-relevant functionality for an enterprise as a whole and is "integratable" by design.

So a service represents business logic. This can be something simple, such as setting the status of a particular DVD to Discontinued or retrieving the list of rented DVDs of a particular customer. But it can also be something more complex, such as ordering more copies of each of the ten best-selling DVDs.

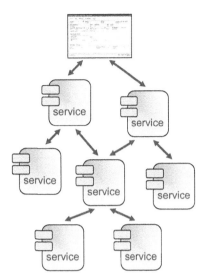

FIGURE 9.1

A service-oriented architecture (SOA) consists of a network of services in which each service represents a certain amount of business functionality.

New systems are developed by creating services and by linking them together to form a *service network* in which they invoke one another (Figure 9.1). Compare this to developing a classic, monolithic application in which all the required logic is programmed inside one application. Because an SOA consists of self-contained services, changes can be made without impacting the whole system. This leads to a very flexible system.

There are two special characteristics of a service. First of all, each service has a well-defined and explicit *interface*. In a way, that interface defines the service. For example, in a hospital environment, the input part of a service interface can be a patient number and its output a complete patient file, including address information, information on prescribed medications, x-rays, and textual descriptions of specialists. As indicated, this interface defines exactly what the service does: it retrieves patient information for one patient. The input and output can be called the *logical interface*.

To be able to invoke a service, it also needs a *technical interface*, which usually consists of an API and a language for specifying the format of the messages to be processed by the service. An example of a popular API is HTTP with SOAP as the message format language (SOAP is a particular XML language). Another example is HTTP with ReST (Representational State Transfer) and JSON (JavaScript Object Notation) as the language for the messages; see [49] for a description of ReST and JSON.

The second special characteristic of a service is that, through its interface, it hides the internal workings, what business logic is executed, how it's executed, and what the implementation looks like. For example, a service might be a piece of code written in Java or C# that performs calculations, some SQL code retrieving data from a data store, or an interface to an internal procedure or function belonging to a legacy application written in Cobol. Figure 9.2 shows that some services access applications and databases to get the work done, others call other services, and still others access nothing and do their own processing. Whatever the implementation of the service is, it's completely hidden for the consumers of the service. In other words, through their interfaces, services offer encapsulation (see Section 1.5.1) and abstraction (see Section 1.5.2).

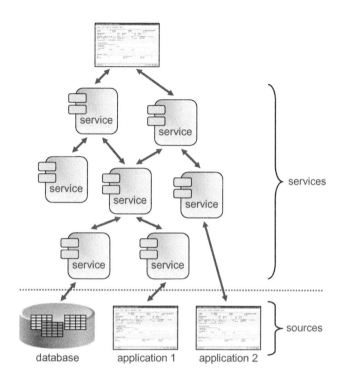

FIGURE 9.2

Services can access applications, databases, other services, or any other source.

Different approaches exist for developing services. The approach where all the code is written by hand is the most labor-intensive, because developers have to develop all the necessary logic and also all the code the services need to communicate with one another. A more productive approach is by deploying a so-called *enterprise service bus* (ESB). Usually, an ESB is a product that supports technology for safely and securely sending messages back and forth between services, for creating service interfaces more easily, and so on. ESBs can be acquired from many different vendors, including IBM, JBoss, Microsoft, Oracle, Progress, and SAP.

The main reason why organizations invest in SOA is summed up quite well in one of Thomas Erl's books (see [47]): "SOA represents an architectural model that aims to enhance the agility and cost-effectiveness of an enterprise while reducing the overall burden of IT on an organization."

9.3 Basic Services, Composite Services, Business Process Services, and Data Services

SOA services can be classified in different ways. One way is based on where they reside in the service network and the kind of functionality they offer. We describe the following four types: basic, business process, composite, and data services.

Basic services: Basic services (sometimes called *raw services*) offer entry points into existing applications and other types of systems. These services allow modules, functions, procedures, or components operating inside existing applications to be invoked. For example, a basic service can invoke a Java component that retrieves the address of a customer or a module that is part of an old Cobol application that determines the existing stock level of a product.

It's not uncommon for a basic service to have a slightly technical interface resembling the interface of the internal application module it invokes. This type of interface is sometimes called a *parameter-oriented* or *value-oriented interface*. The input consists of one or more values, and the output consists of a number of values as well. For example, a basic service can have the key value of a DVD release as input parameter and the title as output parameter.

Basic services hide the real technical interface offered by the applications. The result coming from the applications might not have the right coding, values, and structure. So it has to be transformed. In addition, the basic service is responsible for creating the output of the service. All the basic services together offer a standardized interface (logical and technical) to all the resources, making it easier to invoke and reuse the logic of those applications.

Business process services: Business process services form the top layer of the service network. Examples are the processing of an incoming order, the hiring process of a new employee, and the shipping of goods. These services are normally executed by so-called *business process engines*. They represent the real business processes of an organization. Not all SOA projects include this layer of services.

Composite services: This group of services forms the middle layer of the service network. Usually, they are located between the business process services and the basic services. The reason these composite services exist is granularity. Business process services need access to stored data and to the functionality offered by existing applications. Technically it's possible that business process services invoke basic services directly. However, as indicated, the interfaces of the basic services are probably too technical and too detailed. This would imply that quite some code has to be added to the business process services for invoking the basic services. In addition, a large portion of that code is repeated in multiple business process services. To avoid that problem, an intermediate layer of services is introduced consisting of composite services. Composite services usually offer an interface that is more oriented toward the needs of the business process services. They offer a more *document-oriented interface*. As comparison, if a basic service returns the address of a patient, a composite service returns a whole patient file. Thus, a composite service has an interface on a higher granularity level than a basic service.

To create these more document-oriented interfaces, it's common that a composite service accesses mutiple basic services and joins the data from multiple applications—hence the name *composite*. In other words, composite services are responsible for the federation of data coming from different services and systems (see also Section 1.5.3).

Data services: Data services are somewhat similar to basic services in that they also reside at the bottom of the service network. However, the difference is that data services are used for, as their name suggests, querying and manipulating data. Whereas basic services access the applications (if technically possible), data services in most cases access data stores directly and bypass the applications entirely. Besides retrieving data from a data store, a data service is also responsible for cleansing and transforming the values to a result that the consumers expect and need. It also assigns a structure to the result of the service.

The last two classes of services, the composite and data services, can be developed using a data virtualization server. This is the topic of the next two sections.

9.4 Developing Data Services with a Data Virtualization Server

The previous section describes a few of the tasks a data service has to perform. Here is a more complete list:

1. *Input:* Incoming input data which might be in a SOAP/XML or JSON format has to be parsed and checked to ensure that all the required data is there and that all the data values are correct.
2. *Data access:* Database statements have to be created and executed to retrieve data from a data store.
3. *Functional logic:* Data returned by the data store has to be cleansed and transformed so all the values are according to all the applicable standards. In fact, this is not much different from all the necessary data transformation and data cleansing when data is copied from production systems to a data warehouse. In addition, extra logic, such as calculations and checks, might have to be performed.
4. *Output:* The result, which is in tabular format if it's coming from an SQL database server, has to be given the proper hierarchical structure and has to be placed in the right SOAP or JSON format.
5. *Security:* A data service has to guarantee that all the applicable security rules are implemented. If a particular user is not allowed to access a piece of data, the data service should prohibit access to it.

Whatever the technology and/or programming language used, somehow all this functionality has to be built into each data service.

Roughly speaking, data services can be developed in two ways. The most obvious approach is by developing custom-code that performs all the above tasks. For example, a data service can be developed in a language such as Java or C# as a component which accesses an SQL database (Figure 9.3). The drawback of this approach is that most of the tasks are coded by hand. Some of it, such as parsing the incoming XML document, can be handled by calling Java functionality, and some can be implemented by ESB functionality. Still, no task is done automatically.

Alternatively, a data service can also be developed using a data virtualization server (Figure 9.4). In this case, a virtual table is defined that includes all the data the data service has to return when

data
service

database

FIGURE 9.3

Data services for accessing a data store developed with custom-code.

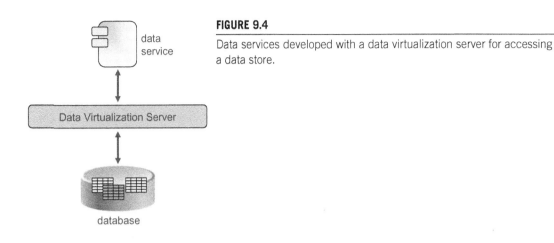

FIGURE 9.4

Data services developed with a data virtualization server for accessing a data store.

invoked. Section 3.9 contains a description of how such an interface on a virtual table is defined. When the virtual table with its mapping is defined, including all the required transformations, the only thing left to do is create the proper hierarchical structure for the data and to publish the virtual table as a service with one or more technical interfaces. This means that Tasks 1, 2, and 4 are automatically handled by the data virtualization server, and a high-level programming langusage is used for Task 3. Task 5 is purely a matter of setting the right privileges: which user/application is allowed to use the new data service?

The advantages of using data virtualization over a custom-made solution are the following:

- *Increased productivity*: Developing a data service with a data virtualization server requires less development time than when a custom-made solution is developed. Developers of data services using a data virtualization server only have to focus on defining the mappings for virtual tables. They don't have to deal with most of the technical issues (Tasks 1, 2, and 4), which is where the developers using programming languages have to spend time on. Having to spend less time on technical details and having to purely focus on the required transformations improve productivity.
- *Improved maintenance*: Because there is less code, maintenance is less complex. In addition, if the structures of the tables in the underlying data store change, the synchronization feature of the virtualization server notices that and will ask whether the change has to be propagated (see Section 4.3). This feature is not supported when the services are hand-coded.
- *Interface independency*: If code is written by hand, probably only one technical interface is implemented. Supporting an extra interface requires a serious development effort. With a data virtualization server, allowing consumers to invoke a service using other technical interfaces is purely a matter of publishing another API for the existing virtual table (see Section 3.9). In other words, the functionality of what a service should do is developed independently of the technical interfaces for invoking it.
- *Security independency*: All the specifications related to security are specified in the data virtualization server. They can easily be changed without having to change the service itself. In fact, the technical advantages of using a data virtualization server for developing data services are identical to those for using data virtualization in general. These advantages are listed in Section 1.7.

Most data services are used for querying data. However, some allow inserts, updates, and deletes of data. A data virtualization server does allow the contents of virtual tables to be manipulated, although some restrictions apply. (The restrictions are described in Section 3.11.) Designers have to be aware of those restrictions when designing and developing data services for manipulating data.

9.5 Developing Composite Services with a Data Virtualization Server

The task of a composite service is to combine the results of multiple services into one. This section discusses various ways to implement composite services. A composite service performs the following tasks:

1. *Input:* Incoming input data, which might be in a SOAP/XML or JSON format, has to be parsed and checked that all the required data is there and whether all the data is correct.
2. *Service access:* Code has to be executed to access other services. If some of these services are not available, decisions have to be made on whether or not to proceed.
3. *Functional logic:* Data returned from the invoked services has to be combined into one result. Additional logic, such as calculations and checks, might have to be performed.
4. *Output:* The result should be given the proper hierarchical structure and should be placed in the right SOAP or JSON format.
5. *Security:* The composite service has to guarantee that all the applicable security rules are implemented. If a particular user is not allowed to invoke the service, it should prohibit that.

Figure 9.5 shows the approach taken when a composite service directly invokes the underlying services, which are usually basic services, data services, and other composite services. This type of composite service performs all the five tasks.

A wide range of languages can be used to implement composite services this way, ranging from classic programming languages, such as Java and C#; via more XML-related languages, such

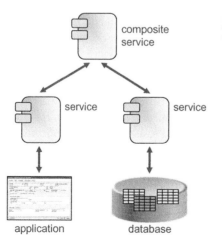

FIGURE 9.5

Composite services accessing other services directly.

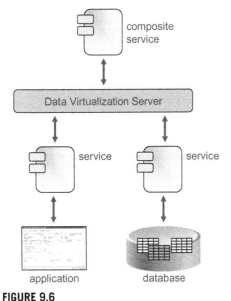

FIGURE 9.6

Composite services accessing other services using a data virtualization server.

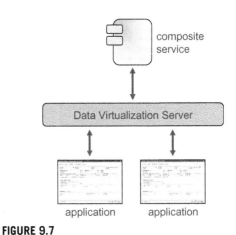

FIGURE 9.7

Composite services accessing a data virtualization server for integrating data coming from the applications.

as XSLT and XQuery; to *BPEL* (business process executing language). The rest of this section is devoted to developing composite services using data virtualization.

When a data virtualization server is used to implement a composite service, the designers have a choice. They can let the data virtualization server access applications or databases through a set of services (Figure 9.6), they can let it access the applications straight on (Figure 9.7), or they can decide to have the composite services access the databases (Figure 9.8) straight on. A data virtualization server supports the technology to access all of those sources. Let's discuss all three.

When a data virtualization server sits between the composite services and other services, it completely handles Task 1. For each of the invoked services, a wrapper is defined (Task 2). One virtual table is defined for combining the data from the different services (Task 3). The effect is that the data virtualization server presents all the data coming from the underlying services as one virtual table. This virtual table is published as a service (Task 4). Task 5 is, as with data services, purely a matter of setting the right privileges.

The advantage of accessing applications directly might be efficiency; it might be that the extra service layer in between the data virtualization server and the applications is too slow. If a composite service invokes a basic service that accesses an application, the result from the application is first transformed by the basic service and subsequently by the composite service. From the perspective of performance, accessing applications directly might be the preferred approach. A disadvantage of this approach is that every composite service accessing a particular application needs to understand how that application works. If basic services or data services are used, that kind of functionality is encapsulated by these services and doesn't have to be repeated in the composite services. By going straight to the applications, there is little reuse of that functionality.

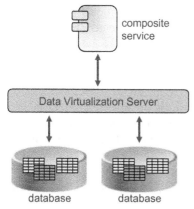

FIGURE 9.8

Composite services accessing a data virtualization server that integrates data from databases.

Whether applications can technically be accessed by a data virtualization server directly, strongly depends on how the applications have been developed. For example, if they have been developed in a modular fashion using Java or C#, modules within the applications can easily be accessed through technical interfaces, such as RMI and JCA. No service interface is needed. However, some applications are so highly nonmodular that finding an entry point is impossible.

Another factor that can complicate accessing an application is when application modules do more than the data virtualization server wants. Imagine an application module that inserts new orders into the system and that automatically invokes another application module that inserts some extra data in the database. This might be unknown to the data virtualization server and may not be the intention. This can be especially disastrous for the integrity of the data when it's updated.

In both cases, when applications have a nonmodular structure and execute more functional logic than expected, accessing them directly may not be the preferred approach. In that situation, letting the data virtualization server access the applications through basic services is recommended.

With the next approach, databases are accessed directly and thus bypass the applications (see Figure 9.8). This is a very efficient approach. The only risk is that the developers building the mappings to extract the data may not understand all the details of the structure and the contents of the data stores. This can lead to a situation where the data is retrieved in an incorrect manner. And if in the future the database structure and the application are changed, the data virtualization server has to be warned about this. Keeping the functionality in the applications and the mappings synchronized is a challenge.

If a composite service is accessing multiple data stores, updating data can lead to a distributed transaction. Whether or not this is supported depends on what the data stores themselves support and what the data virtualization server supports. For example, if the data stores can't be part of a distributed transaction, the data virtualization server can't implement a distributed transaction (see also Section 3.11).

9.6 Services and the Internal Data Model

Section 3.10 describes how different data virtualization servers use different internal data models, such as the relational, extended relational, or object-oriented data model. Which data model is used has an impact on how services are developed and on their performance.

If a data virtualization server is used to develop a composite service and if that data virtualization server uses a relational data model internally, two data model conversions are executed. First, the data coming from the invoked services is transformed from hierarchical to relational (the data is flattened), next the transformations and integrations are executed, and finally the relational result is transformed to a hierarchical structure for the published service. In other words, two data model conversions are executed, first from hierarchical to relational and then from relational to hierarchical.

Those data virtualization servers supporting an extended relational or an object-oriented data model might be somewhat more efficient in this respect because there may not be a need to execute two data model conversions. With these products it's possible to keep the data coming from the invoked services in a hierarchical form, and this form is transformed to the structure the composite service requires. So only one real transformation is executed: from hierarchical to hierarchical.

Whether having fewer data model transformations is really more efficient depends on how, in general, transformations are implemented in the data virtualization servers. What counts here is the old adage "The proof of the pudding is in the eating." But potentially, two data model conversions require more processing time than one.

Data Virtualization and Master Data Management

10.1 Introduction

The quality of decision making depends to a large degree on the quality of the data used to make the decision. Incorrect data can negatively influence the quality of decision making. One area in IT that deals with the quality of data is *master data management*. Therefore, master data management has a close relationship with data integration and thus with data virtualization.

This chapter describes the advantages of exploiting data virtualization technology in a master data management system. It starts with explaining the need for master data, what master data management is, and why it's important to most organizations. The role of master data management for data integration is explained, and the chapter ends with ways data virtualization and master data management can operate together. For those interested in more detailed and extensive descriptions on master data management, see [50] and [51].

10.2 Data Is a Critical Asset for Every Organization

For many organizations, data is a critical asset. Would a bank, an insurance company, or an airline still be able to operate if it could not access its data? Most likely not. Data has become indispensable for organizations for their day-to-day operations, for being able to manage their organization, and also for being cost effective and competitive. One might think that, therefore, organizations treat this asset carefully. Unfortunately, most often the opposite is true. In some organizations, data is seriously neglected. Next we discuss four types of reoccurring problems that clearly show this neglect of data.

- Quite often, different production systems hold *conflicting versions* of the data. For example, the Sales system indicates that a particular customer is based in the city of Boston (see customer Palmer in the first table in Figure 10.1), whereas the Finance system has that same customer located in New York (see customer Palmer in the second table in Figure 10.1). Which one is the correct version? Did the customer move from New York to Boston, but the change was never made in one of the systems? Or is the Boston address just wrong because Palmer was never based in Boston? Another classic problem is if in one system products are classified based on an old set of product group codes, while in another system a new set of codes has already been introduced. Again, this is an example of conflicting versions of the data. Which is correct, and when was it correct?
- Another frequently occurring problem that shows how carelessly organizations treat data is when different departments and/or systems use (slightly) *conflicting definitions* for the same concept.

Customer table in Sales System

ID	Name	Initials	Date Entered	City	State
12345	Young	N	Aug 4, 2008	San Francisco	CA
23324	Stills	S	Sep 10, 2009	New Orleans	LA
57657	Furay	R	Oct 16, 2010	Yellow Springs	OH
65461	Palmer	B	Nov 22, 2011	Boston	MA
...	...	...	...	...	...

FIGURE 10.1

Two tables with customer data from two different production systems: Sales and Finance.

Customer table in Finance System

ID	Name	Initials	Date Entered	City	State
C5729	Young	N	Sep 16, 2007	San Francisco	CA
LA781	Stils	S	Dec 8, 2010	New Orleans	LA
J7301	Furay	R	Jan 10, 2008	Yellow Springs	OH
K8839	Palmer	B	Feb 11, 2009	New York	NY
...	...	...	...	...	...

For example, the reservation system of an airline is using a different definition for the concept of a flight as the crew planning system. Maybe in the reservation system a flight is formed by all the hops made to get a set of travelers from one destination to another, while in the crew planning system a flight always consists of one hop only. Additionally, travelers might be using a completely different definition.

- The third problem relates to key values. In some organizations, *inconsistent key values* are used in different systems to represent one and the same object. For example, in the Sales system, customer Young has 12345 as a key value, but in the Finance system, C5729 is used to represent him (see Figure 10.1). A reason for this can be that the company recently acquired another company. Each company had its own customer management system. The two companies do share the same customers, but the keys assigned to those customers are different. Bringing data together from different systems with inconsistent key values is hard and sometimes close to impossible.
- *Incorrect data* is the fourth type of problem. (This topic is discussed in more detail in Section 8.2.) An example of incorrect data is the spelling of the name of customer LA781 in the Finance system (see Figure 10.1); his name should be spelled with two l's.

The problems described in this section—conflicting versions, different definitions, inconsistent key values, and incorrect data—make integrating data difficult. When a business intelligence system is developed, data from all kinds of systems is brought together and is integrated using data virtualization or ETL/ELT technology. In this book we indicate how particular data-related problems can be solved. But certain data integration problems can't be solved by applying software only. For example, the problem of inconsistent key values can only be solved if someone studies the data and decides that 12345 and C5729 represent one and the same customer. Fuzzy matching algorithms can be applied to determine whether they represent the same customer, but there is no 100 percent guarantee that the result is correct.

10.3 **The Need for a 360-Degree View of Business Objects**

The need for organizations to have a complete view of particular business objects (sometimes called core business entities) keeps increasing. Examples of such business objects are the products a retailer sells, bank accounts and loans, the policies of an insurance company, an airline's airplanes and flights, the trucks of a transport company, and, of course, the most classic business object: the customers. In the sample database, customers and DVD releases are examples of business objects.

A complete view shows a business object from every angle possible. All the data an organization has available on a business object is brought together and presented in an integrated fashion. Normally, such a complete view is called a *360-degree view*. For example, a 360-degree view of a customer may include the products he has purchased in the past, the contracts he has signed, any complaints he has made, the tweets he wrote about the company, the number of times he patronized the store, and which managers have handled his accounts. A 360-degree view can be quite comprehensive.

A 360-degree view gives an organization a better insight into who that customer is and how valuable he is. This can make an organization more competitive, costs can be reduced, and new sales opportunities may become visible. For example, if we only analyze how much a customer has ordered, we may qualify him as a good customer. But if we look at the number of times he has made complaints and weigh the amount of work involved in handling all those complaints, we might conclude that he is also a very costly customer. And by bringing all the data together, it might become apparent that he is not a good customer at all. The driving force of creating a 360-degree view is usually business oriented.

Adding extra data that is not stored in the production systems can be helpful in creating a real 360-degree view. For example, relationships between customers may not be maintained in the production systems, although they may exist in reality. For example, one customer is a subsidiary of another (in case the customer is an organization), or maybe one customer is married to another customer (if customers represent people). To complete the 360-degree view, those relationships can be crucial. Imagine if the return on a particular customer is less than the total investment, an organization may want to get rid of that customer. But do they want to get rid of him if he's a subsidiary of their largest and most profitable customer? Probably not.

In most organizations, data on business objects is not stored in one system but is spread out over many systems. In a perfect world, creating a 360-degree view is relatively simple. All the data related to a business object is joined, and the 360-degree view is presented. Unfortunately, that perfect world doesn't exist in most organizations. As indicated, due to inconsistent key values, conflicting versions of the data, different definitions, and incorrect data, this can even be close to impossible. For example, if the customer's addresses are merged together from different systems to create the 360-degree view and they aren't the same, which version is the correct one?

Initially, it sounds like a simple request—create a 360-degree view of a business object—but technically it can be a tour de force. Master data management helps solve the problems described in this chapter. Before we explain what master data management is, let's define the term *master data*.

10.4 **What Is Master Data?**

Master data is data on *core business objects* of an organization. Core business objects are usually the focus of the business processes and are crucial for an organization's operation. Master data on

Master Customer table

ID	Version	Sales ID	Finance ID	Date Entered	Name	Initials	City	State
MD12	1	12345	C5729	Sep 16, 2007	Young	N	San Francisco	CA
MD13	1	23324	LA781	Sep 10, 2009	Stills	S	New Orleans	LA
MD14	1	57657	J7301	Jan 10, 2008	Furay	R	Yellow Springs	OH
MD15	1	65461	K8839	Feb 11, 2009	Palmer	B	New York	NY
MD15	2	65461	K8839	Nov 22, 2011	Palmer	B	Boston	MA
...	...	...	...	...	...	...	...	...

FIGURE 10.2

Example of master data.

business objects include definitions, properties, occurrences, and taxonomies. Each business object requires a precise definition acceptable to anyone within the organization. Examples of properties are the address, the company name, and the status of a customer; the sales price of a product; and the title, the studio, and the rating of a DVD release. The two other aspects—occurrences and taxonomies— require some explanation.

Master data also includes all the *occurrences*, so it's not restricted to descriptive information. For example, the correct home address and the correct email address of each customer and the correct spelling of each customer's name can all be master data. In addition, correct historical data is also seen as master data, such as the previous correct address of a customer and the date on which the customer moved.

Figure 10.2 is an example of a table that contains master data. This table holds the master data related to the two tables from Figure 10.1. Among other things, this table contains the customer IDs of both tables, the correct spelling of customer Stills, and two correct versions of customer Palmer showing that he first lived in New York before he moved to Boston. From the two timestamps the older one is picked.

Note the frequent use of the word *correct* in the previous two paragraphs. Managing master data is all about managing correct data, so master data is sometimes referred to as the *single version of the truth*. Regardless of which version of the data other systems store on a particular customer, the master data indicates what the organization sees as the correct version of the data. In fact, that's why it's called *master* data. So if there are discussions about, for example, what the correct address of a customer is, the address indicated as master data is regarded as the correct version.

Master data also includes how business objects are identified in production systems. To use the same example again, if for a particular customer different key values are used in various production systems, the master data indicate what those key values are and in which system they are used. This allows for integrating data from different systems even if the key values are inconsistent.

Master data also includes *taxonomies*. Taxonomies indicate the different types of relationships that can exist between business objects. These can be relationships between business objects of the same type—such as one customer is a subsidiary of another or one employee is married to another. Subset relationships are also part of taxonomies, such as all the canceled flights form a subset of all the flights. Relationships between business objects of different types can exist as well, such as orders having relationships with deliveries and customers having relationships with products. The fourth type of relationship is sometimes referred to as an *aggregation*. For example, a project plan consists of activities and assigned resources. All can be business objects on themselves. For more detailed descriptions on taxonomies, see [52] and [53].

Not every piece of data is considered master data. For example, many experts don't consider *transactional data* to be master data. Typical for transactional data is that it represents an event, an action, or a process. A customer renting or buying a DVD is an example of transactional data. But the difference between master data and nonmaster data is not always clear cut. A gray area does exist.

In addition, what can be considered to be master data by one organization might not be seen as master data by another. For example, in one organization, employee data is master data, but passport-related data is not. The latter is considered a property of employee. However, for the government agency responsible for registering and printing passports, the data on passports is undoubtedly considered master data.

Here are some typical characteristics of master data:

- Master data is usually shared by many processes within the organization, many functional groups, and/or many applications. Data introduced for just one system is normally not considered to be master data.
- Master data is typically stored in various data stores. That's also one of the reasons why master data management is needed to identify the real master data.
- Master data is usually nontransactional. Transactional data usually include a timestamp to indicate when the activity took place. Note that master data experts have different opinions on this.
- The properties of business objects are subject to change, but they usually change slowly. For example, a customer's address might change, but it will change infrequently. Compare this to the properties of transactional data that usually do not change; the event has happened, and that's the end of the story.
- Master data should not be confused with *reference data*. Although reference data can be seen as a subset of master data, not all the master data is considered reference data. Examples of reference data are product group codes and their descriptions and the list of all the countries. Reference data is normally used to classify and describe data. For example, the product group code of a product describes to which group it belongs. In that respect, reference data can also be used to classify master data. In the world of technology, the terms *lookup table* and *code table* are sometimes used to refer to reference data.

10.5 **What Is Master Data Management?**

Master data does not just fall out of the sky, and it doesn't grow on trees. An organization has to work hard to organize all its master data properly. In fact, it requires a *lot* of hard work. Informally said, all this work is called *master data management*. David Loshin (see [50]) defines master data management more precisely as follows:

> *Master data management is a collection of best data management practices that orchestrate key stakeholders, participants, and business clients in incorporating the business applications, information management methods, and data management tools to implement the policies, procedures,*

services, and infrastructure to support the capture, integration, and subsequent shared use of accurate, timely, consistent, and complete master data.

Master data management is all about managing master data and keeping it "accurate, timely, consistent, and complete." Like business intelligence, master data management is not a tool, and it's not something that can be bought. Instead, it's an activity or a process with no ending. Once started, work on master data never stops. In this respect, master data management is very much like business intelligence.

To keep master data accurate, timely, consistent, and complete, master data management involves many practical and time-consuming tasks, such as:

- Identify sources of master data.
- New data inserted in the production systems has to be extracted and studied to see if it represents new master data or whether existing master data has to be updated.
- Incorrect data has to be transformed and cleansed to become master data. This is somewhat similar to what happens when data is copied from production systems to a data warehouse.
- Taxonomies have to be developed and maintained. When new data is entered, the taxonomies have to be extended or changed. Working on taxonomies requires knowledge of the data and the business.

10.6 A Master Data Management System

Organizations need dedicated systems to help manage master data; these are called *master data management systems* (MDMS). MDMSs are offered by vendors such as IBM, Microsoft, Oracle, and SAP. Applications that need access to master data perceive an MDMS as a simple system that can be treated like a black box (Figure 10.3). These applications retrieve master data through common

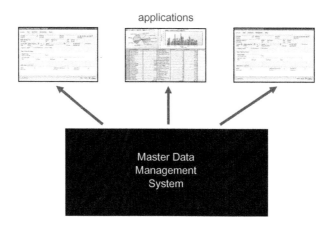

applications

Master Data
Management
System

FIGURE 10.3

To applications that need master data, a master data management system is like a black box they can use to retrieve it.

technical interfaces. For example, for a particular customer, the correct address and the key value used in a particular production system can be retrieved.

If we open the hood of these products, most of them have a comparable architecture (Figure 10.4). Each MDMS consists of three core modules: the management module, the run-time module, and the load module. All the master data, including all the definitions, taxonomies, and occurrences, is stored in a dedicated data store managed by the MDMS. With the *management module,* specialists can organize all that master data. New master data can be inserted, existing master data can be changed, taxonomies can be updated and extended, and so on.

The *load module* is used for retrieving new data from other systems and for loading it in the MDMS. With respect to their functionality, most of these load modules are comparable to ETL tools. Important to note is that specialists can study the incoming data before it's added.

The *run-time module* is used by applications to retrieve master data. Most of the products support multiple technical interfaces for accessing the master data stored in its database. A very common interface is SOAP, and some support an SQL/JDBC interface. These interfaces are necessary to create, for example, the 360-degree view of a business object. Note that an MDMS does not supply all the required data for the 360-degree view because that would imply that it contains the sum of all the data stored in all the production systems. Instead, it holds all the correct master data plus the key values that represent those business objects in various systems. This makes it possible to, for instance, retrieve the transactional data to complete the 360-degree view.

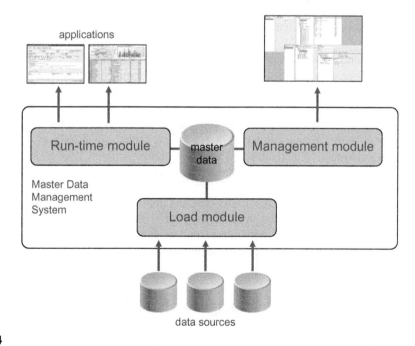

FIGURE 10.4

The modules of a master data management system.

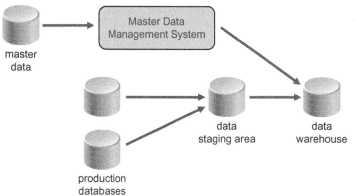

FIGURE 10.5

A master data management system can act as a data source for a business intelligence system.

10.7 **Master Data Management for Integrating Data**

Data extracted from an MDMS doesn't have to be cleansed anymore, and it already has the right form. Even complex integration issues, such as dealing with inconsistent key values, incorrect data, and different versions of the data, are solved in the MDMS. For example, if two customer tables from two different systems have to be joined and those tables use different key values, the MDMS can be accessed to make the join possible. Only data from other sources, such as transactional data, still has to be processed.

A business intelligence system can exploit an MDMS when treating it as a source (Figure 10.5). The business intelligence system can assume that the data extracted from the MDMS is correct; it doesn't need a lot of cleansing or transformations. All this work has been done when loading that same data in the MDMS. This definitely simplifies the development of a business intelligence system.

The same story applies to a business intelligence system based on data virtualization. To integrate data from different systems, a data virtualization server can exploit an MDMS as if it's one of the many data sources (Figure 10.6). The effect is that, for example, a virtual table is defined in the data virtualization server that contains for each customer the different customer key values for each source system.

Most MDMSs are designed to manage master data and don't always offer the fastest access to the data stored in their own master data data store. When a data virtualization server accesses the master data via such an MDMS, performance might, therefore, be somewhat slow. A periodically refreshed cache is probably necessary to obtain the proper performance.

10.8 **Integrating Master Data Management and Data Virtualization**

The previous section shows how master data management and data virtualization can work side by side. This section describes what the benefits can be if master data management and data virtualization are integrated more tightly.

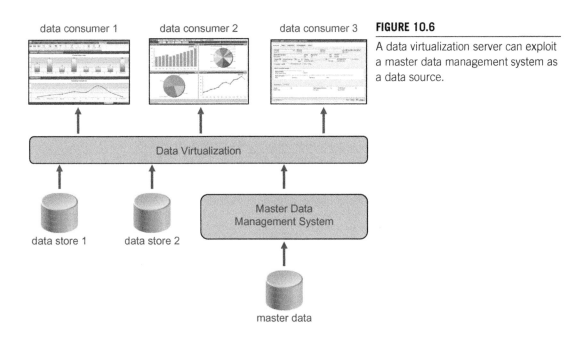

FIGURE 10.6

A data virtualization server can exploit a master data management system as a data source.

As indicated in this chapter, most products available for developing master data management systems store all the master data in their own dedicated data store. This implies that most of the data in such a data store is stored redundantly, because the original data is stored in the production databases as well. For example, customer master data might be duplicated from a production database. As an example, the master data table in Figure 10.2 contains most of the data also stored in the two tables in Figure 10.1. Note that the data stored by an MDMS is slightly different from the data stored in a production system because the former has probably been cleansed and corrected. Still, it is duplicated data.

This duplication of master data can lead to the following two problems:

- Storing duplicate data costs resources. Especially if there are many occurrences of a specific business object, such as all the customers of a large telephone company or all the members of a popular social media network, the extra amount of storage space needed is significant. The master database might become too massive and, therefore, hard to manage. The question arises whether storing master data redundantly is really necessary in a situation where most of the data in the production systems is correct.
- The master data has to be updated when the original data is updated. For example, if a new customer is introduced, this customer data should be copied to the MDMS. This requires a technical solution based on ETL, ELT, or replication.

These problems can be minimized if not all the master data is stored in an MDMS redundantly, but if some is stored in the MDMS and some remains in the production systems, and data virtualization is used to integrate both to form one logical master data store. Technically, there are two ways to do this. Figure 10.7 shows the first way, where the MDMS sits on top of a data virtualization

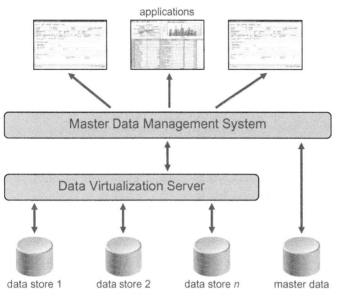

applications

FIGURE 10.7

A data virtualization server as data
source for the master data management
system.

server. Some master data, such as descriptions, definitions, and new relationships, is still stored in a dedicated data store, and large portions of the master data (the occurrences) are not copied from the production systems but are extracted from those systems in an on-demand fashion by a data virtualization server.

In this architecture, the MDMS determines whether to physically store all the master data or only the minimal amount necessary and to have the data virtualization server retrieve the remaining data from the proper production databases. For applications that need access to the master data, nothing changes. Master data is still retrieved via the MDMS. Currently, this approach is only possible if the MDMS supports any type of database server, including data virtualization servers.

In the second approach, all the data (including master data) is accessed via a data virtualization server (Figure 10.8). Applications can access all the data via the data virtualization server directly or via the MDMS. In this situation, the data virtualization server knows where all the data is including all the master data. Master data is made available in the same way as nonmaster data. Management of definitions, taxonomies, and so on are still handled through the management module of the MDMS, but all the data is retrieved via the data virtualization server.

The key difference between this and the previous approach is that many of the transformation rules, normally defined in the MDMS, are now implemented as mappings in the data virtualization server. The primary role of the MDMS is management of the master data—in other words, the management module is the dominant module. The importance of the run-time module diminishes. Most of that work is taken over by the data virtualization server.

Figure 10.9 shows what the impact of this approach might be on the customer master data table used in this chapter. The only columns left are the ones that can't be derived automatically from the data in the original two tables. Data such as names, initials, states, and cities is removed and are not duplicated in this solution.

applications

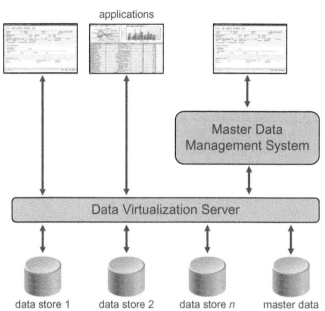

FIGURE 10.8

A data virtualization server used by applications to access master data.

Master Customer table

ID	Version	Sales ID	Finance ID	Date Entered
MD12	1	12345	C5729	Sep 16, 2007
MD13	1	23324	LA781	Sep 10, 2009
MD14	1	57657	J7301	Jan 10, 2008
MD15	1	65461	K8839	Feb 11, 2009
MD15	2	65461	K8839	Nov 22, 2011
...	...	...	...	...

FIGURE 10.9

The master data table that includes only the data not stored in the production systems.

To make this possible, within the data virtualization server a virtual table has to be defined that has the same contents as the master data table in Figure 10.2. The mapping to construct this virtual table would look like this:

```
DEFINE    V_CUSTOMER_MASTER AS
SELECT    MC.ID, MC.VERSION, MC.DATE_ENTERED, SC.NAME, SC.INITIALS
          CASE
              WHEN MC.DATE_ENTERED = SC.DATA_ENTERED THEN SC.DATE_ENTERED
              WHEN MC.DATE_ENTERED = FC.DATA_ENTERED THEN FC.DATE_ENTERED
              ELSE NULL
```

```
              END AS DATE_ENTERED,
              CASE
                 WHEN MC.DATE_ENTERED=SC.DATA_ENTERED THEN SC.CITY
                 WHEN MC.DATE_ENTERED = FC.DATA_ENTERED THEN FC.CITY
                 ELSE NULL
              END AS CITY,
              CASE
                 WHEN MC.DATE_ENTERED = SC.DATA_ENTERED THEN SC.STATE
                 WHEN MC.DATE_ENTERED = FC.DATA_ENTERED THEN FC.STATE
                 ELSE NULL
              END AS STATE
   FROM       MASTER_CUSTOMER AS MC,
              SALES_CUSTOMER AS SC,
              FINANCE_CUSTOMER AS FC
   WHERE      MC.SALES_ID = SC.ID
   AND        MC.FINANCE_ID = FC.ID
```

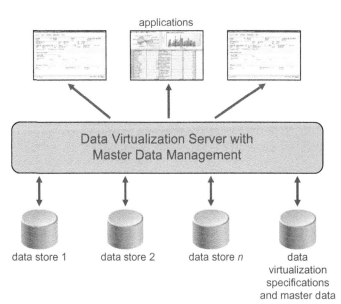

FIGURE 10.10

A data virtualization server with integrated master data management features.

Some typical master data management decisions have been implemented in the mapping of this virtual table. First of all, the customer name and initials are retrieved from the table in the Sales system and not from the Finance system. In other words, names and initials in the Sales system are seen as master data. This means that for customer MD13, the name Stills is selected. Second, the selected date entered, the state, and the city all come from the Sales or the Finance system. If the date entered in the master table is equal to that of the Sales system, then the date entered, state, and city of the Sales system are selected; otherwise the values are taken from the Finance system. Again, this is a typical master data management decision, and here it is implemented in a virtual table.

This second approach does solve some of the problems described above. First, if there is a lot of production data, not all of it has to be duplicated anymore. Problems such as different versions of the data can also be solved by defining mappings that implement the decision on which value to take. Second, no solution has to be developed that copies all the data from the production systems to an MDMS. All the transformations handled by that solution are now implemented in the virtual tables.

But the ideal approach is if the vendors of data virtualization tools add master data management capabilities to their products (Figure 10.10). In this approach, data virtualization and master data management come together into one product.

The directory of such a combined product contains all the typical data virtualization specifications, such as mappings, virtual tables, and wrappers, plus all the master data specifications, such as taxonomies, definitions, and properties of business objects. In Chapter 13 we return to the topic of merging master data management and data virtualization.

Data Virtualization, Information Management, and Data Governance

11.1 Introduction

This chapter describes the impact deploying data virtualization technology within business intelligence systems has on certain data-oriented tasks within an organization. These tasks fall within the domain of *information management*. According to Wikipedia (on January 2, 2012), the definition of information management is:

> *Information management is the collection and management of information from one or more sources and the distribution of that information to one or more audiences.*

Examples of tasks that fall within this domain of information management include the following:

- Information modeling
- Database design
- Data profiling
- Data cleansing
- Data governance

For each of these tasks, this chapter describes the effects of deploying data virtualization. Some background knowledge on these tasks is expected. Each of the topics addressed in this chapter probably deserves an entire book. We are only touching the surface of each of these topics to give readers a general, high-level understanding of the impact that data virtualization has.

11.2 Impact of Data Virtualization on Information Modeling and Database Design

Data virtualization has an impact on certain aspects of how databases are designed. To show clearly where and what the differences are, this book considers this design process to consist of three steps: *information modeling*, *logical database design*, and *physical database design*.

One of the tasks when developing a business intelligence system is to analyze the users' *information needs*. On which business objects do they need reports? What are the properties of those business objects? On which level of detail do they need the data? How do they define those business objects? This is information modeling, which is about getting a precise understanding of the business processes, the data these processes need, and the corresponding decision-making processes. It's an activity that requires little to no knowledge of database technology. What's needed is business knowledge. The more an analyst understands of the business and its needs, the better the results of information modeling. This step is sometimes referred to as *data modeling*, *conceptual data modeling*, or *information analysis*. The term *information modeling* is used in this book because it's the most commonly used term.

The result of information modeling, called the *information model*, is a nontechnical but formal description of the information needs of a group of users. Usually, it consists of a diagram describing all the core business objects, their properties, and their interrelationships. Diagramming techniques used are normally based on *entity-relationship diagramming* (see, for example, [54]). Another diagramming technique used regularly in business intelligence environments is based on multidimensional modeling (see [55]).

In the second step—logical database design—the information model is transformed to tables consisting of columns and keys that are implemented in a staging area, data warehouse, or data mart. These tables will hold the users' information needs. This is a semitechnical step. Normally, the result is simply a description or model of all the tables with their columns and keys structures.

The third step—physical database design—focuses on finding the most effective and efficient implementation of these tables for the database server in use. In this step, database specialists study aspects such as which columns need indexes, whether tables have to be partitioned, and how the physical parameters of table spaces should be set. They can even decide to restructure tables to improve performance. For example, data from two tables is joined to form a more denormalized structure, or derived and aggregated data is added to existing tables. The result of physical database design is a *database model* showing all the tables, their columns, and their keys. An example of such a database model is shown in Figure 11.1.

Compared to logical database design, physical database design is a very database server-specific step. This means that the best imaginable solution for an Oracle database server doesn't have to be the best solution for a Microsoft database server.

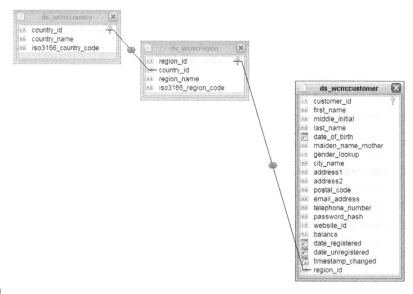

FIGURE 11.1

An example of a database model.

For business intelligence systems with a more classic architecture, early on in the project designers decide which data stores are needed. Should the system be built around a data warehouse, is a staging area needed, and should data marts be developed? These decisions don't have to be made when data virtualization forms the heart of a business intelligence system. Initially, only a data warehouse is created, so no data marts or personal data stores are developed at the start of the project. For performance reasons, they might be created later on.

Using data virtualization has impact on information modeling and database design:

Impact 1—Less Database Design Work: When a business intelligence system is developed, that three-step design process has to be applied to all the data stores needed. So information modeling and logical and physical database design have to be performed, for example, for the data warehouse, the staging area, and the data marts. An information model has to be created, and a database model has to be developed for each of these data stores. For a system based on data virtualization, information modeling is still necessary, but database design only applies to the data warehouse because there are no other data stores. Because there are fewer data stores, there is less database design work.

Impact 2—Normalization Is Applied to All Tables: In a classic system, different database design approaches are used: normalization is quite often applied to the data warehouse, whereas the data marts usually receive a star schema or snowflake schema (see Section 2.6). Compare this to all the tables of a data warehouse in a system based on data virtualization, where initially they receive normalized structures. The reason they are normalized is that this is still the most neutral form of a data structure—neutral in the sense that it can support the widest range of queries and reports. Next, virtual tables are designed (according to the rules in Chapter 7). But for these virtual tables, no physical database design is needed because there are no data stores.

Impact 3—Information Modeling and Database Design Become More Iterative: An iterative approach for information modeling and database design is easier to deploy when data virtualization is used. The initial design of a data warehouse doesn't have to include the information needs of all the users, and new information needs can be implemented step by step. But why is this easier to deploy? When new information needs are implemented, new tables have to be added, columns may have to be added to existing tables, and existing table structures might have to be changed. In a system with a classic architecture, making these changes requires a lot of time. Not only do the tables in the data warehouse have to be changed, but the data marts and the ETL scripts that copy the data must be changed as well. And changing the tables in the data marts leads to changes in existing reports as well. Reporting code has to be changed to show the same results.

This is not the case when data virtualization is used. If the information needs to be changed, the tables in the data warehouse have to be changed, but this doesn't apply to data marts and ETL scripts. Those changes can be hidden in the mappings of the virtual tables accessed by the existing reports. The consequence is that the extra amount of work needed to keep the existing tables unchanged is considerably less. The changes to the real tables are hidden for the reports. This is why a more iterative approach is easier to use when data virtualization is deployed.

Impact 4—Logical Database Design Becomes More Interactive and Collaborative: Usually, logical database design is quite an abstract exercise. The designers come up with a set of table definitions. In the eyes of the business users, especially if they don't have a computing background, those definitions are quite abstract. It's sometimes difficult for them to see how those tables together represent their information needs. The main reason is that they don't always think in terms of data structures but in terms of the data itself. For example, a designer thinks in terms of customers and invoices, while a user thinks in terms of customer Jones based in London and invoice 6473 which was sent to customer Metheny Metals. Therefore, it can be hard for a user to determine whether the table structures resulting from logical database design are really what he needs.

It would be better if the data structures plus the real data are shown so the users can see what those tables represent. When data virtualization is used, a logical database model can be implemented as virtual tables. The advantage is that when a virtual table is defined, its (virtual) contents can be shown instantaneously—in other words, both the analyst and the user can browse the contents and the user can confirm that what he sees satisfies his information needs. Logical database design becomes a more collaborative and more interactive process.

Impact 5—Physical Database Design Decisions Can Be Postponed: Physical database design changes in two ways. First, instead of having to make all the right physical design decisions upfront, many can be postponed. For example, if a report is too slow, a cache can be defined. That cache can be created instantaneously, and no existing reports have to be changed for that. A more drastic solution might be to create a data mart to which the virtual tables are redirected.

The assumption made here is that derived data stores are not needed initially and therefore require no physical database design. Second, there is less to design. If, indeed, because of data virtualization, fewer databases have to be designed, then there is less physical database design work to do. In a classic architecture where data warehouses and data marts have to be designed, only the first is designed. This makes it a simpler process.

Impact 6—Denormalization Is Less Negative: When designing real tables, denormalization leads to duplication of data, increases the size of a database (in bytes), slows down updates and inserts, and can lead to inconsistencies in the data. These have always been seen as the main disadvantages of denormalization. Every database designer knows this, and it's on page one of every book on database design. If denormalization is applied when designing virtual tables, these assumptions are not true, and these disadvantages don't apply anymore. The point is that a virtual table doesn't have a physical content. So if a virtual table has a denormalized structure, no redundant data is stored, the database doesn't increase, it does not by definition slow down updates and inserts, and it does not lead to inconsistent data. However, if a cache is defined for a denormalized virtual table, then the cache does contain duplicated data.

11.3 Impact of Data Virtualization on Data Profiling

One of the tasks of information management is *data profiling*. The purpose of data profiling is to understand the business meaning and business value of data and to discover *incorrect data*. If incorrect data has been identified, the organization can decide whether or not it can and should be cleansed. This is usually a matter of comparing the costs of cleansing versus the benefits of having reports based on correct data (which is not always an easy task).

Data profiling techniques can be classified in two groups: *column profiling* and *join analysis*. Column profiling techniques involve discovering patterns in values and extracting statistical data, such as the number of null values, the maximum and minimum value, and the number of numeric and alphanumeric values. With join analysis, the populations of two columns (possibly from different tables and data stores) are compared: Do their populations overlap? Some of these techniques are explained here.

With the simplest column profiling technique, quantitative meta data on the contents of the columns of a virtual table is derived. Figure 11.2 shows an example of the result of such a profiling exercise on the CUSTOMER table. The right-hand side of the same result is presented in Figure 11.3. The result

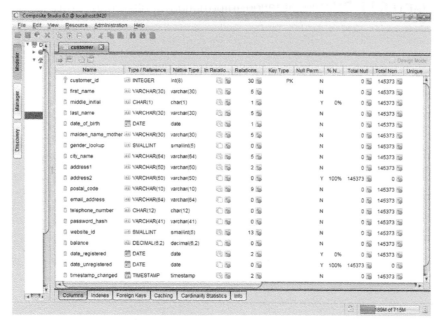

FIGURE 11.2

With data profiling, quantitative meta data on the contents of columns of a virtual table can be analyzed (left-hand side of result).

Reprinted with permission of Composite Software.

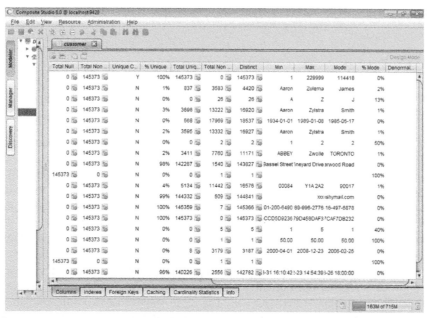

FIGURE 11.3

With data profiling, meta data on the contents of columns of a virtual tables can be presented (right-hand side of result).

Reprinted with permission of Composite Software.

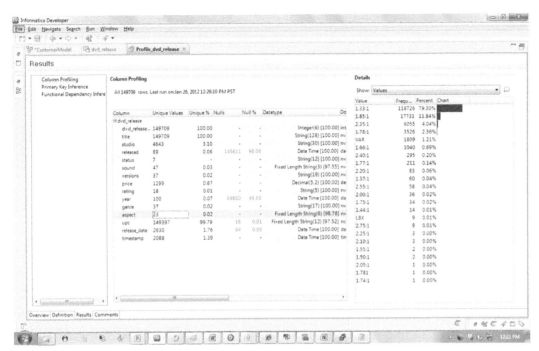

FIGURE 11.4

The contents of the ASPECT in the DVD_RELEASE table has been profiled and shows some incorrect values (right-hand side of diagram).

Reprinted with permission of Informatica Corporation.

contains for each column, among other things, the number of null and nonnull values, the uniqueness of values, the number of distinct values, and the minimum and maximum values. In one overview an analyst can see whether all the data is what he expects it to be.

Another profiling technique analyzes the individual values of a column. Imagine that a developer has defined a virtual table on a source table and he expects only to find the values A, B, and C in a particular column. By using column profiling, the developer can quickly and easily check whether those are really the only values in the underlying source table. This exercise could show that some undocumented values exist in that column, meaning the developer has to come up with a solution on how to handle those unexpected values. Should they be filtered, flagged, or transformed?

For example, the ASPECT column in the DVD_RELEASE table contains a limited number of different values (Figure 11.4). Some of them are not correct, such as 1:781 (it should be 1:78:1), 2:05:1 (it should be 2:50.1), LBX, and VAR. By using column profiling, it's easy to detect these incorrect values.

Pattern analysis is another form of column profiling. Figure 11.5 contains the result of a pattern analysis applied to the column POSTALCODE. The result shows that two different patterns exist in this column: one consisting of five digits and one consisting of four digits. In addition, there are a few null values in that column. It's up to the developer to determine whether all these values are correct or, for example, whether the four-digit numbers are incorrect.

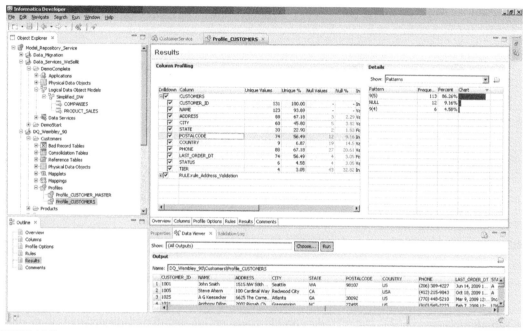

FIGURE 11.5

The result of a column profiling exercise.

Reprinted with permission of Informatica Corporation.

Before two tables are joined, pattern analysis can be used to determine whether the values of the joined columns really match. Imagine we want to join two tables on columns containing telephone numbers. The problem may be that in one of the columns brackets are used in the telephone number, such as `(123)456789`, and in the other the format `123-456789` is used. With pattern analysis, we can determine whether it makes sense to join the columns or whether the values have to be transformed first.

Figure 11.6 presents the result of a join analysis. In this example, the contents of the CUSTOMER_ID column in the ORDERS table is compared with the CUSTOMER_ID values in the CUSTOMERS table. Each value in one column is checked to see whether it appears in the other column. The result is presented with a Venn diagram, which can show that the set of values in one column is a subset of the other, that the two sets are identical, that they overlap, or that they have no overlap whatsoever. The Venn diagram at the top right-hand side of the figure shows that for this example there is no problem because the values in the ORDERS table all appear in the CUSTOMERS table.

But imagine that a developer wants to join the source tables CUSTOMERS and ORDERS in the columns called CUSTOMER_ID and that join analysis indicates that there are values in CUSTOMER_ID in the ORDERS table that don't appear in the CUSTOMERS table. This means that some orders exist with no matching customer, which must be incorrect. This is an important piece of information. For developers and business users, it's important to be aware of such problems, and a decision has to be made on how to fix it.

FIGURE 11.6

The result of a join analysis is presented as a Venn diagram.

Various tools are available that offer data profiling features ranging from dedicated tools to modules within ETL tools. Data virtualization servers support data profiling functionality as well, as can be seen in this section's figures. In this case, the data profiling techniques operate directly on the virtual tables. When the profiling techniques access the virtual tables, only then is the data to be profiled retrieved from the data stores. There is no need to extract data from a data store first, file it somewhere, and then activate the profiling. In other words, data virtualization servers support *on-demand data profiling*.

Using data virtualization has the following impact on data profiling:

Impact 1—No Loss of Time Due to Switching between Tools: Deploying data virtualization does have an impact on the data profiling exercise. In a classic environment, when a designer wants to profile data, he starts up a data profiling tool, connects to the proper database, and requests the tool to profile the data. Imagine that he detects incorrect data in some table, so he will have to discuss it with the users to determine what to do. If it's incorrect data and if the solution is to include extra logic in the ETL scripts to handle that incorrect data, it will take some time before one can see whether the change is the right one. The reason is that after the script has been changed, the script has to be run again to get the transformed data in the target database, and only then can the effect of the change be seen and can the result be studied. If it's not the correct effect, then he has to come up with a different solution. It's very common for the designer to have to switch several times from the data profiling tool to the other tools, and vice versa, losing a lot of time in the process.

Impact 2—Integrated Data Profiling: As indicated, in most data virtualization servers, data profiling is an integral part of the development environment. When source tables are imported and wrappers and virtual tables are defined, designers can activate the data profiling module to verify the quality of the data in the source tables. In addition, when virtual tables are defined, developers can study the virtual contents of the virtual tables to see whether the mappings have the desired result. Literally, the developer can profile the virtual data and source data, change the mapping, and right away be able to study the impact on the outcome of the new mapping. In other words, data virtualization products support *integrated data profiling*. There is no loss of time due to going back and forth between tools.

Impact 3—Collaborative Data Profiling: In addition, because data profiling is more integrated, it can lead to a closer collaboration between designers and business users. When a virtual table is defined, they can study the contents of the virtual table together. The designer can study the data profiling result from a technical standpoint, while the business user can analyze it from a business standpoint. There will be no need for the designer to first do his work, plan a meeting with the user, discuss the results, go back to implement some changes, and then plan another meeting. In other words, data virtualization makes *collaborative data profiling* possible. This shortens the overall time to get the right virtual table definitions.

To summarize, the impact of using data virtualization on data profiling is that the latter becomes a more integrated step in the design process and makes it a more collaborative process that involves the business users more heavily.

11.4 Impact of Data Virtualization on Data Cleansing

In business intelligence systems with a classic architecture, the data cleansing operations are usually implemented in the ETL scripts responsible for copying the production data to the data warehouse or, if no data warehouse exists, to the data marts. If a data virtualization server accesses only the data warehouse and the data marts, the same approach for data cleansing can be implemented.

It's a different situation when a data virtualization server accesses the production databases and the staging areas as well. The reason for this might be to retrieve the latest version of the data or the lowest level of detail of that data. This data probably hasn't been cleansed and is therefore inconsistent with the data in the data warehouse. To avoid this problem, the same data cleansing operations have to be implemented in the mappings of the virtual tables, or data cleansing has to be moved upstream (see Section 8.2 for guidelines on how to do this). In other words, the impact of data virtualization on data cleansing is that the need for *upstream data cleansing* increases.

In general, it's better to do as much of the data cleansing as close as possible to the point of entry: the production systems. In the ultimate situation, production applications make it impossible to enter incorrect data. Changing these systems in such a way that they check more of the incoming data is, however, easier said than done. Some of those applications are old, and the code is not that easy to maintain. Also, some of them have been purchased, which means the application code is inaccessible. But deploying data virtualization in a business intelligence system does mean that organizations have to reconsider how much data cleansing they must do in their production systems and whether more cleansing should be added.

11.5 Impact of Data Virtualization on Data Governance

The last, but certainly not the least, important task of information management is *data governance*. Data governance is defined by Wikipedia (on October 5, 2011) as follows:

> *Data governance is a set of processes that ensures that important data assets are formally managed throughout the enterprise.*

All these processes ensure that data can be trusted by the data consumers and that someone or some department can be made accountable for any adverse event that happens because of low data quality. In other words, people are made responsible for the quality of the data. Data governance is about putting people in charge of fixing the data and preventing issues with the data so the enterprise can become more efficient. People assigned to data governance are called *data stewards*. They are the guardians of the data. If something is wrong with the data, they are held accountable.

Overall, deploying data virtualization in a business intelligence system has a positive impact on various aspects of data governance:

Impact 1—Less Proliferation of Meta Data Specifications: From a data governance perspective it's important that the definitions of business objects are organized in one system. This has always been a recommended approach, because no one wants to have a definition of a business object replicated in multiple systems. This also applies to the implementations of those definitions. Unfortunately, in many classic systems the implementation of what a business object is, such as a customer or an invoice, can end up in many systems. For example, if we consider the CUSTOMER table and if we look at all the code and specifications needed to get the data from the source systems to that table, that code can be everywhere. All the code needed to get the data from the source systems, via the staging area and the ODS, into the data warehouse is part of the implementation of the definition of the business object customer. This proliferation of meta data specifications is detrimental for data governance. One key advantage of data virtualization is that many of these meta data specifications are brought together under the control of a data virtualization server. In other words, data virtualization doesn't only integrate and centralize data, it does the same for meta data, leading to less proliferation of meta data specifications. This is good for data governance, because the meta data specifications become more manageable for the data stewards.

Impact 2—Fewer Copies of the Data: As indicated throughout this book, when data virtualization is used in a business intelligence system, a simpler architecture can be developed, meaning less duplication of data. Having fewer copies of the data simplifies data governance. More copies make data governance a bigger challenge.

Impact 3—Centralized Data Access: When data virtualization isn't used, any data consumer accessing the data stores performs data access independently. It's hard to determine which data consumer is accessing which data store and how. It's like a stadium that has 50 entrances, which makes it hard to monitor everyone who comes in. With data virtualization, the goal is to have all access to the data stores be handled by a data virtualization server: one centralized point of entry to all the data. This makes it easier to manage the data access aspect. This is good for data governance because it will be easier to guarantee that every data consumer sees the same data. The reason is simple: If different data consumers are retrieving data from the same data stores, those data have undergone the same transformations and conform to the same definitions.

Impact 4—Improved Data Consistency: When all the data consumers access data via a data virtualization server, it's easier to guarantee data consistency. Compare this to different data consumers accessing different data marts. In such an architecture, it's technically more complex to enforce that the same transformations are applied if data is duplicated in several data marts.

Impact 5—Improved Auditability: An aspect of data governance is auditability. Fewer data stores and less data duplication make auditing easier. This is probably a general rule: The fewer duplicated components in a solution, the more transparent the solution is for auditing. With data virtualization there is less need to develop data stores, and the amount of stored, duplicated data is mimimized.

Impact 6—Improved Flexibility: Another difference is flexibility. If a business object is implemented as some real table, changing its definition is hard because the structure and the contents of that real table may have to be changed as well. This can have a serious impact on the data consumers using the data in that table. Therefore, designers are always taught to design flexible table structures that are as generic as possible because a change in the implementation can be quite expensive. It's almost as if the definition of the business object has been set in concrete. This certainly does not apply to virtual tables. These can be changed easily. This is one of the reasons why systems based on data virtualization are more flexible. Being able to implement changes more easily helps data governance considerably.

The Data Delivery Platform— A New Architecture for Business Intelligence Systems

12.1 Introduction

This chapter does not describe another aspect or feature of data virtualization, nor does it explain an application area; instead, it describes the *data delivery platform* (DDP). The DDP is a flexible architecture for designing and developing business intelligence systems. The architecture is an alternative to the business intelligence architectures described in Section 2.8.

We include this architecture in this book because it's based on the same principles and concepts as data virtualization: abstraction, encapsulation, decoupling, on-demand transformation, and so on. In fact, the simplest way to develop a business intelligence system with a DDP-based architecture is with a data virtualization server. This chapter covers the following topics:

- What the DDP does
- The definition of the DDP
- Comparison between the DDP and the other BI architectures
- The requirements of the DDP
- Differences between data virtualization and the DDP

Note: In 2010, in a series of well-received articles published at BeyeNetwork.com, I introduced the DDP (see [56] and [57]). More articles were written about the same topic in the months that followed. In this chapter all that material has been summarized, extended, restructured, and edited.

12.2 The Data Delivery Platform in a Nutshell

The *data delivery platform* (DDP) is a flexible architecture for developing business intelligence systems in which data consumers and data stores are decoupled from each other and where meta data specifications are shared (Figure 12.1).

Two concepts are key in this sentence: *decoupling* and *shared meta data specifications*. In a DDP-based business intelligence system, the data consumers should not be aware of where, how, and in which data store the data is held; all the data storage aspects should be hidden for these data consumers. They should not know or concern themselves with whether the data they're using are coming from a data mart, a data warehouse, or maybe even a production database. They should not be aware that data from mutiple data stores has to be joined, nor should they know which data store technologies are being accessed: an SQL database, a web service, or maybe a NoSQL database. In addition, the structure of the data stores should be hidden as well. Data consumers should see the data in the

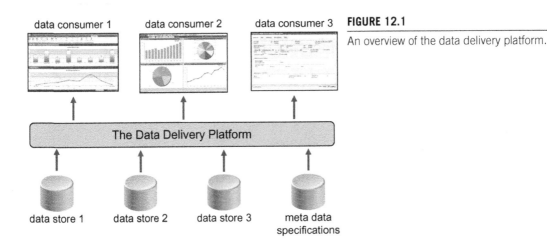

data consumer 1   data consumer 2   data consumer 3

The Data Delivery Platform

data store 1   data store 2   data store 3   meta data
specifications

FIGURE 12.1

An overview of the data delivery platform.

way that's convenient for them, and they should only see relevant data. This is achieved by decoupling data consumers from data stores.

The primary goal of decoupling is to get a higher level of flexibility. For example, changes made to the data stores don't automatically mean that changes have to be made to the data consumers as well, and vice versa. Or replacing one data store technology by another is easier when that data store is "hidden" behind the DDP.

Some examples of meta data specifications are definitions and descriptions of business objects, logic to transform the data coming from production systems to a structure suitable for reporting, cleansing rules, relationships between business objects, and integrity rules. In many business intelligence systems, these specifications are spread out over the reporting and analytical tools, the ETL tools, the database descriptions, and so on. Spreading them out like this has several disadvantages. First, the specifications are replicated. Especially in cases where different user groups use different reporting tools, many specifications have to be repeated and specified in the proprietary languages of those tools. Keeping all those specifications consistent becomes a challenge. Second, the logic for transforming production data is broken into many small fragments. These fragments end up everywhere in, for example, replication code, ETL scripts, database stored procedures, and reporting logic. To get a complete view of how the data is transformed from source to target is, again, a challenge. In a DDP-based system, all these specifications are shared. They are kept in one central place, which leads to fewer consistency problems and to no (or less) fragmentation of logic. To summarize, the focus of the DDP is on decoupling and on making meta data specifications shared.

Note: From reading the previous chapters and this section, it must be clear that there is a close relationship between DDP and data virtualization. What that relationship is exactly, is described in the coming sections.

12.3 **The Definition of the Data Delivery Platform**

The definition of the DDP is:

The data delivery platform is a business intelligence architecture that delivers data and meta data to data consumers in support of decision making, reporting, and data retrieval, whereby data and meta data stores are decoupled from the data consumers through a meta data–driven layer to increase flexibility, and whereby data and meta data are presented in a subject-oriented, integrated, time-variant, and reproducible style.

Let's explain some of the terms used in this definition.

The first sentence states that the architecture "delivers" data. The DDP is not restricted to deliver only data stored in production systems and/or data warehouses and data marts. Nor should it be limited to structured data. The DDP can deliver any type of data: internal and external, structured and unstructured, operational and historical, and so on.

It's important that the architecture is able to deliver meta data and that it is *meta data driven*. The workings of this architecture should be guided by technical meta data on virtual tables, mappings, and wrappers, and it should also contain more business-oriented meta data, such as definitions, taxonomies, and descriptions. All this meta data should be reusable and accessible by all types of tools accessing the DDP. In other words, it should be an open solution that can deliver data and meta data.

The terms *subject-oriented*, *integrated*, and *time-variant* are copied from Bill Inmon's definition for *data warehouse* (see Section 2.5.1). These terms have the same meaning in the definitions of both DDP and data warehouse. However, the term *nonvolatile* has been replaced by *reproducible* in the DDP definition. Inmon uses the term *nonvolatile* in his definition because users of reports usually want to see consistent results. Practically speaking, when a user runs a report a few times a day, he wants to see the same result. However, data stores can be designed in such a way that they are volatile and can still present consistent results. Therefore, in the definition of the DDP, the term *reproducible* is used instead. If the same report result can be reproduced, even on a volatile data store, the DDP satisfies the needs of the users.

As indicated, two concepts are fundamental to the data delivery platform: *shared meta data specifications* and *decoupling* of data consumers and data stores. Both of these concepts lead to a number of advantages. Because the DDP leans heavily on data virtualization, the list of advantages that applies to the latter applies to the DDP as well (see Section 7.3). Therefore, we restrict ourselves to repeating them:

- Increased speed of report development
- Easier maintenance of meta data specifications
- More consistent reporting
- Cost reduction due to simplification
- Increased flexibility of the architecture
- Easier data store migration
- Seamless adoption of new technology
- Transparent archiving of data

12.4 The Data Delivery Platform and Other Business Intelligence Architectures

The DDP can be seen as a separate business intelligence architecture, just like the architectures described in Section 2.8. It can also coexist with them. For example, Figure 12.2 shows how the DDP can work with the CIF (corporate information factory), and Figure 12.3 shows how it can be used in conjunction with the data warehouse bus architecture.

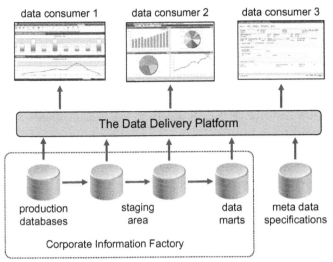

FIGURE 12.2

The data delivery platform can coexist with the corporate information factory architecture (inside the dotted box).

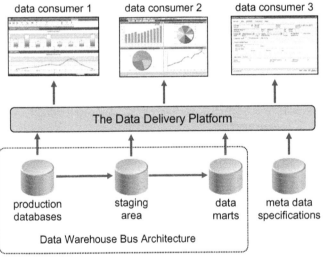

FIGURE 12.3

The data delivery platform can coexist with the data warehouse bus architecture (inside the dotted box).

What all these architectures have in common is that they try to deliver the right data at the right moment with the right quality level to the data consumers. The difference is that the DDP can be seen as an architecture that complements the other business intelligence architectures. By adding the DDP to those architectures, they become more flexible. One can also state that the importance of data storage is deemphasized in the DDP, and the focus is shifted to flexibility (through decoupling and shared meta data specifications).

12.5 **The Requirements of the Data Delivery Platform**

When does a business intelligence system have a DDP architecture? Is supporting a data virtualization server sufficient, or is it a little bit more complex than that? Having a definition like the one in Section 12.3 is important for describing a particular concept as accurately as possible. In addition, a definition can help to explain what that concept is. Having a clear definition can also avoid endless discussions, or otherwise different people might have different opinions about what that specific concept is.

However, even if the definition of a concept is perfect, it's hard to include all the requirements of that concept in its definition. For example, Section 2.5.1 contains Bill Inmon's popular definition for the term *data warehouse*. Although this definition is widely used, and although most specialists have a good understanding of all the terms used in the definition, it still leaves many questions unanswered. For example, should the tables in a data warehouse be normalized or not? Should all the tables be stored physically, or is a more virtual solution acceptable as well? Should all the data be organized in tables at all? Does the term *data* include unstructured data? The definition doesn't answer those questions, and that can lead to conflicting interpretations, misunderstandings, and confusion.

Inmon is aware of this, and therefore in some of his other articles and books, he describes some additional requirements. For example, in his article "What a Data Warehouse Is Not" (see [58]), he writes, "A much more rational way to build the data warehouse is to use the relational model." By this he means that a requirement for a data warehouse is that its table structures are normalized and are not designed as star schemas or snowflake schemas. In other words, a database that contains tables that are not properly normalized cannot be called a data warehouse. Other requirements can be found in other books and articles.

Thus, having additional requirements (in addition to a definition) is not uncommon for describing a concept in more detail. The main reason these requirements are needed is that it's very hard to come up with a definition that describes exactly what a particular concept is, is still understandable, and isn't a full page long. This is definitely true for nonmathematical concepts such as a data warehouse. In general, it's unfortunate that in the IT industry, we don't have more precise definitions, such as $E = MC^2$, but alas.

To avoid confusion and misconceptions with respect to the data delivery platform, this section lists the minimal requirements of a DDP-based system. The list should also give a more detailed understanding of what the DDP is and what it isn't. In addition, if an organization wants to develop its own DDP-based business intelligence system, the list also informs them about the minimal requirements.

To bring some structure to these lists, they have been classified in nine categories:

1. Requirements related to the deliverable data
    a. A DDP-based system should be able to deliver operational and historical data to data consumers.
    b. A DDP-based system should be able to deliver internal and external data to data consumers.
    c. A DDP-based system should be able to deliver structured, semistructured, and unstructured data to data consumers.
2. Requirements related to data stores and data access
    a. A DDP-based system should support access to a large heterogeneous set of data store technologies and systems, including relational database technology, content and document management systems, MDX-based database technology, XML-storage technology, message

queues, archive, streaming database technology, HTML-based websites, web services, spreadsheets, and textual documents.

b. A DDP-based system should be able to process a wide range of query languages, including SQL, XQuery, MDX, SOAP/XML. The more languages that are supported, the more reporting and analytical tools can query the DDP and the easier it is to migrate an existing business intelligence application to the DDP.

c. A DDP-based system should support a wide range of open APIs for passing the queries from the data consumers to the DDP, including ODBC, JDBC, OLE DB, OLE DB for OLAP (ODBO), XML for Analysis (XMLA), XQuery API for Java (XQJ), and ADO.NET.

3. Requirements related to querying and data consumers

a. A DDP-based system should allow any combination of query language and API to access any data store. For example, it should be possible to write an MDX query that joins a relational database and an MDX database, or an SQL query that joins a spreadsheet with a relational database.

b. A DDP-based system should support a pull-model and a push-model for transporting data from the data stores to the data consumers (see also Section 13.2.5).

4. Requirements related to meta data

a. A DDP-based system should support a registry for storing additional meta data that is not stored in any other (meta) data store. However, the DDP does not enforce that all meta data is stored and managed by the DDP itself. In fact, the DDP should be able to process meta data the way it processes data itself: if needed, it should use a data virtualization approach to deliver meta data.

b. A DDP-based system should make meta data accessible to any type of tool.

c. A DDP-based system should deliver meta data to data consumers in the same way it delivers the data to the data consumers.

d. A DDP-based system should support all types of meta data, including technical, business, and operational meta data. In fact, the more meta data–driven the DDP is, the better.

e. A DDP-based system should allow for different definitions of data elements for different users.

5. Requirements related to acquisition and integration of data

a. A DDP-based system should support acquisition (extracting data from data stores) and integration of data in every possible form, including on-demand, scheduled, and replication.

b. A DDP-based system should support all the common types of transformation operations, including name changes, joins, selects, aggregations, splits, projections, and cleansing.

c. A DDP-based system should support lineage and impact analysis.

6. Requirements related to features to improve performance, scalability, and availability

a. A DDP-based system should support advanced caching techniques to minimize interference and to reuse query results.

b. A DDP-based system should support features for controlling which data elements are to be cached and when.

c. A DDP-based system should support distributed join optimization techniques to optimize query performance.

d. A DDP-based system should be able to monitor queries and other performance-related aspects, and it should also be able to show usage (which user is using which tables). These features are needed for managed self-service business intelligence as well.

    e. A DDP-based system should allow for the definition of usage limitations. Available limitations might lead to canceling a query before it is executed to avoid queries consuming too many resources.

7. Requirements related to data quality
    a. A DDP-based system should support simple and advanced operations for cleansing the data.
    b. A DDP-based system should support data profiling capabilities.

8. Requirements related to security
    a. A DDP-based system should support single sign-on.
    b. A DDP-based system should support authentication techniques.
    c. A DDP-based system should support authorization features (which users are allowed to access which data and when). It should be possible to specify rules for authorization up to the individual data value level.

9. Requirements related to transactions
    a. A DDP-based system should support updates, inserts, and deletes on all the data stores that allow those operations.
    b. A DDP-based system should support heterogeneous distributed transactions.

To summarize, a business intelligence system has a DDP-based architecture if it adheres to the definition of the DDP and if it meets the preceding requirements.

Final remark: This list of requirements does not include *nonfunctional* requirements such as those related to performance, availability, scalability, and concurrency. The reason is that in general these requirements do not determine whether something adheres to a particular definition. For example, whatever the definition of the word *car* is, even if a car is incredibly slow, it's still a car; in fact, even if it's broken and not drivable, it's *still* a car. Or if my computer crashes, it's still called a computer, because it still adheres to the definition of computer and to the additional functional requirements. Similarly, if the query performance of a particular data warehouse is bad, it's still a data warehouse; a data mart with availability problems is still a data mart; and likewise, a DDP-based system is still a DDP-based system even if problems occur related to aspects such as performance, availability, scalability, and concurrency.

In most cases, nonfunctional requirements apply to specific solutions and are subjective. The car I drive is fast enough for me, but maybe it's too slow for other drivers. The same applies to a DDP-based business intelligence system developed for a specific organization. Its query performance might be fast enough for them, but maybe it's too slow for another. It all depends on what the organization wants and needs. But whatever the performance is and whatever the organization thinks of it, it's still a DDP-based business intelligence system. It's the responsibility of the vendors and the developers to build and deliver solutions that conform to the nonfunctional requirements demanded by organizations and users.

12.6 **The Data Delivery Platform versus Data Virtualization**

Although a DDP-based system can be developed in many different ways and with many different technologies, today a data virtualization server is the most obvious choice. The DDP is to a data virtualization server what SOA is to an ESB. Data virtualization servers support the right features to decouple the data consumers from the data stores and to manage meta data specifications centrally. But in principle other types of abstraction, encapsulation, and federation technologies can be used.

In this respect, the DDP is not much different from other business intelligence architectures; a business intelligence system based on the data warehouse bus architecture is also more than just a matter of installing a database server.

The current data virtualization products make developing a DDP-based system easy. It's just that some of the requirements of the DDP have not been implemented (yet) by those products. For example, the push-model for queries has not been implemented by most current data virtualization products (Requirement 3.b). This makes it impossible to build a report that is automatically refreshed if data in a data store change. Another example is that most data virtualization servers don't support usage limitations (Requirement 6.e). These extra features have to be developed separately or bought as separate tools. In other words, to create the ultimate DDP-based business intelligence system, just buying and using a data virtualization server are not enough.

To summarize, the DDP is an architecture, and data virtualization is an implementation technology. Using the syntax of the C programming language, one can say, DDP = data virtualization++.

12.7 Explanation of the Name

Why is it called a "data delivery platform?" Why *data*, *delivery*, and *platform*? Let's begin with *data*. Why not use *information*? Quite often, the terms *data* and *information* are used interchangeably. Some analysts, however, feel that there is a fundamental difference between the two. For them, *data* becomes *information* when the receiver considers it as something new. Whether or not something is information can therefore only be decided by the receiver. If someone tells me that Neil Young was one of the founders of the band Buffalo Springfield, then that's data because I already know that. But if they tell me that Neil Young also played with the Beatles for a few months (if that were true), then that would be information. But I'm the one who decides if it's information. The same applies for a more business intelligence–like example. If a report shows that the number of sales in a particular region is decreasing, and the user already knows this, it's data, but if it's something he didn't know, it's information.

So all the data, regardless of how it's presented, is just that: *data*. That means that it's difficult (and probably close to impossible) for an information system to present information and to know beforehand that it's really information. Therefore, the term *data* was chosen instead of *information* because a DDP-based business intelligence system doesn't know beforehand whether the data sent to a data consumer is information.

The second term is *delivery*. The purpose of the DDP is to support a broad spectrum of applications requiring access to data. On one end of the spectrum, it should support high-end analytical applications analyzing massive amounts of data, and on the other end, it should support applications requesting something simple like a customer's address. For any application that needs data, the DDP delivers the data in the right form and through the right language and API: the DDP delivers data.

The term *platform* is usually used in the IT industry to indicate a foundation on which applications can be developed and can run. An operating system is an example of a platform or an application server. The DDP had the same role: It's the foundation for any application that needs access to data. It's not a solution by itself nor is it an application. Therefore, the term *platform* is included in the name.

12.8 **A Personal Note**

Quite regularly I am asked whether I "invented" the DDP architecture. The answer is no. As Sir Isaac Newton—physicist, mathematician, astronomer, natural philosopher, alchemist, and theologian—once said, "If I have seen a little further, it is by standing on the shoulders of giants." The DDP is like that. Many great thinkers in years past proposed the idea of data virtualization, or something similar. The giant I credit most is David Parnas, who introduced the notion of information hiding in the 1970s (see [6]). But I also must thank all those people who introduced and were involved in developing the concepts of object orientation, abstraction, encapsulation, component-based development, and service-oriented architectures. They all saw the need for separating the application from the implementation. In my eyes, all those vendors involved in introducing data federation and data virtualization products years before the DDP was introduced are giants as well. It's unfortunate that a large part of the IT industry hasn't recognized the value of those products for such a long time. The DDP is the result of a lot of work by many. I just combined it and added a teaspoon of my own thinking. I would like to thank all those giants for the work they did.

The Future of Data Virtualization

13.1 Introduction

At the time of writing this book, data virtualization is in the spotlights. In 2009, data virtualization was still a technology that was not on the radar of most organizations. It's now moving more and more to the forefront. New products are being released, organizations are implementing their first systems based on data virtualization, and many are studying whether they can benefit from the technology. The general expectation is that data virtualization is rapidly becoming mainstream technology.

This fast-growing acceptance is clearly shown in a study performed by The Bloor Group in 2011 (Figure 13.1; see [59]). In this study, respondents were asked what middleware sofware they had already implemented or were implementing. In total, 59 percent of them were seriously involved with data virtualization: 14 percent had already implemented data virtualization, 14 percent were currently implementing it, and 31 percent were planning to implement data virtualization. If we compare this to the percentages for master data management and data governance, which have been around much longer, we have to conclude that data virtualization is being adopted much faster than those two.

Due to the need for agility, the ability to quickly develop new and change existing systems is leading organizations to a solution based on data virtualization. This need for agility is also clear when reading Judith Davis and Robert Eve's book on data virtualization (see [60]). This book includes ten case studies of organizations using data virtualization. One of them is Chicago-based Northern Trust, a leading provider of investment management, private banking, wealth management, and worldwide trust and custody services. After adopting data virtualization, the time it requires them to implement a new outsourcing customer reduced by 50 percent: from six to nine months to three to six months. Another one is Qualcomm Inc., a global leader in next-generation mobile technologies. Before using data virtualization, introducing a new application with the need to access five different systems could take six months. With data virtualization, virtual tables presenting the same data can be developed in days, improving development speed and agility dramatically.

The effect of the increasing popularity and the speedy adoption by the market is that development of the products will continue by their respective vendors. New features will be added, existing features will be expanded and enhanced, and performance and scalability will be improved.

This chapter gives an overview of which new features and improvements we may expect to see in the coming years. Note that most of the features described in this chapter have not been implemented yet by the majority of the vendors.

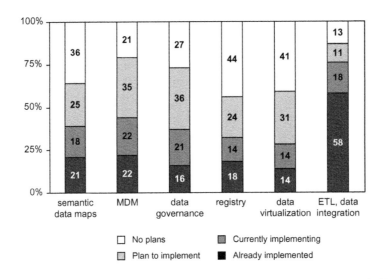

FIGURE 13.1

The acceptance of data virtualization is increasing rapidly.

Source: The Bloor Group, 2011.

The chapter is divided into four sections. The first one contains my view on the future, and the next describe the views of the CTO's of three data virtualization server vendors: Composite Software, Denodo Technologies, and Informatica Corporation.

13.2 The Future of Data Virtualization According to Rick F. van der Lans

13.2.1 New and Enhanced Query Optimization Techniques

Chapter 6 describes some of the query optimization techniques supported by most of the data virtualization servers. In many cases, the optimizers of these products are able to find the best strategy for processing a query and for retrieving the data from the data stores, but there will always be queries for which the most efficient processing strategy isn't found. This leads to poor query processing times. Therefore, it's important that research into discovering new and better query optimization techniques is crucial and should continue.

All this research and development is not only important for improving the performance of these slower queries but for other reasons as well. One reason is that the amount of data collected and stored by organizations keeps increasing. More and more organizations build systems that process massive amounts of data. For example, a European utility company is installing 55 million meters in as many houses that measure and report energy consumption every 15 minutes. This means that every 15 minutes, 55 million measurements are processed and stored. This amounts to over 5 million records per day and close to 2 trillion records per year. This amount of data can clearly be classified as *big data* (see Section 2.9.2). More and more organizations are developing production systems with comparable amounts of data. To be able to operate succesfully in these big data environments, new techniques for query optimization have to be studied.

Another reason is that query demands are mounting: organizations are finding that more and more queries and more complex queries are executed. The user community that needs to query the data is growing as well. More queries and more complex queries mean that research has to focus on techniques for efficiently executing queries concurrently.

If we look at some of the optimization techniques described in Chapter 6, some of them have to be improved as well. For example, the push-down technique has to be improved (see Section 6.6). The more processing of a query that can be pushed down to a database server, the more processing that is done in Stages 4, 5, 6, and 7 and less in Stages 8 and 9. The more processing is done close to the stored data itself, the better it is, because it minimizes the amount of data that the data stores have to retrieve from disk (Stage 6), and it reduces the amount of data transmitted back from the data stores to the data virtualization server (Stage 8).

To execute distributed joins, more techniques have to be invented. More SQL injection techniques have to be implemented because this type of technique can seriously minimize the amount of data transmission between data stores and the data virtualization server (Stage 8).

This need for improving query optimization techniques for data virtualization servers is not very different from the similar need for more and better query optimizers for SQL database servers. Since the day these database servers were introduced, new query optimization techniques have been invented, and this research and development process hasn't stopped since. Note that improving the performance of database servers automatically has a positive impact on the performance of data virtualization servers because regardless of how smart and efficient a data virtualization server is, its performance is always determined by the performance of the underlying database servers; it forms Stages 4–7 of the processing of a data virtualization server query.

13.2.2 Exploiting New Hardware Technology

Certain hardware improvements will have a significant impact on the performance of data virtualization servers. Therefore, vendors of data virtualization servers have to strive to fully exploit some of them, such as the following:

- More and faster internal memory
- Faster processors
- Faster networks

Internal memory is becoming cheaper and cheaper by the year. The effect is that servers come with much more internal memory than in the old days. For example, at the end of 2011, Oracle introduced their Oracle Exalytics In-Memory Machine. This machine comes with 1 terabyte of RAM. This amount of memory would have been unthinkable a few years earlier. The general expectation is that this trend of increasing internal memory will continue in the coming years.

A data virtualization server can exploit more internal memory to improve query performance in multiple ways. The caching mechanism in particular can benefit from this hardware development. Imagine that if a 1 terabyte of internal memory is available, then many of the cached virtual tables can be kept in memory and don't have to be written to disk at all. This would mean that accessing data in a cached virtual table requires no I/O; all the data is retrieved from internal memory, thus seriously improving query performance.

It's not unthinkable that in the future, data virtualization servers will be released as *appliances*, much in the same way some database servers are released. A *data virtualization appliance* would be a dedicated machine with a large amount of internal memory on board and with a data virtualization server preinstalled. Every hardware and software component of such an appliance would be tuned toward running that data virtualization server. It would have fast communication capabilities to retrieve data from data stores, and it would have its own technology on board to store cached data on disk (or in memory).

The second hardware technology that will have a positive impact on the performance of a data virtualization server is faster processors. Faster processors will directly impact the performance of all the stages, but primarily Stage 8. Especially in cases when a data virtualization server has to execute many transformations within the mappings, more processor power helps.

Finally, data virtualization servers will have to exploit network technology better and better. The time needed to transmit data can form a significant portion of the overall query processing time. The amount of data to be transmitted between the data stores and the data virtualization server can seriously impact the total performance (Stage 6). It's one of the research areas of query optimization. Faster networks have a direct and positive impact on overall performance, especially if large amounts of data are processed.

13.2.3 Extending the Design Module

Section 1.12 indicates that the design module of a data virtualization server is used by analysts, designers, and possibly users, to enter and manage virtualization specifications, such as mappings, wrappers, virtual tables, and their respective definitions and descriptions. All these specifications are stored in a dictionary managed by the data virtualization server.

Most of the design modules of current data virtualization servers only allow designers to enter specifications on those objects needed to operate. But they can't enter other types of specifications, such as business glossaries, data models, and taxonomies. The expectation is that in the future many new features will be added to the design modules of data virtualization servers. In general, a data virtualization server will support more and more features currently supported by tools, such as data modeling, master data management, and business glossary tools (Figure 13.2). Data virtualization servers should be able to support the whole process of information management, including information modeling, data governance, and logical database design, and not just the implementation phase.

Here is a list of some of the features that can be expected to be added to data virtualization servers.

Features from data modeling tools:

- To support the analysis phase of a project, data virtualization servers should allow analysts to enter data models without having to "link" the entities to implementation artefacts, such as wrappers and virtual tables. Currently, most products only support implementation models and no pure analysis models. In a way, by supporting features for analysis, the design modules of the data virtualization servers will slowly take over the role of more classic data modeling tools.
- Besides definitions, it would be useful if more descriptive specifications can be entered.

Features from master data management tools:

- If indeed master data management and data virtualization will slowly merge (see Section 10.8), the need to be able to enter master data becomes important. Currently, data virtualization

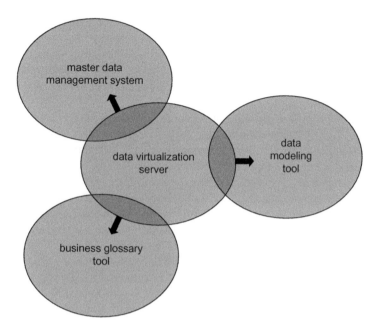

FIGURE 13.2

Data virtualization servers will inherit features currently supported by master data management systems, data modeling tools, and business glossary tools.

servers don't manage data (except for the cache data). That's the responsibility of the data stores themselves. To support master data management, it should be possible to enter data (including master data) that is managed by the data virtualization servers, such as the keys of the various business objects, historical data, and correct data. It should also support an environment to manage that data logically and technically.

- Designers should be able to enter taxonomies. This leads to new (meta) data that is not stored in any source system but in a data virtualization server and will have to be managed by it.

Features from business glossary tools:

- To make data virtualization servers useful for business users and business analysts as well so they can also enter specifications, we expect these tools to support the functionality offered by *business glossary tools*. Users should be able to enter their definitions of business concepts in their own language, and they should be able to search for virtual tables and other meta data specifications based on their business glossaries.

We also expect data virtualization servers to be enhanced with new concepts, besides virtual tables, wrappers, and mappings. One of those new concepts is the integrity rule (see Section 8.2.3). For every application area where data virtualization is used, the importance of data quality is increasing. A data virtualization server can help implementing the integrity rules, but in most products it means implementing them as logic inside the wrappers and mappings. In other words, the concept of an integrity rule doesn't exist explicitly; only the designers know that a particular piece of code is the implementation of an integrity rule. In the future it has to be possible to define integrity rules independently of the mappings. It should be possible to link them to the virtual tables. A data virtualization server should know when to enforce those rules. It should also support an automatic form of flagging and filtering. All this will ease the development and maintenance of integrity rules and will improve the quality of the data presented to the data consumers.

Another valuable concept is *reusability* of transformation logic. For example, in most data virtualization servers, it's not possible or difficult to write transformation logic that can be reused in different virtual tables. For example, in many products, it's not straightforward to define some logic that transforms telephone numbers to the correct format and that can be applied to multiple columns containing telephone numbers. The odds are that the same logic has to be duplicated a few times (for each column with telephone numbers once). The only form of reusable specifications supported by most data virtualization servers is by placing logic in virtual tables that are used by other virtual tables (see Section 3.7). Support of patterns, functions, or templates would definitely help to minimize duplication of logic; it would increase the level of reusability of specifications.

Currently, data virtualization servers offer features that are useful for any type of application area, including business intelligence and service-oriented architectures. This also applies to expected new features such as integrity rules and reusable specifications. But to make the designers of a business intelligence system more productive, the products have to support more common and well-known business intelligence–related concepts. For example, a data virtualization server should understand the concept of a slowly changing dimension. It should know how to derive a star schema from a set of normalized tables, and it should support features to model history. Making data virtualization servers more business intelligence–aware increases productivity.

13.2.4 Data Quality Features

Organizations are more and more aware that it's crucial to improve the quality of their data. Section 7.5.2 indicates that when data virtualization is deployed, it's recommended to solve data quality issues as close as possible to where the data is entered. This is called upstream data cleansing.

Still, a data virtualization server has to be able to deal with incoming data that is not according to the integrity rules. Therefore, we expect that data virtualization servers will support more and more features to detect incorrect data and to cleanse incorrect data. Currently, most products are somewhat behind what ETL products offer in this respect. They have some catching up to do.

The following are some expected features:

- More powerful cleansing operations, such as those supported by dedicated data cleansing tools, including fuzzy matching, address checking, deduplications of rows, proper casing of names, telephone number matching, and language and nationality identification
- Dedicated concept for explicitly specifying integrity rules (see Section 8.2.3)
- Standard solution for working with translation tables (see Section 8.2.7)

13.2.5 Support for the Push-Model for Data Access

Most data virtualization servers operate according to what is called a *pull-model* for data access. With a pull-model, a data virtualization server retrieves data from the data stores when it is asked for by a data consumer. In other words, a data virtualization server "pulls" data from the data stores. For most data consumers, this is the appropriate way of accessing data.

Some data consumers, however, need the opposite: a *push-model*. With a push-model, data is pushed automatically from the source to the data consumers, which is usually done when the source data changes. For example, new data is added, or existing data is changed or deleted. When such a change occurs, that data is automatically sent to the data consumer.

A popular example of the push-model is RSS feeds on the Internet. Someone can register for a feed, and if something happens, the data (probably a message) is pushed to the receiving application. Replication technology is also an example of push-technology. When source data is changed or added, the replicator automatically copies it to another application or data store. The TV system as we know it can be seen as more of a push-model than a pull-model, while PO boxes are more like pull-models; owners have to visit their PO box to see if something has been dropped in the box.

For processing queries from data consumers, most data virtualization servers support only the pull-model. The data virtualization server only starts working when asked for by a data consumer or when it's scheduled.

Lately, in the business intelligence community, the interest for the push-model has increased. Especially in cases where operational business intelligence applications are developed, a push-model can be very beneficial. Imagine an application that continuously monitors the amount of spill of a factory process. Suppose that when that percentage of spill is above a certain level, a notification has to be sent to a manager so that proper actions can be taken. Evidently, this type of application can be developed with a pull-model. It would mean that data is periodically retrieved to determine what the percentage of spill is. If it's below the acceptable level, nothing happens, but if it's above, a notification has to be sent out. This periodical querying of the same data is sometimes called *polling*. Polling can be quite inefficient, especially when the data is retrieved to determine the percentage of spill, and the percentage is not above the acceptable level, so no action needs to be taken. Technically, too often data is queried unnecessarily. With a push-model, data is not periodically checked but is pushed to the data consumer when the data, in which the data consumer is interested, has changed.

Because of the increasing need for push-based business intelligence applications, the vendors of data virtualization servers will have to implement this type of technology. It has to be possible to push data from the data stores through the mappings (for necessary transformations and integrations) to the data consumers. The expectation is that this will be a serious technological challenge for most of these products.

Note: The push-model is usually implemented using the *publish-subscribe framework*. In this framework, applications (the subscribers) register for particular messages, and the source is the sender (the publisher) of those messages.

13.2.6 Blending of Data Virtualization, Extract Transform Load, Extract Load Transform, and Replication

Data virtualization, ETL, ELT, and replication are alternative solutions for transforming and integrating data. Regardless of their differences, they have certain things in common. For all three, many comparable specifications have to be entered before data can be processed. For example, for all of them, the structure of the source data, the structure of the target data, and the transformations have to be defined. The biggest difference between the three is how they process those transformations.

With data virtualization, it's done on-demand; with ETL, it's performed in a scheduled fashion; and with replication, the data is copied when the source data change.

The expectation is that in the future these integration forms will blend together. Designers will first design the logic on how to do the necessary transformations and integration, meaning defining source and target structures and transformation specifications. They will be able to use on-demand data profiling capabilities to study whether the transformations they have defined are logically correct. And when everything works according to the requirements, the designers will have the option of choosing between the different implementation forms. For some of them, extra specifications have to be added. For example, for ETL, the refresh rate has to be specified, and for data virtualization, a cache with a refresh rate has to be specified.

In fact, there will be at least six different implementation forms:

- ETL
- ELT
- Replication
- Data virtualization without caches
- Data virtualization with caches
- Data virtualization with the push-model

Depending on the requirements of the data consumers and the capabilities of the data stores, the designers can pick the right technical solution.

The advantage of this blending of the different approaches is that switching between them becomes much easier. First, an ETL solution can be selected, and afterward, if, for example, processing power has increased, a switch to data virtualization can be made. This can be done without having to change any of the transformation specifications. Another advantage is that all the forms of data integration are handled by one product. Currently, if replication is the proper solution for copying data between the production systems and the staging area, and ETL is ideal for copying data between the staging area and the data warehouse, and for the rest, data virtualization is needed, it can well be that three different products from three different vendors are needed. These three products won't share specifications. Being able to handle all this from one product is strongly recommended.

To summarize, in the future, data virtualization servers will have to support all the different implementation forms. So instead of having to switch to another product and redevelop all the transformation and integration logic, it will just be a matter of switching to another implementation form.

13.3 The Future of Data Virtualization According to David Besemer, CTO of Composite Software

Today, enterprise IT is under siege. Business users are far more demanding as agility, mobility, and cost drive their IT agenda. Data's exponential growth and bring-your-own-device's omnipresent delivery make information overload the status quo. Further, IT complexity is out of control as we layer new big data stores, such as Hadoop; new use cases, such as predictive analytics; new styles of deployment, such as cloud; and more on top of byzantine on-premise IT infrastructures. These macro-level business and technology drivers are revolutionizing IT as we know it, forcing an entirely new enterprise IT infrastructure, with a dramatically expanded data virtualization deployment at its center.

13.3.1 **The Empowered Consumer Gains Ubiquitous Data Access**

Business users' expectations have changed dramatically. No longer will large IT backlogs and less than Apple- or Google-level application interfaces be tolerated. The Data Warehousing Institute recently identified five factors driving businesses toward self-service BI (see [61]):

- Constantly changing business needs (65 percent)
- IT's inability to satisfy new requests in a timely manner (57 percent)
- The need to be a more analytics-driven organization (54 percent)
- Slow and untimely access to information (47 percent)
- Business user dissatisfaction with IT-delivered BI capabilities (34 percent)

To meet their requirements in the future, business users will use lightweight applications that are quick to adopt and easy to personally adapt. Mavens and super-users will guide solutions by influence rather than IT standards. Losing its applications development role, IT's function will shift dramatically, becoming the provider of ubiquitous data access and management services for these applications.

Data virtualization is "the technology that offers data consumers a unified, abstracted, and encapsulated view for querying and manipulating data stored in a heterogeneous set of data stores." So literally, by definition, data virtualization is the ideal infrastructure to service this ubiquitous data access and management requirement.

13.3.2 **IT's Back Office Becomes the Cloud**

The big data phenomenon is well underway as volumes, varieties, and velocities extend far beyond traditional transactional data with the staggering expansion of unstructured data such as emails, tweets, video, and more, as well as log data from RFID, GPS, websites, and more. Today's IT back office is not well suited to support data at this scale, but tomorrow's must be!

Further, corporate data will be increasingly distributed beyond the enterprise across multiple cloud infrastructure-as-a-service, software-as-a-service, and data-as-a-service providers. Cisco projects a 12-fold increase in cloud data center traffic over the next five years (see [62]). These data distribution trends, combined with big data's disruptive force, are driving cloud computing's ascension as the next-generation of enterprise computing.

13.3.3 **Data Virtualization of the Future Is a Global Data Fabric**

To meet these increased ease-of-use requirements, unprecedented data volumes, ever-widening heterogeneity, extreme low-latency expectations, and always-on service levels, data virtualization technology of the future will advance in myriad ways—some revolutionary, some evolutionary. Data virtualization's transformation from an enterprise-scale data layer to a global data fabric is the most radical of these changes. So let's focus on it.

Imagine a system that not only automatically understands where increasingly mobile users are and what kind of data they typically use but will also automatically access, transform, combine, and stage that data for them, mere moments ahead of when they need to consume it. Some organizations are already doing exactly this—for example, Netflix does this with its online streaming services. (And Netflix's users love it.)

If this can be done for movie viewers today, then why can't it be done for enterprise data consumers tomorrow? The data virtualization technology of tomorrow will make this scenario an everyday reality. Its deployment will be called a *global data fabric*. Here is how it will work:

- Consumer use of data will expand and become increasingly mobile. Nearly all their data will be provided via data fabrics.
- Lightweight data virtualization servers along with high-speed caches will be deployed in cloud data centers globally to optimize query and transaction processing and manage data close to the always-on, mobile consumers.
- Heavier-duty data virtualization servers closer to the data sources will optimize query and other workloads, in conjunction with distributed source system resources, to provide always-on data services from anywhere within the enterprise or across the cloud.
- Extending internal networks, content delivery networks from third-party managed service providers will intelligently route traffic and caches to further mitigate latency. Service provider–type systems management and billing techniques will replace today's enterprise IT methods.
- Data virtualization optimization techniques will advance to support this global data fabric topology. And new optimizations will be invented to leverage an ever-widening array of high performance, fit-for-purpose data management systems.
- Classification terms such as *structured*, *semistructured*, and *unstructured* will no longer be relevant, instead replaced by improved meta data and modeling automation that provide consumers with the insights into dimensions that truly matter—for example, data quality, granularity, freshness, and stability.
- And numerous visibility and control functions will be added to provide data governance at this scale.

13.3.4 Conclusion

Significant business and technology drivers are revolutionizing IT infrastructure for consumers, IT's back office, and the critical services layer and technology that spans the middle. Global data fabrics, the data virtualization technology of the future, will be the critical enabler for this revolution. Enjoy the journey.

13.4 The Future of Data Virtualization According to Alberto Pan, CTO of Denodo Technologies

Like many of the very best ideas in the history of computer science, data virtualization comes from an old concept that has matured to become mainstream. Actually, E. F. Codd started the most influential paper in the history of data management as follows (see [63]): "Future users of large data banks must be protected from having to know how the data is organized. . . . Application programs should remain unaffected when the internal representation of data is changed and even when some aspects of the external representation are changed." This illustrates one fundamental principle of computer science that is at the root of data virtualization: Applications should be independent of the complexities of accessing data. They should not have to bother about where data is located, how it is accessed, or what its native format is. They should also be independent of changes in any of those aspects.

Nevertheless, the proliferation of distributed architectures and the explosion in the volume of accessible data have created a situation where applications are probably more concerned about data access complexities than ever before. In addition, other requirements have also driven the evolution of data management technology in the enterprise. They can be summarized as the four "V's" identified by recent analyst research: (1) support for *volumes* to cost-effectively manage big data and reduce physical consolidation and replication; (2) support for *velocity* to cope with real-time and event-driven data delivery; (3) support for *variety* of data types, from structured to unstructured, external or internal to the enterprise; and (4) management support for the *variability* of data consuming methods, service levels, security policies, and other governance issues.

At Denodo we see data virtualization as the technology catalyst to address all the preceding requirements in conjunction with other tools. Data virtualization minimizes replication, allows real-time or batch data delivery, has the potential to abstract the heterogeneities of structured and unstructured data, and can provide a single entry point for management and governance. This conviction is the basis of the following predictions.

Data virtualization will be enterprise-wide: Currently, data virtualization is still frequently used as a tool for increasing productivity and time to market in specific projects or for specific business purposes. This is good, but it ignores the fact that data virtualization does much more than what data federation or EII ever did. The full vision of abstracting applications from data access complexities requires a more comprehensive approach where data virtualization acts as a generic and unified data access layer used by all applications (or, at least, by most of them) to interact with all sources, including persisted consolidated data stores and event-driven messages.

Having a true single enterprise-wide entry point for data access also enables a number of data governance and monitoring tasks. For instance, you have a single point to enforce access rules, to limit resources usage by users and applications, or to dynamically throttle the access to critical data sources to guarantee performance.

Data virtualization's integration model needs to go beyond the pure relational model: Codd's relational model has served us very well and will continue to do so for years to come. Its solid theoretical foundation and wide industry support guarantee it a central role in data virtualization. Nevertheless, mapping the data models of data services, NoSQL systems, multidimensional databases, API-based applications, web information, and semantic information (among others) to the pure relational data model may be simply asking too much. Data virtualization tools need to use an integration model that extends the relational model to accommodate some concepts that repeatedly appear in other data models (e.g., hierarchical data, limited query capabilities, and lack of predefined schema) in order to really provide easy-to-use and high-performance integration of all those data sources.

Data virtualization will allow more data access paradigms: While many applications can do perfectly well with conventional structured queries executed through JDBC/ODBC or web service interfaces, fulfilling the needs of all enterprise applications, mobile and end user needs also require supporting other data access paradigms.

The most obvious example is the "search" paradigm typically found in the unstructured world. Supporting this paradigm and combining it with the structured query paradigm when needed is a must for dealing with unstructured and structured content in a unified way.

It will be also crucial to support the "browse" paradigm by providing a single point to browse *all* the data and metadata of the enterprise ecosystem, for both humans and applications. Notice the emphasis on *all*. The data resources in your corporate databases are not only related among them, but they are also related with data resources maintained by accessible, external applications. For instance, your leads may have twitter accounts that you want to browse, or financial information about your customers may be available through an external web service, and so on. To this respect, Denodo predicts that data virtualization technology will establish a tighter relationship with the RESTful architectural principles that, among other benefits, provide a powerful and scalable way of browsing the relationships among data resources.

Finally, pull-based data access is not enough for all cases. Support for the push-model will also be required (more about this in the next section).

Data virtualization will be the predominant overall framework for all data management: The term *data virtualization* is sometimes used (wrongly in our opinion) to refer to a particular style of data integration, typically real-time federation. The correct, broader context of data virtualization emphasizes the abstraction and decoupling principle (a la E. F. Codd) between all data sources, all consumers, all data delivery styles, and all data management functions.

From this architectural point of view, data virtualization provides the overall framework that includes real-time, cached, and traditional batch-based data integration (e.g., ETL), the last being simply the particular case of data virtualization where all the data is consolidated. What is important is that data virtualization will become the core framework, and whether the functionality comes from modular components of a data virtualization platform or separate products is not so important.

In addition, many real-world messaging tasks can be modeled as a process that takes a message from an input queue, transforms it in some way (possibly using data from other systems along the way) and places the result in an output queue. Those are really real-time data integration tasks and also the basis for supporting push-based data access. The data virtualization layer will support this as well.

Similarly with data quality and master data management, while some efforts will continue to be stand-alone, it will increasingly be done as part of the unified data layer that enterprise-wide adoption of data virtualization enables. The capabilities for data quality and MDM can come from advanced data virtualization platforms as well as continuing to leverage specialty tools.

In-memory databases are also a perfect fit to become part of a data virtualization layer, effectively providing a high performance, application-neutral cache layer for data access.

A corollary of all this is that future uses of data virtualization will further increase the need for supporting hybrid approaches combining on one hand real-time access, batch access, and mixed data access (some data for a view is cached, and some is not), and on the other hand in-memory data access, disk data access, and network data access.

In summary, we think data virtualization has the potential to finally fulfill Codd's vision, enormously reducing the complexities associated to data access and management in a world characterized by the massive production of heterogeneous and distributed data. Of course, the future is always uncertain, and probably some surprises are still waiting for us along the way, but we can be sure of one thing: It will be a fascinating journey.

13.5 The Future of Data Virtualization According to James Markarian, CTO of Informatica Corporation

Exponential growth in traditional transactional data, plus new information from social media, call detail records, sensors and devices, and geolocation systems, has made it imperative that businesses take the lead in harnessing data to derive new insights for competitive advantage. To turn these new insights into business opportunities, both business and IT executives are being challenged to rethink their information management practices, break down organizational and data silos, and improve business/IT collaboration.

While many companies know that data is key to driving competitive advantage, they also know that they may not be as effective as they could be at transforming it into a useful asset. The data is there, but it's fragmented across systems; it's in the cloud, it's on the desktop, it's on mobile devices, and it's in a variety of data sources. In fact, it's everywhere, and it's duplicated again and again. It's often not available when it's needed, and when it is available, it might be full of errors or it does not deliver the value desired to improve operations and increase revenue. And, as data grow, the cost to manage it only increases.

This is particularly true in the case of business intelligence, the top priority for the CIO. According to Forrester Research Inc. (see [64]), "As data volumes and information complexity continue to skyrocket, traditional business intelligence tools try hard to keep up with ever-increasing and changing demands. But it's an uphill battle—and business intelligence tools and applications do not always keep up the right level of pace and advancement. As a result, the rift between business requirements for on-demand information and real-time decisions, and business intelligence applications and IT support staff's ability to support them, continues to grow."

According to the report:

- 66 percent of BI requirements change on between a daily and monthly basis
- 71 percent of the respondents said they have to ask data analysts to create custom reports for them
- 36 percent of custom report requests require a custom cube or data mart to answer the request
- 77 percent of respondents cited that it takes between days and months to get their BI requests fulfilled

It is clear: In order to turn data into new insights, and thus opportunities, businesses need to pay greater attention to data integration to provide more actionable, trustworthy, and timely information in their BI projects and initiatives. They need to put data integration and business user–driven self-service to work for uncovering new insights that the business needs and can trust. Doing this will drive growth, reduce costs, and deliver innovations through spotting patterns and trends, while meeting compliance and risk mandates more effectively. But how do you accomplish this?

13.5.1 How to Maximize Return on Data with Data Virtualization

Here are some critical factors that organizations must consider in order to maximize their return on data:

- They must be more business-focused and think from a perspective of an end-to-end business use of information and associated processes.
- They must employ self-service and business-IT collaboration best practices to enable the business to own their data, while IT retains control and governance.
- They must employ agile data integration techniques that *cut wait and waste* in the process, while complementing traditional approaches to BI.
- They need to define user-driven service-level agreements (SLAs) around data latency, accuracy, consistency, availability, and uptime, and they must understand system implications.
- They must use data to complement their business strategy and technical infrastructure, instead of reinventing the entire wheel.

Of late, data virtualization has evolved as an agile data integration concept to enable more agile BI. However, traditional BI approaches, including data integration, data warehousing, and other complex data processing initiatives, are not going away anytime soon. This is because data will continue to be heterogeneous, dirty, and semantically different across systems. To succeed, data virtualization must coexist—reuse and complement existing infrastructures and investments made to solve these problems rather than just be a Band-Aid for a small subset of special use cases. It must also involve the business user early and often to ensure that the data is trustworthy.

13.5.2 Beyond Looking Under the Hood

The trick is to gain competitive advantage by accelerating the delivery of critical data and reports and to be able to trust and consume them instantly. But data virtualization must be done right to support the critical success factors. Very often, data virtualization borrows heavily from its data federation legacy. The primary use case of data federation is to access and merge already cleaned and conformed data in real-time, leaving the heavy lifting for other processing logic to make this possible. So the time advantage gained is lost as one realizes the federated data had to be prepped for federation. As a result, the ROI simply disappears.

So do go beyond looking under the hood, and ask a few hard questions. To what extent does the solution support data transformation? Is it nominal, limited to what you can do programmatically through SQL or XQuery? Is there any data profiling, or will you require staging and further processing? Is it profiling of both logic and sources, just sources, or neither? Are data cleansing and conforming simplistic, hand-coded, or nonexistent? How about reuse? Can you quickly and easily reuse virtual views for any use case, including batch? To do data virtualization right, it requires a deep and thorough understanding of very complex problems that exist in the data integration domain.

So what's our perspective? Simply put, data virtualization must take a page from the world of virtual machines. Data virtualization must do the heavy lifting of accessing, profiling, cleansing, transforming, and delivering federated data to and from any application, on-demand. It must handle all the underlying data complexity in order to provide conformed and trusted data, reusing the logic for either batch or real-time operation, whether through SQL, SOA, REST, JSON, or new acronyms yet to be specified. Data virtualization must be built from the ground up on the *cut the wait and waste* best practices discussed in the book *Lean Integration* by Schmidt and Lyle (see [65]).

By starting with a logical data model; giving *business* and *IT* role-based visibility to the data early in the process; enabling data profiling on federated data to show and resolve the data integrity issues; applying advanced transformations, including data quality in real-time to federated data; and completely and instantly reusing the integration logic or virtual views for batch or real-time, you can cut the wait and waste throughout the process. By leveraging optimizations, parallelism, pipelining, identity resolution, and other complex transformational capabilities that you can find only in a mature data integration platform, data virtualization can enable more agile business intelligence.

Finally, with enterprises generating huge volumes of data, the types of data changing enormously, and the need for shorter data processing speeds, data virtualization can maximize the return on data. You can ensure that immediate action is taken on new insights derived from both *big data* and existing data. You can combine on-premise data with data in the cloud, on-demand. With the world becoming more mobile, you can provide access to disparate data by provisioning it to any device. Done right, data virtualization can give you the agile data integration foundation you need to embrace what we call secular megatrends: *social*, *mobile*, *cloud*, and *big data*.

Bibliography

[1] Bouman R, van Dongen J. Pentaho solutions; business intelligence and data warehousing with Pentaho and MySQL. John Wiley and Sons, Inc.; 2009.

[2] The Aberdeen Group, Agile BI benchmark report; March 2011.

[3] Clark T. Storage virtualization: technologies for simplifying data storage and management. Addison-Wesley Professional; 2005.

[4] Schulz G. The green and virtual data center. CRC/Auerbach Publications; 2009.

[5] Berard EV. Abstraction, encapsulation, and information hiding, *itmWEB.com*, www.itmweb.com/essay550.htm, 2006.

[6] Parnas DL. On the criteria to be used in decomposing systems into modules. Commun ACM December 1972;15(12) Recently republished in *Software Fundamentals, Collected Papers by David L. Parnas*, Addison-Wesley Professional, 2001.

[7] Blair G, et al. Object-oriented languages, systems and applications. New York, New York: Halsted Press; 1991.

[8] Rumbaugh J, et al. Object-oriented modeling and design. Englewood Cliffs, New Jersey: Prentice-Hall; 1991.

[9] Codd EF. Relational database: a practical foundation for productivity, turing award lecture. Commun ACM February 1982;25(2).

[10] Ross DT, et al. Software engineering: process, principles, and goals. IEEE Comput May 1975;8(5).

[11] Roebuck K. Enterprise service bus (ESB): high-impact strategies—what you need to know: definitions, adoptions, impact, benefit, maturity, vendors. Tebbo; 2011.

[12] Broughton E. Periscope: access to enterprise data. TUSC; 2005.

[13] Selinger PG, Adiba ME. Access path selection in distributed database management systems. Proc Int Conf Databases July 1980.

[14] Daniels D, et al. An introduction to distributed query compilation in R*. IBM RJ 3497 April 1982.

[15] van der Lans RF. Introduction to SQL, 4th ed. Addison-Wesley; 2007.

[16] Walmsley P. XQuery. O'Reilly; 2007.

[17] Turban E, et al. Decision support and business intelligence systems, 9th ed. Prentice Hall; 2010.

[18] Ponniah P. Data warehousing fundamentals for IT professionals, 2nd ed. John Wiley and Sons; 2010.

[19] Evelson B. Topic overview: business intelligence. Forrester Res November 21, 2008.

[20] Luhn HP. A Business Intelligence System. IBM J October 1958.

[21] Power DJ. A brief history of decision support systems. DSSResources.com, Version 4.1, March 10, 2007.

[22] Davenport TH, Harris JG. Competing on analytics; the new science of winning. Harvard Business School Press; 2007.

[23] Inmon WH. Building the data warehouse. QED; 1990.

[24] Inmon WH, Strauss D, Neushloss G. DW 2.0, The architecture for the next generation of data warehousing. Morgan Kaufmann Publishers; 2008.

[25] Kimball R, et al. The data warehouse lifecycle toolkit, 2nd ed. John Wiley and Sons, Inc.; 2008.

[26] Inmon WH, Imhoff C, Battas G. Building the operational data store. John Wiley and Sons, Inc.; 1996.

[27] Simsion GC, Witt GC. Data modeling essentials, 3rd ed. Morgan Kaufmann; 2004.

[28] Linstedt DE. Data vault series 1—data vault overview. The Data Adm Newsl July 1, 2002 http://www.tdan.com/view-articles/5054/.

[29] Codd EF. Further normalization of the database relational model. In: Courant computer science symposium 6, Database systems; May 1971.

[30] Codd EF. Normalized database structure: a brief tutorial. In: ACM SIGFIDET workshop on data description, access and control. San Diego, California; 1971.

[31] Kent W. A simple guide to five normal forms in relational database theory. Commun ACM February 1983.

[32] Inmon WH, Imhoff C, Sousa R. Corporate information factory, 2nd ed. John Wiley and Sons, Inc.; 2001.

[33] Ariyachandra T, Watson HJ. Which data warehouse architecture is most successful? The Data Warehouse Ins 2006 also published in *Business Intelligence Journal*, Q1 2006.

[34] Pendse N. Keynote at trends in business intelligence 2006. Array Publications; 2006.

[35] Loshin D. Effecting data quality improvement through data virtualization. Knowledge Integrity, Inc.; June 2010.

[36] Hewitt E. Cassandra: the definitive guide. O'Reilly Media; 2010.

[37] White T. Hadoop: the definitive guide, 2nd ed. Yahoo Press; 2010.

[38] Chodorow K. MongoDB: the definitive guide. O'Reilly Media; 2010.

[39] Anderson C. CouchDB: the definitive guide. O'Reilly Media; 2010.

[40] Date CJ. Relational database writings 1991–1994. Addison-Wesley Publishing Company; 1995.

[41] Bernstein PA, et al. Concurrency control and recovery in database systems. Addison-Wesley Publishing Company; 1987.

[42] Gray J, Reuter A. Transaction processing: concepts and techniques. Morgan Kaufmann Publishers; 1993.

[43] Hasan W. Optimization of SQL queries for parallel machines. Springer; 1996.

[44] Yu CT, Meng W. Principles of database query processing for advanced applications. Morgan Kaufmann Publishers; 1997.

[45] Eckerson WW. Data quality and the bottom line: achieving business success through a commitment to high quality. The Data Warehouse Inst 2002.

[46] Erl T. SOA principles of service design. Prentice Hall; 2008.

[47] Erl T, et al. Web service contract design and versioning for SOA. Prentice Hall; 2009.

[48] Lublinsky B. Is REST the future for SOA?, www.infoq.com, August 11, 2011.

[49] Allamaraju S. Restful web services cookbook: solutions for improving scalability and simplicity. Yahoo Press; 2010.

[50] Loshin D. Master data management. Morgan Kaufmann Publishers; 2009.

[51] Berson A, Dubov L. Master data management and data governance, 2nd ed. McGraw-Hill Osborne Media; 2010.

[52] Hedden H. The accidental taxonomist. Information Today; 2010.

[53] Stewart DL. Building enterprise taxonomies. Mokita Press; 2011.

[54] Hoberman S. Data modeling made simple, 2nd ed. Technics Publications; 2009.

[55] Golfarelli M, Rizzi S. Data warehouse design; modern principles and methodologies. McGraw-Hill; 2009.

[56] van der Lans RF. A definition of the data delivery platform, *BeyeNetwork.com*, J http://www.b-eye-network.com/view/12495, January 10, 2010.

[57] van der Lans RF. The requirements of the data delivery platform, *BeyeNetwork.com*, http://www.b-eye-network.com/view/12582, February 4, 2010.

[58] Inmon WH, What a data warehouse is not?, *BeyeNetwork.com*, http://www.b-eye-network.com/channels/1134/view/11352, October 29, 2009.

[59] The Bloor Group. A new awareness: the age of architecture has arrived. The Bloor Group; 2011.

[60] J.R. Davis and R. Eve, Data virtualization, going beyond traditional data integration to achieve business agility, Nine Five One Press, 2011.

[61] The Data Warehouse Institute. Self-service business intelligence. TDWI Best Practices Report July 2011

[62] Cisco. Cisco global cloud index: forecast and methodology, 2010–2015, Cisco; 2011.

[63] Codd EF. A relational model of data for large shared data banks. Commun ACM June 1970;13(6).

[64] Forrester Research. Best practices for breaking through the BI backlog; April 2010.

[65] Schmidt JJ, Lyle D. Lean integration: an integration factory approach to business agility. Addison-Wesley Professional; 2010.

Index

Printed and bound by CPI Group (UK) Ltd, Croydon, CR0 4YY

03/10/2024

01040319-0007